Heavy Hitter I.T.
Sales Strategy

Other Books by Steve W. Martin

Heavy Hitter Sales Linguistics
Heavy Hitter Sales Psychology
Heavy Hitter Sales Wisdom
The Real Story of Informix Software and Phil White
Heavy Hitter Selling

Heavy Hitter I.T. Sales Strategy

Competitive Insights from Interviews with
1,000+ Key Information Technology Decision
Makers and Top Technology Salespeople

Steve W. Martin

TILIS Publishers

TILIS Publishers
24881 Alicia Parkway, #E293
Laguna Hills, CA 92653
www.tilispublishers.com

Ordering Information
Orders by U.S. trade bookstores and wholesalers. Please contact Cardinal Publishers Group: Tel: (800) 296-0481; Fax: (317) 879-0872, www.cardinalpub.com.

Cataloging-in-Publication
Martin, Steve W.

   Heavy hitter I.T. sales strategy : competitive insights from interviews with 1,000+ key information technology decisions makers and top technology salespeople / Steve W. Martin.

      p. cm.
      ISBN 978-0-9797961-6-6 (hardcover)
      ISBN 978-0-9797961-7-3 (e-book)
      Includes index.
1. Selling--Anecdotes. 2. Selling--High technology. 3. Selling--Technology. 4. Information technology. 5. High technology industries--Management. 6. Selling--Technological innovations. 7. Success in business. I. Heavy hitter I.T. sales strategy : competitive insights from interviews with one thousand plus key information technology decisions makers and top technology salespeople. II. Title.

HF5439.H54 M37 2014
658.8/2--dc23   2014947558

Printed in the United States of America

First Edition

19 18 17 16 15   10 9 8 7 6 5 4 3 2

Cover design: Kuo Design

Interior design and composition: Marin Bookworks

Editing: PeopleSpeak

Contents

Introduction: How to Read This Book

This book is for senior technology salespeople and sales leaders, those who have been in the field for five-, ten-, and fifteen-plus years. It is based on my experiences working with over 150 technology companies and extensive research that included three types of interviews:

- Interviews with several hundred technology vice presidents of sales about their sales organization goals, challenges, and their strategies to exceed their revenue targets. You will find excerpts from these interviews in part I, "Sales Organization Strategy."

- Interviews with over one thousand key information technology (IT) and business services decision makers as part of the sales effectiveness consulting and win-loss analysis research I conduct on behalf of my clients. Listening to these evaluators share their honest thoughts about how they made their decisions and why they selected the vendors they did was always fascinating. You will find excerpts from these interviews throughout the book.

- Interviews with over one thousand Heavy Hitters (top technology salespeople) who sell for the world's best technology companies. I never grow tired hearing how these Heavy Hitters defeat their archrivals and close large deals. You will find excerpts from these interviews in part IV, "Sales Call Strategy," and part V, "Personal Communication Strategy."

The interview excerpts are a fundamental part of the book and provide important competitive insights. While they include the interviewee's actual title, the names of vendors have been replaced with "Vendor A" or "Vendor B" like below.

I am relatively hard on salespeople in general. A lot of big companies say, "Your account rep is your account rep." We end up choosing not to spend money with companies like that. For example, we were doing six million dollars a year with Vendor A. Over a three-year period we went to zero dollars with them specifically because of account management. It wasn't because we lacked telling them about this problem. It was because of their lack of responsiveness to make changes that work in our best interest. Their senior management wasn't listening or didn't care.

—*Chief Information Officer*

PART I

Sales Organization Strategy

1. Technology Sales Organization Stages

The technology company life cycle starts as an entrepreneurial idea that becomes a reality during the adolescent stage. As the company continues to grow, it enters the adult stage, where the business has established the organizational infrastructure to achieve a measurable market presence and significant revenue growth. The company exits the adult stage and enters the stability of the middle-age stage, where it enjoys sustainable growth balanced with organizational control. As the company continues to age, it enters a senior stage where the goal is to stay relevant and avoid decline.

Sales organizations can also be classified according to their maturity. Every sales organization can be classified based upon whether it is in a build, compete, maintain, extend, or cull stage. The build stage is when the sales organization is first establishing itself. If successful, it will proceed to a high-growth compete stage, and then to maintain stage that is contingent upon stable, predictable success. As the sales organization ages, it will either extend its prior success and enjoy longevity or suffer decline and be forced into the cull stage where it must reduce its size. Figure 1.1 shows the interrelationship between the sales organization stages and the company life cycle.

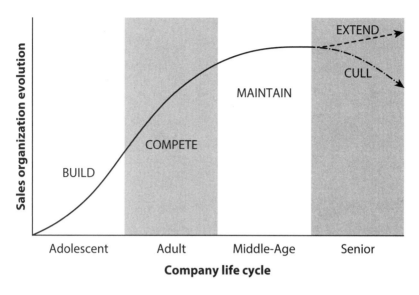

Figure 1.1 Interrelationship between sales organization stage and company life cycle

Adolescent

In the build stage, the organization is establishing its presence and the foundational infrastructure. The sales engagement model is created and continually refined through the iterative process of meeting with early customers. This is a key learning period based upon trial and error, ranging from what type of salespeople should be hired to determining the specific messages that appeal to prospective customers.

Adult

As the sales organization grows, it enters the compete stage and early adulthood. In this stage, the sales organization is engaged with head-to-head competitors, most of whom are well-established and typically larger in size. The sales organization continues to grow rapidly with a large injection of new sales team members.

Similarly, engineering is extending product functionality and adding ancillary products to complete the vision of the product road map.

Middle-Age

The sales organization enters the maintain stage when the market share between competitors becomes more fixed. Because the market has coalesced around a handful of competitors, the untapped greenfield sales opportunities that existed in the compete stage are gone. Now the company must increase its market share and grow at the expense of the competition.

Senior

As the organization continues to age it enters the senior stage. Here the sales organization's goal is to extend the company's market position by increasing the vendor's strategic importance at existing accounts and to remain competitive so new prospective customers can be won. Conversely, when the sales organization passes the tipping point of effectiveness, it enters the cull stage and is forced to downsize in conjunction with its diminished market presence. The positions of some well-known technology companies are plotted on the company life cycle chart in figure 1.2.

> In the past we would lose a deal for a reason that had nothing to do with the product. Our company wasn't well known, and a larger competitor would throw some FUD [fear, uncertainty, and doubt] into the account and we would lose. Those things have gone away now that we are well known.
> —*Vice President of Sales, Maintain Stage Company*

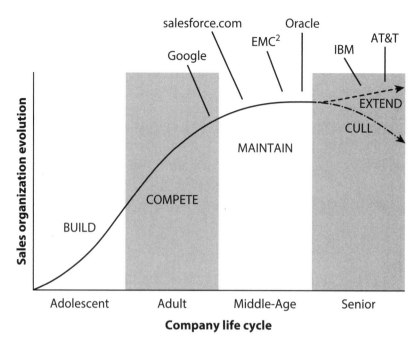

Figure 1.2 Well-known companies' life-cycle positions

2. Technology Sales Organization Challenges

The top sales challenge is always exceeding the monthly, quarterly, or yearly revenue target. However, the sales challenges that inhibit a company from achieving revenue growth vary based on the sales organization stage. This is due to the "push" versus "pull' market characteristics of each stage. For example, in the build stage, a small group of salespeople must push themselves into new accounts and introduce their solution and its benefits. Conversely, a well-known company in the maintain stage is pulled into new sales opportunities because of its market position. Figure 2.1 highlights the different sales organization challenges in the build, compete, maintain, extend, and cull stages.

> Our salespeople are experienced and they can get the meeting with the CIO. The challenge comes in when I tell them I don't want you to talk to the CIO anymore. I want you to talk to the Chief Marketing Office or Chief Financial Officer.
> —*Vice President of Sales, Maintain Stage Company*

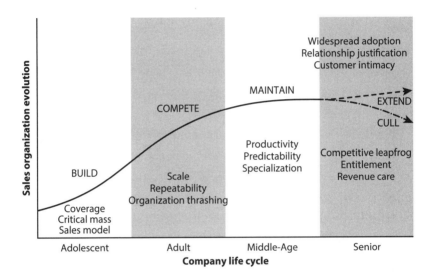

Figure 2.1 Sales organization stage challenges

Build Stage

The top sales challenge in the build stage is creating sufficient sales coverage to push the product into the market. It takes time to hire, train, and build a critical mass of capable salespeople who can penetrate new accounts. During this stage, the sales model is first established, whether the sales organization will sell directly via outside field salespeople, over the phone with inside salespeople, or through channel partners.

> There is a big difference in focus between a small, medium, and large company. Let's assume the markets are equal and each can sell their solution to twenty thousand prospects. In mature markets, big companies will tend to verticalize across all industries. For the small player, it is a Catch-22. If you go after all these markets, you are in trouble. What investment does it take to accomplish this? Do you have the resources to accomplish this?
> —*Vice President of Sales, Build Stage Company*

> We are continually learning from every sales cycle and adapting our message to be more effective when we are in front of customers. We are trying to create a repeatable sales process, but our product focus is changing as much as our sales model.
> —*Vice President of Sales, Build Stage Company*

Compete Stage

The compete stage challenge revolves around quickly scaling the sales organization so that it can compete effectively against more established competitors in existing markets or grab as much market share as possible in greenfield markets. In this stage, the sales organization begins to develop its collective intuition about where it can win new business and where it is likely to lose. If the knowledge and attributes of how business is won are not instilled into the new salespeople, "organization thrashing" occurs. The newer salespeople will chase business they cannot win and waste precious presales resources because there isn't a repeatable sales model. They won't make their quotas and are likely to either be let go or choose to leave because they lack a sufficient pipeline of business to make commissions. In this situation, organization-thrashing occurs because of the continual replenishment of new and underperforming salespeople.

> One of the challenges we've had is that we've been growing so fast that there has been a lot of territory realignment with the addition of new people. Unfortunately, we aren't upstream on deals, and most of the early deal influence is through our marketing activity. In a perfect world, our salesperson has enough time in the territory to build relationships over time. There is huge value when you get in before the sales cycle starts. I'd say the influence is maybe 35 percent before you get into an actual engagement. We walk into a deal and can tell there is a bias. But if we have a really effective first engagement and understand the customer's needs we can position our company advantages.
>
> —*Vice President of Sales, Compete Stage Company*

> We have been in a land grab, and now we are approaching the next phase of our existence, which is lowering the cost of sales. For example, a $40,000 transaction takes as much time as a $300,000 transaction for one of my field salespeople. We understand what the capacity is for field reps and the limitation on the number of transactions they can manage on a quarterly basis.
>
> —*Vice President of Sales, Compete Stage Company*

Maintain Stage

The sales challenge changes radically during the late compete stage and into the maintain stage. The focus shifts from scaling the organization to maximizing sales productivity by lowering the cost of sales and increasing the average sales price. This may result in moving business from outside sales to inside sales or to less-expensive partner and distributor channels. Another challenge revolves around the predictability of revenue and the size of the sales organization. Since the sales organization is fully staffed and the territory coverage model is complete, the challenge is where to find the additional revenue to meet the growing annual target. Since territories have been split numerous times, the answer revolves around specialization. The sales force is segmented by the size of the company to be called upon, national accounts are segregated, and industry vertical sales specialists covering finance, government, retail, distribution, healthcare, and so on, are created.

> I have to balance capacity with productivity. What this means is, how do we get more leverage from the sales model? When you start a company, it is about going as fast as you can to separate yourself from the pack. Now we have to take the next step as a company and say, "What are the sales per employee? What's the cost per rep? What commissionable costs are we paying?" All of these things become relevant. The only way you can have an impact on those is to increase productivity and lower cost.
>
> —*Vice President of Sales, Maintain Stage Company*

> There is a massive number of transactions under $50,000 and we are changing our pricing methodology under this level to be nonnegotiable. We want those deals to be low-touch as we move into distribution and have our channel engaged on that business as opposed to our own people.
>
> —*Vice President of Sales, Maintain Stage Company*

Extend Stage

Sales organizations in the extend stage seek to deflect the attacks from compete and maintain stage competitors by extending their presence within existing customer installations. Their challenge is to attain such widespread customer adoption that their solution becomes the de facto standard. From an account management perspective, the challenge is to build irreplaceable customer intimacy by understanding the customer's business issues and goals. Even though superior products might be available from competitors, through the building of strong personal relationships and the sharing of best industry practices, the customer feels justified to continue the relationship as opposed to ending it.

> Our sales organization is in the process of changing from regional account management to a global account structure as we mature as an organization. We want to make it simple for someone to have a global relationship with us. It has been a problem for our larger customers because they have to execute different contracts that have to be signed locally and deal with different price lists around the world. We believe we can capitalize on our existing presence and dramatically increase revenues at these accounts.
>
> —*Vice President of Sales, Extend Stage Company*

> Our number one challenge is operational. Our industry is aging. As a result, value drivers versus growth drivers become more important. So where it was just grow your sales organization in double digits on an annual basis, now it's "how do you grow your business faster than your competitors but do so with an ever decreasing cost of sales?" The sales leader's role becomes more operational than the traditional spending 70 percent of your time in front of salespeople and customers.
>
> —*Vice President of Sales, Extend Stage Company*

Cull Stage

In the cull stage, the company has been leapfrogged by competitors who provide superior offerings. How can a demoralized and marginalized sales force be revitalized? The Darwinian answer is to cull the herd and remove the bottom performers and those with disenfranchised attitudes. The attitude of entitlement must be eliminated for the spark of the competitive spirit to be reignited. Equally important, key existing accounts whose run rate revenue is central to the survival of the company are separated out and placed in "revenue care" programs where they receive dedicated account management, customer support, and executive-level access.

> The other shift we are making is getting some of our more experienced and seasoned salespeople, who really know the industry and solutions well, to be a little bit more provocative in their approaches. We want them to add more value to the sales cycle. We have a successful older sales team that is kind of set in its ways. The business and times dictate that we shake this model up.
>
> —*Vice President of Sales, Maintain Stage Company*

> We are trying to leverage technology to decrease sales costs. Instead of bringing technical specialists with the rep to the meeting, we'll conduct a webinar or use Skype, so we bring the specialists into the meeting without physically being there. From a customer standpoint, certain industries like high tech are comfortable with this and most definitely the younger generation is.
>
> —*Vice President of Sales, Maintain Stage Company*

3. Product Sales Complexity Impacts Organizational Structure

The complexity of the solution sold is directly related to the evolution of the technology sales organization. Product sales can be classified by complexity as enterprise, platform cloud-based, and point-specific. Each sales cycle varies in complexity depending upon the number of individuals and departments involved in the selection process, the size of purchase, and sophisticated nature (implementation requirements, daily operation, and underlying technology) of the solution offered.

Enterprise Product Sales Trends

Enterprise sales typically involve large capital expenditure purchases that require long sales cycles. Multiple departments of a company and all levels of the organization (C-level executive, mid-level management, and lower-level personnel) are needed to approve the solution's functionality and its purchase. The Enterprise Resource Planning (ERP) system is an example of an enterprise sale. Figure 3.1 illustrates the organizational involvement by the prospective customer to complete an enterprise sales cycle.

Across the organization

Finance · Marketing · Operations · Manufacturing · Information Technology

Executive · Midlevel · Low-level

From top to bottom

Figure 3.1 Enterprise sales cycle

The enterprise sales cycle requires the establishment of an outside field sales force in the build stage, where each field salesperson is initially responsible for a geographic territory. As the organization moves to the compete stage, the territories are split according to company size, measured by annual revenue or number of employees. The field salespeople are segmented into large account field reps and geography (or "geo") field reps.

During the late adult or early middle-age stage, the territories are split further with the addition of vertical outside field salespeople calling on specific industries such as finance, government, retail, technology, and so on. At this time, new products may be launched to penetrate midmarket accounts. Depending upon the complexity of the solution, the sales force selected to address the midmarket will either be a field-based group located in remote areas or a centralized inside sales group that demonstrates and closes business over the phone. Figure 3.2 shows the progression of the enterprise sales organization structure.

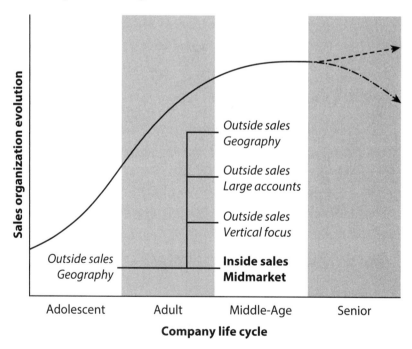

Figure 3.2 Enterprise sales cycle organization evolution

We have geographically distributed enterprise reps that call on large companies and carry $1.5M quotas. Their average deal size is $250K to $300K. Million-dollar deals are not uncommon, so they can make their quota in a deal or two. What we've found is that our competitors are out there selling face to face, and it is a complex sale and if we aren't on-site during the sales cycle, we won't win the business.

—Vice President of Sales, Enterprise Sales Products

The enterprise buyer is expecting you to be on-site showing that you understand and want their business. In the midmarket, there is more openness to being sold over the Internet, but we are still going on-site at least once. I think there is a lot more involvement over the Internet via WebEx and over the phone. The midmarket deals are smaller so you need more activity. When you have so many accounts, you can't afford to spend time traveling to meet with them.

—Vice President of Sales, Enterprise Sales Products

Platform Cloud-Based Sales Trends

The platform cloud-based sale includes a full line of product functionality (or complete stack of technology) that provides a turnkey business solution for the customer over the Internet. Since it is a user-friendly solution designed for the everyday user and average technology consumer, it is sold directly to the business as opposed to the information technology department. A platform cloud-based sales cycle might be instigated by the business users within a department and purchased with the blessing of other interested departments. For example, a sales automation solution may be evaluated by the sales department and purchased with the approval of the IT department as shown in figure 3.3.

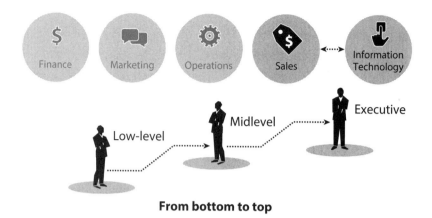

From bottom to top

Figure 3.3. Platform cloud-based sales cycle

The platform cloud-based sales cycle shares many of the same characteristics as the enterprise sales cycle. Different departments and all levels of the organization can be involved. The sales cycles are long and there are significant solution costs. However, the sales organization structure may be different depending upon how the solution evolves. At companies where the solution evolves from a point-specific solution in the build stage to a full product platform in the compete stage, it will be sold primarily over the phone and Internet. As the organization grows and the company tries to penetrate larger accounts, outside field salespeople are added.

At companies where the complete solution is available in its entirety during the build stage, it will typically be sold through field salespeople. When the company later offers a pared-down functional solution to address the mid- and SMB (small to medium business) market, it will be sold through inside sales. However, these reps may make field sales calls depending upon the situation. Figure 3.4 shows the platform cloud-based sales cycle at the adult stage of sales organization development.

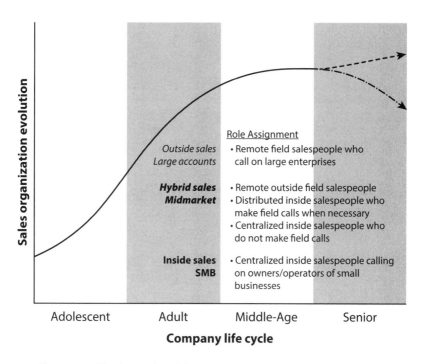

Figure 3.4 Platform cloud-based sales cycle at the adult stage

The sales cycle is different for cloud and on-premise software. The cloud buyer is a business buyer rather than an IT buyer. What you are really selling with the cloud is a solution with a service level agreement attached. With the cloud, we have to deliver 99.9 percent uptime or we are giving money back to the customer. The cloud sales cycle is typically a little shorter and you focus on things like security and service level rather than selling the technology underneath the solution.

—*Vice President of Sales, Platform Sales Products*

We have two cloud sales teams. One team sells to midmarket accounts, where the deal size is twenty to thirty seats. They sell entirely over the phone. The other team goes after large accounts and their model looks more like a commercial software sales model. They have named account sales reps call-ing on accounts in-person.

—Vice President of Sales, Platform Sales Products

Point-Specific Sales Trends

Point-specific sales involve a single solution (or a set of finite complementary functionality offerings) usually targeted to solve the business problems of a single department within an organiza-tion. The purchase decision is typically made by a small number of decision makers, most likely at the lower level of the organization, with decision approval from midlevel management. For example, a résumé tracking system is a point-specific solution sold to the human resources department as shown in figure 3.5.

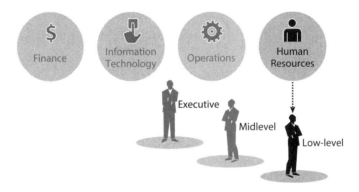

Figure 3.5 Point-specific sales cycle

A point-specific sale can be classified as freeware, simple, or complex. The freeware point-specific sale refers to the initial prod-uct available to the user without any cost. Customers serve them-selves and download the free product from the company website. This limited-use version of the commercially available product is part of a "land and expand" strategy to establish initial product use, and then convert users into paying customers later using inside or outside sales.

The simple point-specific sale is complementary to the customer's existing environment. It is sold as an addition to the way business is being conducted today. The simple point-specific sales primarily utilizes an inside sales model based on geography, which is later verticalized and segmented by company size, with the addition of outside sales field reps calling on large accounts.

The complex point-specific sale may require the customer to break a pre-established relationship with an existing vendor. This entails a "rip and replace" strategy where the existing vendor's products are completely replaced by newer technology or an entirely different way of doing business. This sales effort requires an outside salesperson and expands over time to include named large accounts and vertical overlay salespeople. Midmarket outside or inside sales reps may be added depending upon the complexity of the product. Figure 3.6 shows the sales organization's evolution and the three point-specific sales cycle types.

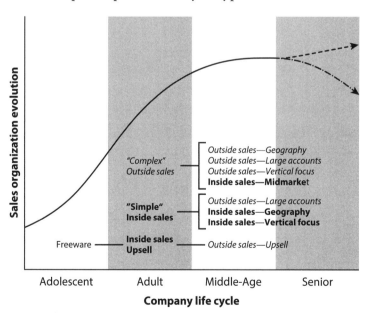

Figure 3.6 Point-specific sales cycle organization evolution

We feel like we figured out the model. Two years ago, we really didn't have an inside sales team and now it's the area that's growing fastest. We have scaled back on the enterprise side. Now we have this formula figured out and we add people to both teams in equal percentages.

—*Vice President of Sales, Point-Specific Sales Products*

For nonenterprise deals of $100K or smaller, they all ultimately move to a phone-based selling strategy. With inside sales, you can drive more head count, onboard them faster, enable them to become more productive quickly, manage them more easily, and do it in a call center fashion. After the $100K number, deal requirements change. Also, some verticals require more face-to-face meetings, such as healthcare, aerospace, defense, and federal government because of regulatory and compliance issues.

—*Vice President of Sales, Point-Specific Sales Products*

4. Attributes of Great Technology Sales Organizations

What separates great from good technology sales organizations? Based on my research, the evidence suggests the best business-to-business sales organizations share specific patterns of organizational structure and behavior. These similarities are defined by the following seven different attributes. Underperforming or weaker sales organizations tend to miss some or all of these critical characteristics.

1. *Strong centralized command and control with local authority.* The greatest single influence on the success of a sales organization is how the sales leaders create the culture and environment

for the people who work for them. The best organizations have strong leaders who exercise authoritarian control, dictate team direction, and establish the codes of behavior that all team members must abide by. Although these tenets are similar to those used within military units to enforce the chain of command, sales leaders prefer to use motivation and the force of their character before employing the power associated with their title.

In addition, the senior leadership team typically does not micromanage the sales teams below. Instead, there is independent and autonomous local decision making that operates within the guidelines and protocols established by the leaders. Rest assured, the actions of the lower levels of the organization always take into account the goals and desires of the senior leaders.

2. *Darwinian sales culture.* The Darwinian sales culture has two aspects. The first is that the next hire by the organization is of such high quality and capability that it challenges the more tenured sales team members to perform at their highest level (so that they do not rest on their laurels). The second is that the sales organization is continually comparing each member's performance against stringent criteria. Weak sales team members who do not contribute their revenue share are quickly let go.

3. *United against a common enemy.* The best sales organizations, those that are driven to succeed against all obstacles, have an archrival whom they resent and fear. This is very important since it drives individual behavior. A higher win ratio occurs because accounts are pursued with greater preparation, higher intensity, and a life or death seriousness.

4. *Competitive but cohesive team.* A sales organization is an amalgamation of cliques. For example, a sales organization may

comprise three areas: North America, Asia-Pacific, and Europe/Middle East/Africa. North American sales may be divided into three regions: east, midwest, and west. Great sales organizations have more than a friendly rivalry between the various regions. Each region is on a mission to prove it is the best. Although all the salespeople and their leaders are intensely competitive individuals by nature, they will support their area and regional teammates when needed. It is likely that the key sales management leaders have worked together before at prior companies. They know, like, and respect each other.

5. *DIY attitude.* Many underperforming sales organizations share something in common. The sales organization tends to blame the other areas of the organization (engineering, marketing, support, and so on) for its own failings. Members of top performing sales organizations not only take ownership for their own success, they have a "do it yourself" attitude. For example, they will not solely rely on marketing to provide leads but build their own pipeline without any expectations of leads from marketing. When problems arise at customer accounts, they will spearhead resolution efforts.

6. *Suspension of negative belief systems.* Sales is a career that experiences tremendous highs and lows. Circumstances can change very quickly. A competitor's new technology may leapfrog yours. The company whose account you worked so hard to close may want its money back because the product isn't working right. The funnel of deals you have been counting on for months can disappear in a few minutes. Sales team members in great organizations do not fixate on negative thoughts that can prevent them from moving forward and taking action. They are not debilitated by bad news or self-defeating rumors heard.

7. *Energy and esprit de corps.* While all sales organizations can be defined as a collection of individuals trying to succeed as a team, there is a tremendous amount of peer pressure inside great sales organizations. If a salesperson doesn't achieve his revenue targets, not only did he fail personally, but he also let his team down. But when salespeople post great numbers, they are honored and respected by the team. This type of culture is different from the individual "every man for himself" environment because it fosters cohesiveness, morale, and a continually high energy level.

Members of great sales organizations don't believe they are in sales by happenstance. They are professionals who believe they are fulfilling their own destiny. As an organization, they are united for a greater purpose than themselves. While the company's goal may be to go public or reach certain revenue milestones, the greatest sales organizations are on a never-ending mission to prove to the world they are the best.

5. Key Technology Sales Organization Metrics

This chapter includes key sales performance metrics based on in-depth interviews and extensive surveys with over one hundred top sales leaders at leading high technology companies and business services providers.

Percent of Organization Achieving Quota

The overall average percentage of technology salespeople that achieved 100 percent of quota last year was 60 percent. However, the number of salespeople who achieved 100 percent varied greatly by sales organization. Twenty-six percent of sales leaders reported that 70 percent or more of their salespeople made quota. Fifty-four percent of sales leaders reported that between 50 and 69 percent of their salespeople made quota. Twenty percent of sales leaders report that less than half of their salespeople made quota.

> If your investors, analysts, or the financial market have you pegged at a revenue number, you will add a buffer onto the overall quota being assigned because you don't want to be "flying skinny" and miss the revenue target. Your internal operating plan will always be higher than the street's expectations. The plan never assumes that you will have quota attainment by all the reps. Quota attainment has navigated between 40-60 percent for us. Ideally, you want 60 percent of the team reaching their goal. The buffer will vary based upon the stage of the company and size. In the early days, you want a real big buffer, but in a larger, publicly held company, it might be lower, at 18 percent or so.
> —*Vice President of Sales*

Quota Attainment Average

The average percentage of salespeople that achieved 100 percent of quota last year varied by industry, as shown in figure 5.1.

Computer software	52%
Cloud and SaaS (software as a service)	61%
Computer hardware	60%
Telecommunications (including managed services and outsourcing)	66%

Figure 5.1 Annual quota attainment averages

Average Annual Quota

The overall average annual quotas were $2.7 million for an outside field salesperson and $985,000 for an inside salesperson. Industry averages are shown in figure 5.2.

	Outside salesperson annual quota	*Inside salesperson annual quota*
Computer software	$3.2M	$1,220,000
Cloud and SaaS	$1.6M	$795,000
Computer hardware	$4.2M	$1,350,000
Telecommunications	$3.3M	$730,000

Figure 5.2 Annual quotas for outside and inside salespeople

Average On-Target Earnings

The average annual on-target earnings, including salary, commission, and bonuses for field and inside salespeople at 100 percent of quota, are shown in figure 5.3.

	Outside salesperson on-target earnings	*Inside salesperson on-target earnings*
Computer software	$240,000	$120,000
Cloud and SaaS	$210,000	$100,000
Computer hardware	$180,000	$80,000
Telecommunications	$150,000	$85,000

Figure 5.3 Average annual on-target earnings for outside and inside salespeople

Sales Force Composition

The average overall sales force composition was 65 percent outside field sales, 25 percent inside sales, and 10 percent channel sales. In figure 5.4 the functional roles are broken down by industry.

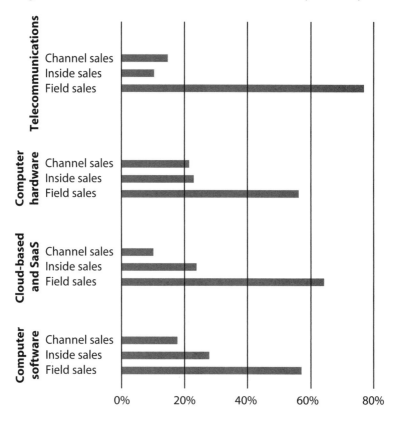

Figure 5.4 Percentage of salespeople by functional role

Vertical Sales Adoption

Sixty-four percent of vice presidents for technology sales organizations indicated they have vertical sales specialists on their sales force (public sector, finance, healthcare, manufacturing, and so on). Seventeen percent do not currently have vertical specialists but plan to do so in the future. Nineteen percent do not plan to verticalize.

> You have to verticalize certain industries, like government, because you need salespeople who understand how to navigate their processes, which are different from commercial organizations. It makes a lot of sense to verticalize around industries like healthcare, telco, and financial services.
> —*Vice President of Sales*

> We can't afford a sales model that is completely based on verticals. It would take too many people. Our salespeople will have one major and one minor vertical. The accounts are made up from companies in those verticals. We make sure the salesperson is trained in detail and knowledgeable on their major vertical, to a lesser degree about their minor vertical, and then on an as-needed basis for everything else.
> —*Vice President of Sales*

SMB Specialization

Sixty-three percent indicated they have specialized inside salespeople that are dedicated to SMB or midmarket sales. Less than one-half of these inside sales reps are allowed to make field sales calls when necessary. Thirty-seven percent do not have SMB sales teams.

> As we grew, we used a sales force matrix strategy by size and type of the company to add more salespeople in the field. For example, we might segment at the $100M revenue mark and have one sales group calling on accounts over $100M and the other calling on accounts under $100M. The second overlay might be geographic region and the third overlay would be the specific industry verticals we target, such as manufacturing,

financial services, and service industries. From this point, you can add microverticals such as automotive, aerospace, and medical to the manufacturing vertical.

—*Vice President of Sales*

Outside and Inside Sales Staff Shift

During the past two years, over twice as many vice presidents of sales reported moving to an inside sales model as opposed to a field sales model as shown in figure 5.5. For 34 percent, the shift was slight, but 12 percent of study participants reported a significant shift from a field sales model to an inside sales model. Twenty-one percent reported a shift from inside sales to a field sales model including 13 percent who reported a significant shift and 8 percent who reported a slight shift.

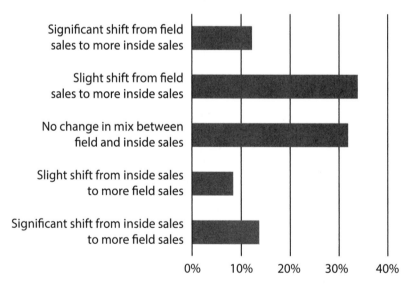

Figure 5.5 Shift in sales staff

Three key factors determine when a sales organization will utilize a field or inside sales model: the sales organization's stage of development, the complexity of the products that are sold, and, to a lesser extent, the sales leader's perception of inside and outside sales model effectiveness. The positive perception of the inside sales model has increased due to many societal shifts, including the technical sophistication of today's buyers and how they research and make buying decisions online.

> Field sales is more strategic, meeting with C-level executives and developing business innovation to help them grow their business, versus inside, which is higher volume and not as in depth the majority of the time.
> —*Vice President of Sales*

> Inside salespeople have to be disciplined, make cold calls, follow up, get volume, and close the deals quickly. Outside people have to develop longer-term relationships, as most transactions are larger and require more sales skills and knowledge of the long-term wants, needs, and expectations of the customer.
> —*Vice President of Sales*

Today, there is a changing perception among technology sales leaders about the strategic role inside sales performs. This is due in part to the benefits sales leaders believe the inside sales model provides in terms of scaling activity, growing the organization, and attacking specific markets. Vice presidents of sales cited several advantages of an inside sales model compared to a field sales model, as shown in figure 5.6.

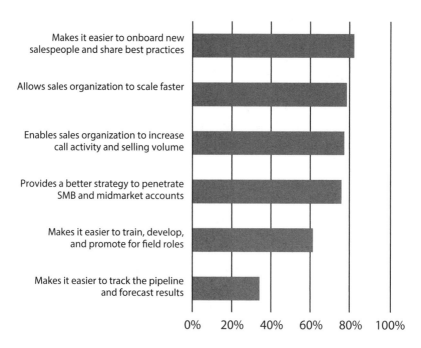

Figure 5.6 Advantages of inside sales model cited by sales leaders

6. Technology Sales Management Styles

The structure and effectiveness of the technology sales department will mirror the sales management style of its leaders. This is because sales leaders naturally imprint themselves on their organization. Therefore, it can be argued that the vice president of sales is the most important person within a company because he is in charge of its most critical assets: customers and the revenue they generate.

Each vice president of sales, like all people, has a unique personality. Some are gregarious. Some are assertive. Some are action-oriented. But even with their individual differences, there are recognized patterns of behavior, which have allowed me to catalog their styles of sales management.

I have found that seven management styles are most prevalent: mentor, expressive, sergeant, Teflon, micromanager, overconfident, and amateur. Most likely, a sales leader will use several different management styles and move from one style to another depending on the situation.

To better understand these management styles, I asked vice presidents of sales from leading high technology companies to estimate what percentage of their time they used a particular style and then rank the applicability of the style to the success in their role on a scale of 1 (least important) to 5 (most important). Figure 6.1 is a summary chart of findings, showing the average results for the study group. A description of each style follows.

Management style	Percent time used	Importance ranking 1 (low) to 5 (high)
Mentor	26%	4.3
Expressive	30%	4.0
Sergeant	18%	3.2
Teflon	10%	2.0
Micromanager	7%	3.3
Overconfident	6%	1.8
Amateur	3%	1.0

Figure 6.1 Technology sales management styles usage and rating

Mentor

Mentors are charismatic leaders and sales experts who measure their success using three criteria: exceeding revenue goals, creating an environment where the entire team can succeed, and helping all team members realize their individual potential. Mentors are confident in their own abilities and possess the business insight to know what needs to be done and how to do it. On average, study participants reported they used the mentor management style 26 percent of the time. As a driver of success, they gave mentor management style the highest ranking of all the styles at 4.3.

Expressive

Expressive managers are people-oriented with a flair for sharing their emotions and amplifying the emotions of those around them. They have a natural ability to put people at ease but are also quite comfortable extolling or admonishing the team. Expressive managers create an environment where a considerable amount of energy is focused on how their organization is thought of and perceived within the company. Study participants indicated they used the expressive style 30 percent on average and ranked the style's importance at 4.

Sergeant

The sergeant is named after the field sergeant in a military organization. Sergeants develop an intense loyalty to their team, perhaps even greater than their personal loyalty to their company. They are hard workers who are constantly worrying about their "troops." They will even sacrifice their own best interests and tolerate personal hardships if they feel it will benefit their team. The sergeant management style was used 18 percent of the time, and its importance was ranked at 3.2.

Teflon

Teflon managers are pleasant, agreeable, and polite people. However, unlike sergeants, they tend not to have deep personal relationships with their sales team members. Another characteristic of Teflon managers is their ability to stay above the daily fray of politics. Regardless of the situation, Teflon managers are even keeled and rarely frazzled. The Teflon management style was used 10 percent of the time and its importance was ranked at 2.

Micromanager

Micromanagers are the most organized and methodical of all management types. They have a strong sense of responsibility to their company and they pride themselves on achieving their revenue goals. They tend to be all-or-nothing thinkers who want things done their way. The micromanager style was used 7 percent of the time and its importance was ranked 3.3.

Overconfident

Overconfident managers tend to be more self-centered. They are charming and gregarious in public and excellent on sales calls. They tend not to be open to feedback and will get the job done their way and succeed at any cost. The overconfident management style was used 6 percent of the time and its importance was ranked at 1.8.

Amateur

The amateur management style is not necessarily equated to someone new to sales management. Rather, the style reflects that the person is outside of his comfort zone in a new management role, working with an unfamiliar product at a new company, or in a new industry. As a result, his management style may suffer an identity crisis until he is able to build back his practical sales experience. Study participants indicated they experienced the amateur management style 3 percent of the time and ranked the style's importance at 1.

Which management style is best? This depends upon the sales organization's stage of development. Running a medium-sized $50 million sales department in the compete stage requires a different skill set than leading a large billion-dollar sales organization in the maintain stage. Culling an inefficient organization requires a specific management style. Nowhere is the sales leader's impact greater than in start-ups, where the vice president of sales must single-handedly build the sales model, recruit the team, and personally persuade customers to buy.

PART II

Sales Cycle Strategy

7. Top Reasons Technology Salespeople Lose

How technology evaluators describe their selection process and why they made their final decision is always fascinating. One of the most interesting parts of these interviews is learning why the competing salespeople lost.

There's a tendency to assume that the losing salespeople lacked the sales prowess that the winner possessed, or their product was inferior in some way. However, in the overwhelming majority of the interviews the evaluators ranked all the competing salespeople and the feature sets of their products as being roughly equal. This suggests that other factors separate the winner from the losers, with some being out of the salesperson's control. These key factors are described below and accompanied by a corresponding win-loss study interview quote.

- *Incumbent advantage.* The incumbent vendor has a huge sales cycle advantage and the tendency is to win business by default. Based upon my research, the odds of unseating an incumbent vendor are typically about one in five.

  It's a pain to switch vendors. It's a pain to analyze whether you should or not. We naturally prefer working with our existing vendors.
  —*Vice President of Purchasing*

- *Inability to remove risk.* Customers are never 100 percent sure they are purchasing the right product. Regardless of their confident demeanor, on the inside they experience fear, uncertainty, and doubt. The ability to remove perceived risk plays a key role in determining who wins the deal.

  It sorts itself out pretty fast—those who will and won't make it with us. We are a big company, so there's always a tendency to go with the big players. Who are your proven big-time customers? What resources do you have to get something fixed?
  —*Chief Operating Officer*

- *C-level executive access.* Because every major purchase involves executive level approval, a salesperson's goal is to connect with a busy executive and conduct a meaningful face-to-face meeting. However, one of the toughest jobs in sales is to penetrate the C-suite and there is a direct correlation of winning to the number of interactions the salesperson has with executives during the sales cycle.

  Every salesperson is trying to get into my office and explain how their wonderful products will save me tons of money. Very few do because most don't understand what it takes to sit across the table from me.
  —*Chief Executive Officer*

- *Business solution focus.* A common theme is that both the winning and losing salespeople knew their products very well. However, winners were better able to prove their value as a business partner with the expertise to solve the customer's problem.

What's *wrong* with salespeople is they're typically selling a product. I don't need a product unless it solves one of my business problems.
—*President*

- *Ineffective messaging.* Successful communication is the cornerstone of all sales. Winners have the ability to tailor compelling messages that resonate with the evaluators across the organization and decision makers up and down the chain of command.

    We are a skeptical group, and they lost the deal during their presentation. They said they were different and much better than what we have, but they didn't provide enough proof. What they said didn't really apply to us.
    —*Chief Financial Officer*

- *Poor presales resources.* The complex sales process is typically a team effort that involves presales technical experts. Losers were often cited as having inferior presales resources, and equally important, the lack of knowledgeable experts who attended meetings throughout the sales cycle.

    The vendor we chose has a group of smart, dedicated, and customer-oriented people. To a great degree, I don't think their products and services are different from their competitors'. They distinguish themselves with their people.
    —*Vice President of Supply Chain*

- *Lack of an internal coach.* A clear difference between winners and losers is the winners developed an internal "coach" within the account. Coaches are evaluators who provide proprietary information about the selection process, status of the competition, and help the salesperson determine his course of action.

Anytime we had a question, the sales rep attacked it. He would get his people on the phone within a day to answer how we could do something. He listened to what we were trying to do and he knew his resources. He earned our trust so we were much more open with him.

—*Chief Information Officer*

- *Out-of-range pricing.* Time after time, interviewees reported they did not pick the lowest cost option. Savvy evaluators realize there will always be a low bidder. However, there is an acceptable price range the prospect is willing to pay and this can be anywhere from 10 to 25 percent higher than the lowest proposal (depending upon industry and products). Solutions priced outside of this boundary are rarely selected.

  Price is always important, but we did not buy the lowest priced solution. Many other factors, including the fit between organizations, render pricing to a secondary factor. With that said, I never want to buy the highest priced solution.

  —*Vice President of Technology*

- *They are outsold!* Winning salespeople establish their credibility and maintain account control. Losers operate in a world based on incomplete information and ineffective sales execution.

  I can tell you what makes a bad rep. They don't come prepared when they see me. They don't understand my business. They don't research what we have in place or understand what challenges we might be facing. They want us to do the legwork and educate them about everything and I don't have the time. If you don't know what you are asking me for and why you are asking about it, forget it. Great reps have done their homework, so when they are in my office they can talk to me knowl-

edgeably. They cut the bull. They don't tell me they can do things they can't. They're honest.
—*IT Manager*

Losing is always a frustrating, humbling, and embarrassing event. If you find yourself in this circumstance, it's time to ask yourself if any of these factors above were at the root cause of your loss.

8. Should We Compete?

As a general rule, it is best to be the first salesperson in an account. The chance to understand a customer's environment first, establish relationships, and set the criteria for the selection process is an obvious advantage. However, it's not always possible to find a customer first, and sometimes arriving first doesn't matter. What matters is the strength of your position versus the competition.

Define your strength compared to your competitor's in one of three ways: you have the advantage, you are equal, or you are outclassed. The three strengths are relationship (the personal relationships you have built in the account), product (the technical merits of your product and perception of your company in the marketplace), and personnel (the quality and quantity of people who are at your disposal to work on the account).

Defining your account strength can be tricky. First, the marketing department's job is to pump out volumes of propaganda proclaiming that every aspect of the company and its product is superior to the competition. Your product's true strength can be ascertained only with direct customer feedback gained in past sales cycles.

The second reason is more complex. While salespeople say they are directly responsible for winning a deal, there is a natural tendency to blame losses on something other than themselves. The true strength of your competitive position directly correlates to the percentage of deals you win. The only way to accurately gauge how you stack up against the enemy is in head-to-head confrontations.

The decision to pursue an account can be a difficult one. One deciding factor is who has set the tempo in the account—you or a competitor. This is particularly important when your product has a long sales cycle that requires a large investment of your time and your company's resources.

Basing the decision on an honest assessment of competitive strength is critical. For example, you should pursue accounts where you have established personal relationships. If you enjoy product and personnel advantages, you should almost always pursue an account, even if you are late into the deal. If you have product and personnel disadvantages, you must be first into the account to win. If you are on equal footing with the competition, you must be on time at the start of the evaluation process to build a relationship advantage. Figure 8.1 illustrates the tempo rules (when you should arrive in accounts) when your products and personnel are at an advantage, equal to, or at a disadvantage to your competitor's.

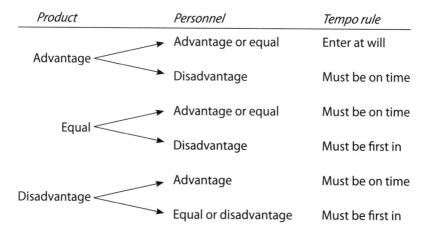

Product	Personnel	Tempo rule
Advantage	Advantage or equal	Enter at will
	Disadvantage	Must be on time
Equal	Advantage or equal	Must be on time
	Disadvantage	Must be first in
Disadvantage	Advantage	Must be on time
	Equal or disadvantage	Must be first in

Figure 8.1 When to pursue the deal

Obviously, many combinations are possible. The decision to work on an account or walk away shouldn't be made solely by the salesperson; it's always wise to get outsiders' opinions. The best people to help you make this call are your sales manager and other members of your team who would work on the account with you. The personnel attribute (whether you are equal, have an advantage, or have a disadvantage) is a direct comparison of your sales skills versus the other competitors'. It also includes the availability, quality, and commitment of the team members (technical presales support, consultants, and management) that will help you win the account. Therefore, it makes sense to get their buy-in before you move forward on any account.

Once engaged in the deal, setting the tempo takes on a new meaning. While a good defense may keep you in the deal, the only way to win is to be on the offense. However, other competitors also want to control the tempo and execute their offensive plans. Meanwhile, the customer wants to dictate the steps taken during the selection process and keep control of the various vendors so they don't run slipshod through the company.

Setting the tempo is the first step in winning the business. Never forget, the only two appropriate positions to be in at the end of the deal are first place, as the winner, or last place, as the first loser. Every place in between is the result of a judgment error.

The sales cycle has a natural evolution. Customers gather information from each vendor. As they gather more information, one vendor begins to look better than the others, its product sounds like it will work better, and the customers feel that vendor will be a better partner. Naturally, that vendor will enjoy an advantage through the remainder of the sales cycle.

However, customers have a dilemma. They still want to collect information from the other vendors to be 100 percent certain they are selecting the right one. Or they may want to complete the evaluation process to show others in or outside their organization (management, colleagues, consultants, or government agencies) that their evaluation was thorough and fair. As a result, they offer the other vendors the customer placebo.

The customer placebo is present in nearly every sales cycle. One vendor is in a unique position of receiving information from the customer that the other vendors don't receive. As the favored vendor and customer spend more time together, a higher level of rapport is developed. While this happens, the customer presents misleading information to the other vendors about their position in the deal, pretending to be more interested in the products than he actually is. Conversely, he may not share critical information or access to company executives as he does with the leading vendor. Unfortunately, the other vendors continue to spend additional resources, time, and effort on an account they have virtually no chance of winning. Figure 8.2 illustrates the impact of the customer placebo.

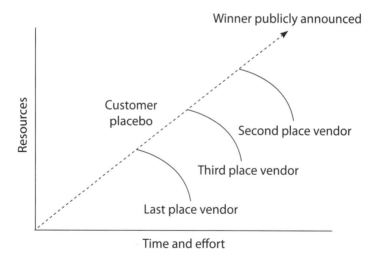

Figure 8.2 Customer placebo

It was an emotional decision. In fact, at the very end when we were making the decision there were days that I really felt the evaluation team was emotionally spent. It was hard on them because we had developed very good relationships with the sales representatives of both firms. I am sure the other solution would have worked for us. If I had to tell you the main reason why we didn't go with them, I am not sure I can. I know I hurt the gentleman who was selling for them, and that disturbs me greatly. Relationships and people's self-worth are very important to me. He truly felt for very good reasons that we were going with him.

—*Chief Executive Officer*

9. Renewal, Persuasion, and Creation Sales Cycles

Technology sales cycles can be classified as transactional or enterprise deals. In transactional deals, the salesperson has only one or two interactions with a potential customer, whereas enterprise deals involve many interactions. For example, simple point-specific product sales are typically transactional deals, while enterprise sales can take many months to close.

The three basic types of sales cycles are renewal, persuasion, and creation deals. Renewal deals involve selling more products and services to existing customers or trying to close a multiyear contract coming up for renewal (such as a three-year cloud application agreement). Persuasion deals are extremely competitive customer evaluations that typically involve the customer creating an RFP (request for proposal) or similar document. In these deals you are usually competing against your archrivals. Finally, in creation deals you target and penetrate a new account to get the customer to use your products for the first time, with the hope the customer will make a much larger purchase in the future.

Each sales cycle requires a different strategy. In renewal deals the goal is to execute a justification strategy, where the customer experiences the benefits from using the solution and working with the vendor to justify renewing the relationship. The salesperson should employ a "sales virus" strategy, where the salesperson continually spreads out to meet everyone in the customer's organization, across all departments and at all levels. He addresses all outstanding issues and provides excellent customer care ensuring the widespread adoption of his solution and its use to the fullest extent by all users. A critical time occurs six months to one year before the actual renewal date. Figure 9.1 shows when the customer begins the decision-making process and decides whether or not to research new vendors or stay with the existing solution.

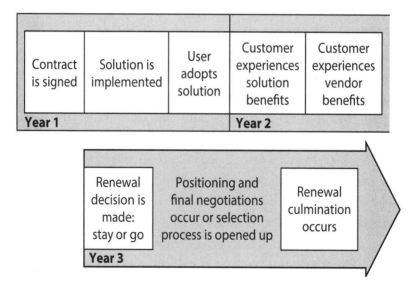

Figure 9.1 Renewal/add-on sales cycle

Persuasion sales cycles are quite different because they are based on the transmission and receipt of information. In essence, they are a series of response-based sales calls where the customer compares your answers to his questions against those from your competitors. As a result, all the salespeople involved in the deal are continually saying to the customer, "We are the best because . . ."

The persuasion sales cycle has four critical moments. The first is prior to the sales cycle starting. The first salesperson to build relationships and influence the selection process criteria obviously has a huge advantage. The second most important moment is the vendor presentation. Why? Because this is one of the few moments during the entire sales cycle when the entire evaluation team, all the key influencers, and senior executives are present. In some cases, it is your only opportunity to win over the senior executives. Therefore, your presentation has to be persuasive to differentiate yourself from the competition, and be flawlessly executed. Since the customer will see presentations from every competitor in a very short period of time of a week or so, the decision is frequently made then but not publicly announced until much later.

The third important moment is the vendor interview. This is one of the few chances you have to develop relationships and uncover the political structure of the account. Asking questions is an excellent way to demonstrate your technical knowledge, domain expertise, and provide evidence that you know best practices of your industry. Questions show your competency and the quality of your company.

The fourth most important moment is after the customer narrows down the solutions and decides to complete hands-on testing of the product finalists or make site visits to existing customer installations. This will determine which vendor wins when the competition between vendors is extremely close. Figure 9.2 shows the four moments during the persuasion sales cycle.

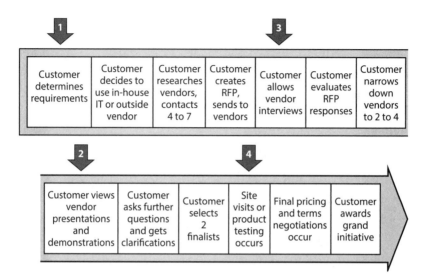

Figure 9.2 Persuasion sales cycle with key moments shown

The truth of the matter is that I knew Vendor A from my previous company. The other vendors never really had a chance.

—*Vice President, IT strategy*

We made our decision after the vendor presentations. It was clear at that point who had the better solution and was more prepared to work with us.

—*Chief Technology Officer*

It became apparent quickly that it would be a two-horse race and we knew who would win.

—*Chief Marketing Officer*

Creation sales cycles are the opposite of the information-based persuasion sales cycle. They are hypothesis sales based upon establishing trust where the salesperson says to the customer, "We can help you do X better. Let us come in and prove it." The salesperson's goal is to win a "beachhead" deal and get the customer to start using his company's product, or start a small project to validate the solution. The hope is that the project will be successful and culminate with a big purchase. Figure 9.3 shows the typical steps of the creation sales cycle.

Account is targeted	Solution is introduced	Sex appeal demonstration is presented	Site survey is conducted	ROI presentation is made	Full validation demonstration is presented

Evaluation or proof of concept pilot is conducted	Rally demonstration is presented	Beachhead project is implemented	Additional projects are earned	Grand initiative is proposed

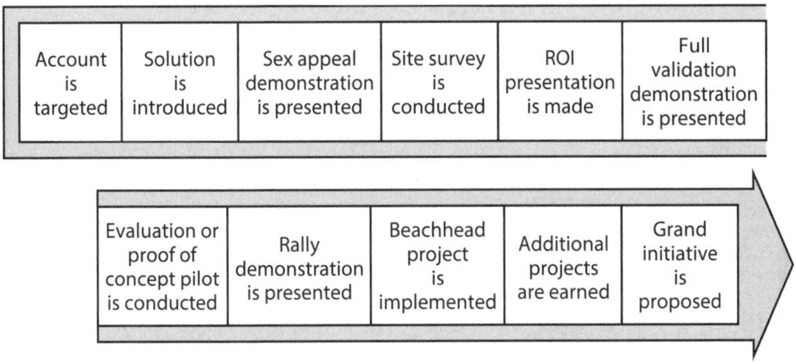

Figure 9.3 Creation sales cycle

We started on a small scale project with them. If you prove one project works, we'll trust you with the next one and the next one.

—*Vice President of Marketing*

It is better to have business level people drive the project. Everyone here looks at IT and says, "They just want to spend money."

—*General Manager*

The creation sales cycle is based upon establishing trust. Unlike the persuasion sales cycle based upon persuasive words, the creation sales cycle is based upon completing actions that create trust, build respect, and form alliances with employees who will promote the solution within their organization. Every interaction is intended to build momentum behind the project's initiative. There are product demonstrations designed to create initial interest and follow-on demonstrations to rally support and validate the breadth of the solution. An extensive return on investment (ROI) analysis should be provided so internal coaches can justify the investment in the solution to their peers and company leadership.

> I have vendors beating on my door saying, "Give us a chance to make your life better." They literally line up at my door to do it.
> —*Senior Director of IT*

10. Technology Sales Cycle Strategy

Technology sales cycle strategy can be defined as the overriding plan to win the business by establishing and maintaining account control. The goals are to neutralize competitors' advantages and place them in a defensive position, while always anticipating "no decision" and motivating the customer to buy. The strategy is based upon executing a series of customer interactions (sales calls, presentations, demonstrations, and so on) and maneuvers. Maneuvers (such as phone calls, letters, and e-mails) are specific actions intended to move a salesperson to the next interaction.

Although maneuvers are typically small steps, they can have a great impact on the deal. Maneuvers include facts and other proof points that put the customer's mind at ease and motivate him to meet with you again. For example, let's say a customer is looking at a competitor's product and hesitates to meet with you. One maneuver is to e-mail the customer an industry article that rates your product better than the competition. After reading the article, the customer decides to let you present your solution. The idea is you have to maneuver into position to make the next interaction. Maneuvers prevent you from remaining at the same stage in the sales cycle or being eliminated. Figure 10.1 illustrates the interrelationships between strategy, goals, customer interactions, and maneuvers.

Strategy	The overriding plan to win the business by establishing and maintaining account control
Goals	Neutralize competitors' advantages and place them in a defensive position; anticipate "no decision" and motivate the customer to buy
Tactics {	**Customer interactions**

Sales calls	Follow-on meetings	Site visits	Product evaluations
Presentations	Demonstrations	Site surveys	

Maneuvers

Phone calls	Letters	Data sheets	Reviews
E-mails	Documents	Specifications	Manuals

Figure 10.1 Technology sales strategy, goals, and tactics

The sales cycle is a sequence of action points, such as sales calls, demonstrations, surveys, and site visits. However, each party has different goals. Your competitors are trying to eliminate you from the next customer interaction. Meanwhile, you are a suitor courting a customer into forming a long-term relationship, akin to a marriage. You accomplish this by scheduling interactions to explain your advantages and the merits of your company. The successful outcome of each interaction provides the opportunity to build momentum in the account, as evidenced by the customer's commitment to spend more time with you through additional interactions as shown in figure 10.2.

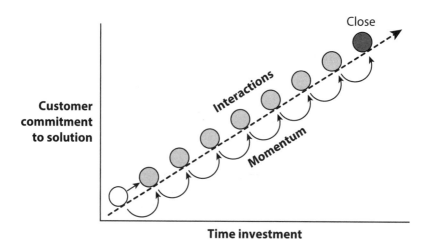

Figure 10.2 Sales cycle interactions and momentum

Customers have a different set of goals. Relationships are expensive and involve investments of valuable time and money. Customers have to spend time to determine whether a product's characteristics are as they have been represented. They have to spend time evaluating other suitors to determine whether they are picking the best possible partner. They have to spend time learning to use the new products they select, implementing them, and most likely, fixing product problems. In addition, customers have to acquire the solution and pay ongoing fees for support. They want to make sure they are selecting the best partner and have found their perfect match.

During a long sales cycle of several months it's easy to focus on individual battles and lose sight of winning the war. The sales cycle is reduced to a series of interactions without an overriding strategy. You become fixated on the next interaction, proceeding from the initial call to the sales presentation, from the presentation to the demonstration, and from the demonstration to the product evaluation. The moment you work on an account without a strategy, you relinquish account control. Worse yet is when the details of the battles—where, when, and how they will be fought—are out of your control because they are determined exclusively by the customer or even a competitor.

Meanwhile, competitors are trying to outdo and sabotage you with their own maneuvers. For example, they provide the customer with believable information that contradicts yours. Therefore, the sales cycle naturally disintegrates into a "he said–she said" type of quarrel. This leaves the customer not only confused but sometimes in analysis paralysis from receiving too much contradictory information, which sets the stage for the dreaded "no decision."

If you find yourself in an account bickering with a competitor, take a step back and ask yourself, What is my strategy to win the account? Is the customer or competition controlling my interactions? Most importantly, am I winning the business? You can chart your position in an account depending upon the amount of information you acquire and the level of rapport you develop with the decision makers and influencers. Figure 10.3 illustrates how to determine your bearings and correlates to your competitiveness to win the business. You are in the position of being blind, competitive, or in control.

> We went through the standard process. We issued an RFP and conducted demonstrations, reference calls, pricing discussions, and negotiations. I'll be the first to admit that sometimes it's who knows somebody. Like any other corporation, if so-and-so at some software company knows our CIO and is a friend, they get their foot in the door. There are some decisions like that.
>
> —*Director of Information Technology*

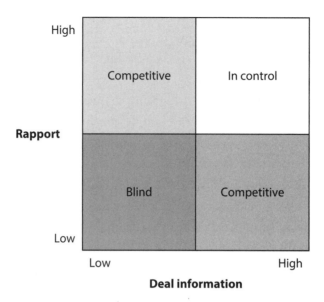

Figure 10.3 Sales cycle quadrant positions

The vertical axis measures the amount of rapport you enjoy with a customer. For example, in a brand new account you would have low or no rapport. A high rapport account would be one where you have personal friendships based on many years of interactions with the customer. The horizontal axis measures the amount of truthful information being shared by the customer. This is an assessment of the quantity and quality of the information you have uncovered and includes unique information the competition doesn't receive.

The "blind" quadrant is where you have little information about the deal and little rapport has been established. You usually find yourself in this unenviable position at the beginning of every new sales cycle. Your immediate goals are to collect information by discovery and start developing rapport. As the sales cycle progresses, if you are unable to collect pertinent information or develop significant rapport, you should stop working the deal.

The amount of information salespeople receive from customers will vary. For example, the evaluation criteria could be extremely well documented. A request for proposal may be three hundred pages long with descriptions about the customer's environment and detailed questions for the vendor to answer. However, this is only the external aspect of the product selection. The internal politics of the selection process isn't publicly revealed. It's by establishing relationships and rapport that salespeople learn the inner workings of the customer.

In the lower right-hand quadrant, you have lots of information but little rapport. The objective is to move quickly to establish relationships and create rapport. Without relationships, the likelihood of winning the deal decreases as the sales cycle progresses.

In the upper left-hand quadrant, you have established rapport but have a low level of information about the customer's requirements or a high level of uncertainty whether the deal will happen. For example, you may have painstakingly developed relationships within the applications group of the IT department of a Fortune 100 company. However, because of the IT department's size and bureaucracy, the application group is unsure of the project's direction and approval. Therefore, even though rapport is high and the application group has identified technical needs, the knowledge of whether there is a deal to be closed is low.

Ultimately, you want to be in the "in control" quadrant. Here, you have established rapport and receive proprietary information that the other vendors aren't. In addition, an interesting paradigm shift occurs in the vendor-customer relationship. The customer begins working with the vendor as a long-term partner while still in the sales cycle. For example, this occurs when issues arise about the functionality of the product and the customer works with the vendor to find an acceptable solution. This shift from being treated like one of the vendors to becoming part of the customer team is very noticeable.

You move from quadrant to quadrant as the sales cycle progresses. Moving from the blind quadrant to a competitive quadrant marks forward progress in the deal. During the sales cycle, you can also experience setbacks that move you back into the position of being blind. For example, if your coach suddenly leaves the company or is reassigned, you are blind again.

An implicit strategy is associated with your position in every quadrant. In each quadrant, execute a strategy that counteracts a competitor or corrects a weakness in your current position. The quadrant strategies shown in figure 10.4 are retreat, attack, confront status quo, leverage relationships, and maintain account control.

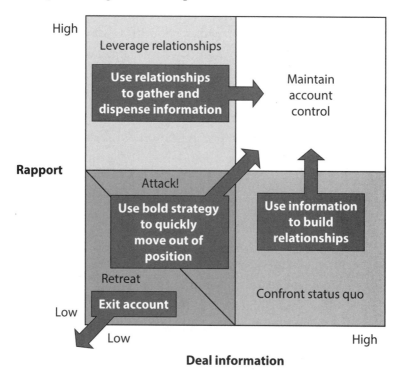

Figure 10.4 Strategy associated with each sales cycle position

Retreat

It takes a lot of discipline to walk away from an account that has involved a heavy investment of time, energy, and emotions. Knowing when to retreat from an account where there is little chance of winning is just as important as knowing when you will win. It makes no sense to work on deals where your involvement is not wanted or appreciated. The salesperson with the poor pipeline continually tries to pry the customer's front door open with his broken foot.

Attack

You will lose the deal if you remain in the attack position for longer than the beginning of the sales cycle. The attack position dictates that the salesperson execute a bold strategy to immediately move from this position. You can attack the customer's business model and processes to make him think differently. Attack the customer's selection process and show him his methodology will not result in the best possible decision. Identify important research steps he is missing and other key considerations that should be included. Bypass the established evaluation process and present your case directly to the customer's key executives. Motivate the customer to spend time with you through a variety of tactics including price discounts, service level guarantees, and other valuable concessions.

Attack the competition and furnish unbiased comparison information that shows you're better. This can include unsuccessful customers, critical industry analyst comments, negative press reports and reviews, and published third-party benchmarks that contrast performance. Provide benchmarks that prove your performance is better. Whatever the attack, it must be bold to interrupt the sales cycle: create fear, uncertainty, and doubt (FUD); and focus the attention back on you. Finally, the attack must be done in the most professional way possible so as to not alienate the customer.

Confront Status Quo

In the confront status quo position, the salesperson has a high amount of information but little customer rapport and few, if any, substantial relationships. In this position, use information to draw attention to your solution to build relationships. Think about all the different types of information you can provide a prospective client:

- Latest industry trends
- Metrics and statistics to benchmark and improve the prospect's business performance
- Best practices and practical advice from current customers
- Information about direct competitors and top performing companies in the prospect's marketplace
- The impact of new technologies and related products on the bottom line
- Developments in other parts of the organization
- Guidance to minimize risk during the selection process
- Information about the other vendors that are being evaluated

Utilize a wide range of colleagues to help you disseminate information and infiltrate the account, such as system engineers, consultants, sales management, company leaders, and channel partners with pre-existing relationships.

Leverage Relationships

In the leverage relationships position, execute a "high and wide" strategy to build deeper relationships up and down the chain of command and across all departments of the company.

Through these different relationships you are able to gather information to assess your position, and the interactions enable you to execute your sales cycle strategy. Most importantly, you can develop internal coaches to serve as your eyes and ears when you are not around.

Your coach can introduce you to other key decision makers and influencers involved in the selection process. These introductions take advantage of the theory of attached relationships, where the salesperson is attached to an existing relationship and bestowed with the same qualities, such as standing, character, and reputation. Assuming the introductory relationship is positive, the salesperson is automatically thought of in the same manner.

Maintain Account Control

Only one competing vendor can be in control of an account at a time. In this position you try to protect yourself from the attack strategies of competing vendors. Strive to fortify your personal relationships to deflect the other vendors. Through the natural strength of this position, take the high ground over the other vendors by engaging in only positive tactics that demonstrate integrity or directly influence the selection process. You are in harmony with the customer and the customer will defend you against others. Once in this quadrant, the goal is to stay there for the remaining stages of the sales cycle. The seven requirements associated with account control are as follows:

1. Intimate knowledge of the selection process, along with the negotiation and procurement processes after the finalist has been chosen
2. Ability to influence the selection process or direct stages of the customer's evaluation

3. Trusted relationships and rapport with evaluation team members and other key sales cycle influencers

4. Ability to persuade people involved in the selection process to follow your advice and recommendations and disseminate information on your behalf

5. Privileged intelligence about the politics of decision making and who is for or against your solution

6. Accurate information about your account standing and whether you are winning or losing

7. Access to managers and senior executives who must approve and pay for the purchase

11. Sales Strategy Creation

Sales strategy can be broken down into three elements. The first element is the different sales cycle factors that define the type of account you are trying to win. The second element is the account control components that serve as the framework to create and execute the strategy. The final element is the purpose behind customer interactions during the sales cycle as shown in figure 11.1.

> Vendor A came in with quite a few people, and from day one they studied our business processes. Then they came back with a demo that really tried to match as much of our process as possible. They also prepared a very thorough RFP response with lots of material about services and references. They showed us they were organized, had real-world experience, and had a high level of professionalism.
> —*Vice President of Technology*

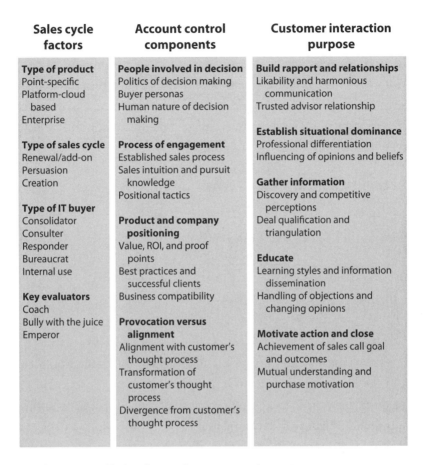

Sales cycle factors	Account control components	Customer interaction purpose
Type of product Point-specific Platform-cloud based Enterprise	**People involved in decision** Politics of decision making Buyer personas Human nature of decision making	**Build rapport and relationships** Likability and harmonious communication Trusted advisor relationship
Type of sales cycle Renewal/add-on Persuasion Creation	**Process of engagement** Established sales process Sales intuition and pursuit knowledge Positional tactics	**Establish situational dominance** Professional differentiation Influencing of opinions and beliefs
Type of IT buyer Consolidator Consulter Responder Bureaucrat Internal use	**Product and company positioning** Value, ROI, and proof points Best practices and successful clients Business compatibility	**Gather information** Discovery and competitive perceptions Deal qualification and triangulation
Key evaluators Coach Bully with the juice Emperor	**Provocation versus alignment** Alignment with customer's thought process Transformation of customer's thought process Divergence from customer's thought process	**Educate** Learning styles and information dissemination Handling of objections and changing opinions
		Motivate action and close Achievement of sales call goal and outcomes Mutual understanding and purchase motivation

Figure 11.1 Technology sales strategy elements

Sales Cycle Factors

The account control factors include the complexity of the product you sell and whether it is point-specific, platform-cloud based, or enterprise. As discussed in chapter 3, each sales cycle varies in complexity depending upon the number of individuals and departments involved in the selection process. The sales strategy will be dependent upon the sales cycle type and whether it is a renewal or add-on, persuasion, or creation (see chapter 9). Strategy is predicated upon the type of IT buyer and which area of the company is driving the decision. Buyer types can be classified as internal use, consolidator, consulter, responder, or bureaucrat (see chapters 17–21). Key evaluators play important roles during the selection process such as a coach, bully with the juice, and emperor (see chapters 23–24). Finally, strategy is predicated upon knowing whether you are behind or in control.

Account Control Components

The second element of strategy is the account control components. The grand strategy should always be based upon an approach to influence the people, politics, and customer's selection process through the strategic positioning of yourself, your company, and your product's unique proof points.

People Involved in Decision

It is critical to identify all the members of the evaluation team and the extended network of influencers and deal approvers in an account. Beyond titles and reporting structure, also seek to understand the politics of decision making and how group decision making will impact the outcome. The complex interrelationships between evaluators and their behavior in group settings are unique to every sales cycle. Specifically, identify each individual buyer's persona (see chapters 55–64) to understand how they process and transmit information, their ability to influence the evaluation group, and the political power they wield. This information is used to plan and execute sales tactics.

Process of Engagement

Most companies have identified a sales process to serve as a framework for the sales organization to engage potential clients.

This playbook provides a step-by-step guide for how the salesperson manages the buying process. The sales process is unique to companies and tailored to the solutions they sell. Figure 11.2 shows examples of the sales engagement process for an on-premises software and mobile application company.

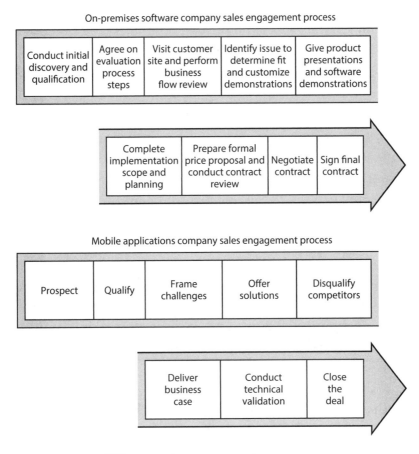

Figure 11.2 Different sales engagement processes

The sales engagement process serves as the blueprint by which the salesperson is ideally working new accounts. However, the salesperson has the difficult task of applying these steps in the real world. The value the salespeople add to the process is their pursuit knowledge and sales intuition based upon previous sales cycle experiences. Sales intuition is the process of comparing a series of past experiences against current circumstances. Think of sales intuition as a highly developed model for making decisions and a powerful heuristic engine constantly learning from every sales call. When a salesperson invokes his intuition, he can recognize account standing and select the best positional sales tactics (see chapter 25) to gain the leadership position.

Product and Company Positioning

To stand out you have to be different. You need a more sophisticated approach that differentiates your solution in the minds of customers. You can't *tell* customers you're unique, different, and one of a kind. You must *demonstrate* it to them, starting with the framework to position your product and company.

Logical arguments alone, no matter how well you present them, will not change skeptics into believers. Finessing customers to change their opinions requires an appeal to their human nature. The positioning of your company and product starts by understanding the strategic, operational, political, and psychological value you provide the evaluators (see chapter 27). This is communicated as you describe how you can solve their problems better than other competitors as the foundation of your sales strategy.

Sales strategy is based upon the creation of intellectual, logical, and psychological appeal. The goal is to build credibility by methodically explaining background information, facts behind your business approach, and your technical superiority that will ensure their success. Sales strategy requires clearly defining the business problem that needs to be solved (or the opportunity that can be created), the cause of the problem (or reason for the opportunity), the possible options that can be utilized to solve the problem (or achieve the opportunity), and the goal realized when the problem is solved (or when the opportunity is realized).

One of the key IT budgeting factors (see chapter 13) that determines which projects will be approved is the investment payback period. IT projects are prioritized by return on investment. Two good rules of thumb are to never assume a purchase is budgeted, and always presume evaluators need your help to justify their purchase internally. Do not expect them to build the business case on their own. Equally important, you don't want your business case presented again. You want to be the person who presents the ROI justification to the key company leaders.

One of the biggest problems most salespeople have is they are too eager to tell the customer about their products. They do not build a story line that piques customer interest. Instead of launching into the product line and technical aspects of the products, the focus should be on the success of existing clients and the best practices you provide. Customer examples (see chapter 52) are very important. Presenting examples from companies that mirror the prospect's business objectives has a powerful impact.

Your strategy should be based upon diagnosing the customer's situation using an unbiased third-party point of view. Do you understand the customer's problem and have the credibility to recommend a solution? Do you understand how to solve their problem from the strategic, operational, and financial perspective (including all costs, ROI, and payback scenarios)? Have you provided real-world results from your existing clients and other tangible evidence that your solution is better than the others? If so, then you have shown your business compatibility and demonstrated you are a fit.

Provocation versus Alignment

The drive to take command of a situation is instrumental to a salesperson's success. Just as a doctor must sometimes prescribe a painful treatment to heal a patient, in some sales situations you must control prospective customers to help them. Conversely, at other accounts you must align with their business strategy and follow their decision-making process explicitly. In the next chapter we'll review when to align, transform, or divert the customer's thought process.

Customer Interaction Purpose

Salespeople work with the unpredictable part of the sales process: people. Their job is to formulate an interaction strategy based upon the people who comprise the organizations they are trying to sell to. This is one of the most important aspects of sales strategy that the salesperson controls.

Every customer interaction can have different purposes. At the foundation are personal likability and rapport. Rapport is a special relationship between two individuals based upon harmonious communication. The salesperson's job is to build rapport with a wide variety of people across the company. You have to communicate with lower-level technical staff, midlevel managers, and most importantly, C-level executives. To do so, you need to change your demeanor and speak different languages depending upon the person you are meeting with. You wouldn't think of talking to a CFO as you would a computer programmer.

The purpose of the interaction is to establish situational dominance where the customer follows your advice. You also want to gather and triangulate information to qualify the opportunity and educate the customer in his learning style to overcome objections. Finally, you need to use the appropriate closing strategy to realize the goal of the sales call. Each of these customer interaction topics is covered in part IV, "Sales Call Strategy," and part V, "Personal Communication Strategy."

12. Provocation versus Alignment to the Customer's Thought Process

In some sales situations, it is necessary to align with the customer's thought process in order to win. These customers are experienced and knowledgeable about their business and technical fields. They are specialists who have buyer personas (see chapters 55–59) that command authority and demand respect. The vetting process they employ is designed to screen out unqualified vendors who don't conform to their established business principles or fit their technical environment. For example, an IT department that spent millions of dollars implementing SAP, Microsoft, or Oracle will probably not entertain vendors that aren't integrated with these solutions.

There are other situations where the customer's thought process must be transformed and gently shaped over the course of the sales cycle. This is based on developing rapport with the customer to gain the control position as described in chapter 10. For example, one top technology salesperson I studied was an extremely curious person by nature. Like a plane crash investigator, he continually analyzed small pieces of information to construct the entire puzzle. He placed himself in the customer's shoes to understand his problems and know when and why he would buy. He was an extremely independent person driven to know how things worked and was not comfortable until all the i's were dotted and the t's were crossed. Gradually, over the course of the sales cycle he gained the customer's respect as a trusted advisor. He was then able to shape the customer's thought process by sharing his expertise, prescribing cures, and suggesting corrective actions.

It may be necessary to divert and separate the customer from his existing thought process and change his way of thinking to stand out from the competition. This requires a realignment of his beliefs through provocation by challenging his preconceived ideas, biases, or decision-making methodology. For example, another top technology salesperson I studied had a strong situational dominance instinct, which includes the propensity to take command in social settings (see chapter 65). He was a verbal warrior who said exactly what was on his mind. However, he was not reckless about his words. Rather, he used them with precision to reach the core of the customer's psyche and reveal the hidden biases and silent objections that are always in the back of someone's mind. He was an accomplished conversationalist who is able to convince customers to change.

The sales linguistic term for this type of mental reorientation is called "pattern interruption." The pattern interruption engages the customer and provokes open-mindedness. The goal of a pattern interruption is to break the customer's current mode of thinking by detaching pre-existing thoughts.

Detaching can be an effective tool in situations where you want to change a behavior quickly. For example, when you greet someone, you will cheerfully say, "How are you doing?" The automatic response is "fine" or "okay." It is the expected and anticipated response attached to that particular question. Let's pretend the response is, "My dog just died." This answer is completely opposite from the expected response. Immediately, you would be detached from being cheerful and become somber or apologetic.

Figure 12.1 illustrates the three paths for working on an account. You can be in alignment with the customer's thought process on how he will solve the problem in order to achieve the goal.

By building rapport and earning the customer's trust you can gradually transform his thought process over time. Or you can perform a pattern interruption early in the sales cycle and completely change the game by diverting the customer's thought process.

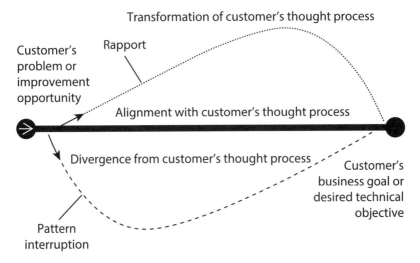

Figure 12.1 Alignment with, transformation of, and divergence from the customer's thought process

The following analogy explains the difference between alignment, transformation, and divergence. A customer wanted to buy a comfortable pen from you because he planned to write a book. A salesperson using alignment might say, "We have a wide range of pens for sale, but this is our most popular because of its ergonomic grip and it will last longer since it contains 30 percent more ink." A salesperson using transformation would say, "Let me study how you write. Based upon this information, I will recommend not only the right pen, but also the paper and pencils that would work best for you." A salesperson employing divergence would say, "What you really want is an iPad. It does so much more than a pen. You can write, edit your thoughts on the fly, and record them for easy retrieval. But most importantly, you can instantly share your important insights with people all over the world via the Internet."

Situational dominance is a personal communication strategy by which the customer accepts your recommendations and follows your advice. In every account, you have an important choice to make. Will you provoke and challenge the customer to think differently about the future by changing how he does business and uses technology? Will you remain adaptable and selectively challenge or align yourself depending upon specific topics as the sales cycle progresses? Or, will you try to align yourself to his current thought process and the manner in which he does business or uses technology today? Figure 12.2 represents the sliding scale of situational dominance.

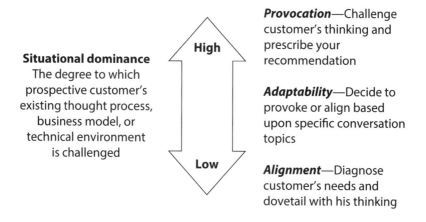

Figure 12.2 Sliding scale of situational dominance

What is the natural situational dominance tendency among technology salespeople? In order to find the answer to this question, two hundred technology outside field salespeople were given a situational dominance test. Half of the salespeople were responsible for new account sales (also called "hunters") and the other half were responsible for install-base sales with existing clients (also known as "farmers"). Test scores indicate that the situational dominance tendency was higher for hunters and lower for farmers. Seventy-five percent of hunters had high or average situational dominance while 43 percent of farmers have slightly below average or low situational dominance as shown in figure 12.3.

	New account field salespeople	Existing client field salespeople
High situational dominance	28%	11%
Average situational dominance	47%	46%
Slightly below average situation dominance	18%	33%
Low situational dominance	7%	10%

Figure 12.3 Situational dominance test results for 200 field salespeople

There is a delicate balance between a salesperson being considered a valuable advisor whose advice is sought out versus alienating the customer by challenging his direction and belief systems. The following quotes are from customers who seek to change their business model. They need the help from outside their organization. They seek provocation from vendors in order to accomplish strategic change. Therefore, a high level of situational dominance should be employed by the salesperson working on these types of accounts.

> As I look at our business, I see our people have been here a really long time. In other words, we have our own version of the truth, and what we know is what we know. We don't have a lot of insight into best practices from other companies. We wanted their sales team to tell us if there was a better way of doing processes and being more efficient. We would like them

to come to us with recommendations and game-changing advances.

—Vice President of Manufacturing

Your people will tell you what you want to hear. It's a little bit like being the emperor who wore no clothes. What I need out of a partner is not just someone who will do what I tell them to do. I need someone who knows as much or more about the marketplace, who can shape my thinking and requests so they can provide the most value.

—President

We classify projects into three different categories; growth, run, and transformation. Transformation projects change the way we do business or establish new ways of doing business that we have never done before. Growth refers to organic year over year growth and run is the base infrastructure needed to run the business. The transformation projects are the most complex and we'll engage our network of vendors to help us plan and successfully complete them.

—Vice President of IT

Never forget you are probably selling to the individuals who charted their current strategic direction and selected the technology they use today. Therefore, there are times when the best strategy is to be aligned with them. For example, the following quotes are from customers who are not amenable to provocation. Rather, they seek solutions that complement their existing thought processes. These selection processes tend to be more tactical as opposed to strategic and usually involve less complexity. These sales cycles are better suited for the alignment or adaptable levels of situational dominance.

We wanted a vendor who was a fit to our business. We are a financial services company that is pretty dynamic in the way we operate, so we had to have a partner who was willing to work in our environment. We are looking for the firm that will understand our business. We are successful because of our business model, not the way any vendor operates. We are looking for the partner who comes to the table and says, "Okay, I get it and we're going to work with you and not impact your business model."

—*Chief Information Officer*

I've had many conversations where a salesperson said, "Did you think about this?" or "We can improve that better than what you're doing." This is simplistic thinking to some extent. There isn't a true understanding of the analysis and decision points that resulted in where we are today. Their assumptions are based upon false pretenses.

—*Vice President of IT*

Vendor A was trying to focus on the bigger picture and we were trying to tactically solve a problem. Their PowerPoint slides showed this grand vision and how all the pieces fit together, and we kept saying we're not doing that, we only want this piece right now. They couldn't bring the conversation from the whole architecture of end-to-end solution to just talking specifics about one product. I tried to tell the salesperson a couple of times I felt like he was missing it with the approach he was taking. He kind of heard and kind of not.

—*Vice President of IT*

I am skeptical of asking for help from salespeople because the answers they come up with naturally revolve around their product. Once we set a direction, how do you help us get

there? They should take a long-term approach, not force-fitting the products they have to sell today.
—*Chief Information Officer*

It is important to understand that people are open to different levels of change. Based upon win-loss sales cycle research, 20 percent of customers are genuinely open to change. Forty-five percent can be persuaded to change, while 35 percent are extremely resistant.

> The sales team didn't prove it would be cost effective, and it was hard for them to prove they would create incremental sales. They need to get some real life examples, customer case studies that spell it out. They tried to explain it, but it wasn't believable.
> —*Chief Financial Officer*

13. IT Budgeting and Organizational Buyer Types

If you are involved in selling enterprise, platform cloud-based, or point-specific solutions, you know the importance of understanding the inner workings of the various departments within a company. Your product might be purchased by the IT department and used by accounting and manufacturing. It might be selected by accounting and used by marketing and other areas of the organization. Or it could be selected solely by IT for its internal use within the department. Many purchase decisions require multiple departments to become involved. It's critical to map out the interrelationships of the departments within an organization, and most importantly, the power of the C-level executive who heads the department involved in the selection process. The organizational structure also determines who will sponsor the project and fund the purchase.

IT Budgeting

One of the most important sales questions is, "Where will the money come from to make the purchase?" In some cases, the answer is easy to find out while in others it is much harder to ascertain. In general, technology purchases are classified as either "lights on" or for "strategic innovation."

Lights-on purchases typically have to do with the operation of the existing infrastructure and are budgeted on an annual basis. For example, the infrastructure operations group has an annual budget to keep the systems and network up and running. This budget includes ongoing costs, expenditures for anticipated growth, and money set aside to replace technologies that become obsolete during the fiscal year. Lights-on expenditures include planned expenditures that are allocated in the annual departmental budget and unplanned expenditures, which require money to be reallocated from the existing IT budget. These surprise expenditures may be the result of drastic change in the business, such as an acquisition or any type of emergency.

> We have a three-year plan that we update on a regular basis. The focus is always on the next year from an operations perspective. There's also a business systems plan, which has a governance body that is led by IT but includes the business stakeholders who look at projects and initiatives from their perspective. Every year there is a pot of money put aside for IT business initiatives. The IT steering committee is made up of our senior executives that validate the prioritization of projects and approves the funding based upon business value and return on investment. When there is an unforeseen IT need or requirement imposed upon us that requires a major IT initiative we essentially rob Peter to pay Paul. The projects that aren't started yet are evaluated and put on hold because overall

funding is finite. We will meet with our strategic vendors to make them aware of our road map for the next year. Our goal is to get them involved to understand where they can add value, whether it's advice on the experiences with customers who have undergone similar projects, industry experience, or helping us understand unforeseen ramifications we might not be aware of.

—*Chief Information Officer*

Organizations constantly search for strategic innovation to increase their revenues and drive down operating costs. Strategic innovation projects are budgeted on an annual basis but also can be added during the course of the year to the list of IT business initiatives. Strategic innovation has a larger scope and the projects impact the entire company. As a result, there is a cross-functional committee comprised of senior leaders from all areas of the organization that approve and prioritize which initiatives will be undertaken. Strategic innovation projects can include approved and planned expenditures for the year, unplanned surprise expenditures that require funds, and "interrupt-driven" initiatives, where business drivers justify the expenditure. Figure 13.1 shows the different types of IT budgeting.

How do I decide whom I will share my strategy with? My best partners have a very good understanding of my company from a technology and business standpoint. They're engrained in the organization and we have discussions about strategy. The other vendors have to earn it.

—*Senior Vice President of Technology*

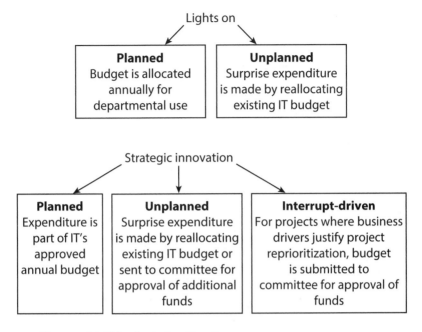

Figure 13.1 IT budget classifications

The type of products that garner executive attention are those that help set strategic direction. These solutions enable the execution of a long-term strategic plan or immediate business benefits in a short payback time frame. The business innovation these projects provide create efficiencies that generate money to the bottom line or significantly increase top line revenues.

There is a continual reprioritization of projects during the year as more interrupt-driven projects are approved. As a result, IT initiatives that have already been blessed by the cross-functional approval committee are tabled and delayed until funds and the resources to complete the project are available. Or, they may be canceled entirely. In the example shown in figure 13.2, ten strategic projects have been approved for the current year. However, during year three additional interrupt-driven initiatives and an unplanned IT expenditure caused project eight to be delayed until next year, and projects nine and ten had to be cancelled.

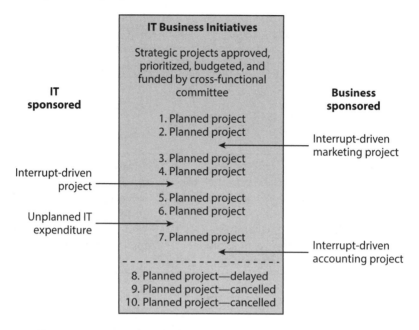

Figure 13.2 Strategic IT initiative planning showing delayed and canceled projects

When you are talking about large projects, the decision is made at the senior executive level. We have a number of governance committees that once projects have been identified as business cases, they are put through a process where we align resources based upon a supply-and-demand model. From there, they are brought to the senior executives and each project is rated on a number of dimensions such as risk, costs, and customer impact. We use a planning tool to optimize our resources and determine where they can be applied. So it is a combination of taking "demand" side projects and resource availability exercise to determine where we can drive the most projects out in a given year. Typically this starts in August and is adjusted quarterly. We'll make sure we are on track for the next six months and then getting some high level project place-holders for the next year. If there is an unexpected expense during the year, such as a major equipment failure or compliance issue we must address, they are dealt with immediately and don't go through the prioritization process. They have to get done. If there's an idea raised by the business that says we can save millions if we do this project for a million, we may hit the pause button on an existing project in order to reallocate resources. We have actually done this on two large projects this year. If we believe the return is so significant we will go out and hire additional resources as to not impact the other projects.

—*Chief Information Officer*

14. The Impact of Procurement

Historically, procurement has played a relatively minor role when it comes to influencing the products that IT used. This was because purchasing agents didn't understand IT and technology in general. However, this has changed in recent years. Now there are procurement specialists who are experts at buying hardware, software, and cloud applications. They belong to associations that teach them how to prepare contracts and negotiate terms. In some organizations, they even report directly to the IT department, such as the following IT procurement specialist who explains his position:

My role is to manage strategic spending for IT as it relates to finance and procurement. This is what products we are going to use and which vendors we are going to work with. For example, on this strategic project here are the four products you are going to use because we want to simplify our IT structure. I see this as IT portfolio management. A business group will contact me and say this is what we need help with and how should we go about it. I provide the templates to help them define what they are looking for and then identify the vendors we'll go after. I'll do the business process fit evaluation and technology evaluation. Once I settle on who we'll use, then general procurement will start the paperwork and contracts, and I will direct the negotiation.

—*Director of IT Financial Procurement*

Titles are very important as they reveal an organization's structure. I am continually amazed at the lackadaisical attitude many salespeople have about understanding the organizational structure of the companies they call on. When they are asked what a person's title is, they will answer, "manager," or something equally nebulous, when they should answer, "manager of application security who reports to the director of application development, who, in turn, reports to the CIO." Knowing the exact titles of the contacts you interface with during the purchasing process and whether they report to procurement, sourcing, or supply chain is critical.

Understanding the different philosophies between procurement, sourcing, and supply chain is important. Sourcing and supply chain buying professionals tend to be more sophisticated than general procurement buyers. They are knowledgeable about lean manufacturing techniques and can be certified in Six Sigma systems and principles. Procurement, sourcing, and supply chain are related to the sophistication of the company's purchasing requirements, the type of products the company creates, and their organizational complexity as shown in figure 14.1.

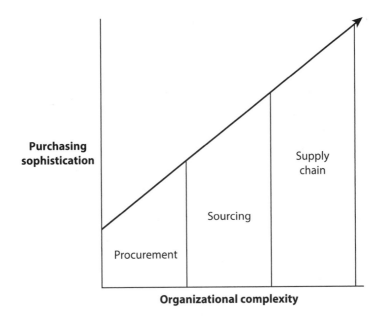

Figure 14.1 Purchasing organization department types

The procurement department's orientation is to consider the products it buys to be commodities. Products are basically interchangeable because there is little differentiation between the competing vendors' offerings. Therefore, price becomes the most important evaluation criteria. Sourcing is more innovative and open to input and recommendations from vendors. As a result, vendors are evaluated holistically, in a different context than procurement—based upon the overall potential of the relationship and its benefits. The supply chain is strategic to the business. The focus is on high-level company objectives at the direction of the senior-most levels of the company. The department establishes mutually beneficial strategic relationships with the vendors who can help it achieve its goals. Note the different orientation in the following quotes from procurement, sourcing, and supply chain managers.

My rule in dealing with salespeople is I like to dictate the relationship.

—*Procurement Manager*

If we are asking for XYZ today, show us you can do it cheaper than our current supplier. But from there, how can we both grow? What cost saving ideas and innovations can you bring to us? Never forget, I'm measured by the money I save the company, from my planned versus actual budget. There's always constant demand to reduce costs. Procurement is more tactical on the day-to-day basis. They execute by the parameters set by sourcing. Sourcing is identifying what we do and how we do it. What are the business requirements we have and how do we change the dynamics of what we are doing today? I qualify suppliers, assess risk mitigation, and establish supplier relationships.

—*Director of Sourcing*

I explained we had three main objectives for the manufacturing of the product. These objectives were passed down by senior management to put on the supply chain. The objectives were to have flexibility, flow, and velocity. Obviously, with a supply base that is 3,000 miles from the facility it is more difficult to accomplish.

—*Supply Chain Manager*

Technology companies that provide solutions that are embedded into products face another challenge. Whom should they call on and when do they need to contact them? During the product development phase, the prospective customer is open to innovation and the strategic involvement of vendors. As the product is defined, prototyped, and the company prepares for its release, they are less likely to innovate and are not open to the strategic involvement of vendors. However, they may be open to the tactical involvement of vendors who offer improvements with very little change effort and risk.

Figure 14.2 shows product development stages and when the various departments within an organization become involved. During the concept development stage, product marketing (product management, brand management, and so on) and engineering (research and development) drive vendor decisions while supply chain issues are considered. As the concept becomes reality, sourcing and operations are involved. Note the time frame difference between general procurement versus sourcing and supply chain. Figure 14.2 should be interpreted as a general guideline because departmental involvement varies greatly by product type and from industry to industry.

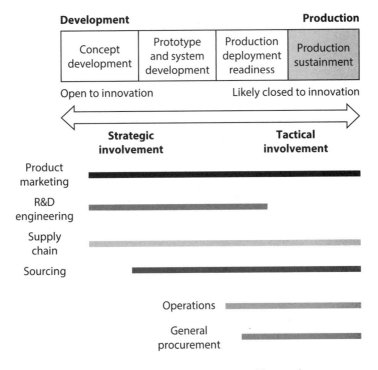

Figure 14.2 When departments are involved in product development

15. How Important Is Price?

Price plays an important role in every sales cycle. Since it is a frequent topic during customer conversations, salespeople can become fixated on the price of their product and believe they have to be lowest. However, technology decision makers have different propensities to buy and the importance of price falls into three categories. Thirty-eight percent of technology buyers studied were "price conscious" and product price was a top decision-making factor. Forty-two percent were "price sensitive" and product price was secondary to other decision-making factors such as technical functionality and vendor capability. Finally, 20 percent of buyers were "price immune," meaning they bought the products they want as shown in figure 15.1. In this case, price becomes an issue only when the solution they want is priced far more than the others being considered, typically above the 15 to 25 percent range.

Figure 15.1 Price as a deciding sales cycle factor

Price is always important, but what is the cultural fit between the organizations? Who has the ability to execute? What is our risk with the vendor? It clearly has some impact but it is not the most important deciding factor. I would say we probably weight price at about 25 percent. However, when you get into

double digit differences in price between vendors, then it starts to become material.
—*Chief Information Officer*

Price sensitivity is different for each company and by industry. While the average company can spend anywhere from 2 to 5 percent of annual revenues on IT expenditures, industries that operate on very small gross margins, such as retail, tend to be price conscious. Conversely, industries where technology is the core of the business, such as banking and finance, tend to be more price immune.

> By the middle of the sales cycle, after the presentations, the group knew who they wanted to go with. The company we chose came out way ahead of the number two and we didn't go with the cheapest solution either. But we didn't want to make that known to them because in the event we couldn't make the negotiation work with our top pick, we could go back to number two.
> —*Corporate IT Manager*

As a salesperson, you are constantly being compared to your competitors. But in reality, you and your company are being compared to all the technology vendors that are doing business. The IT and purchasing departments are continually evaluating your company's product performance, customer service, and support of their account. Price is only one component of measurement and in most cases not the most important.

> We rank vendors not only by spending, but more importantly by strategic significance or if they are commodity-type vendors. This measure is how we feel how critical it is to maintain their services to our company, how easy it would it be to replace them, and what role their organization takes in helping us determine our strategy for our business. Now every vendor wants to be classified

as strategic whether or not they deserve it. The worst place to be is to be thought of as a commodity vendor because we are going to grind you down on price because there is no value add. We specifically dropped Vendor A's ranking because they had been repeatedly pushing their solutions on us. Meaning, they are anything but agnostic. Our opinion is that anyone who truly is a strategic vendor is going to be giving you the best advice and helping you make the best decisions for your organization, regardless of whether or not it involves their products.

—*Chief Information Officer*

16. The Five IT Organization Buyer Types, Liaisons, and Power Users

Five models can be used to define the IT departmental interrelationships that influence a company's buying behavior: departments—and the executives who lead them—are either internal use, consolidators, consulters, responders, or bureaucrats as defined below.

- *Internal use.* The technology solution is evaluated and purchased by IT for use internally within the IT department.
- *Consolidator.* The IT department drives the technology solution evaluation and purchase and controls the implementation rollout to the business user community.
- *Consulter.* The IT department acts much like a consulting organization to the business user community by constantly polling users on their needs and promoting project ideas.
- *Responder.* The business user community drives the technology solution and evaluation with varying degrees of approval from IT.

- *Bureaucrat.* The IT department's priority is to maintain the status quo through rules and standardization.

Before analyzing each type of department in the following chapters, we must first define some company roles. Liaisons serve as intermediaries between departments. There are business liaisons, whose official function is to ensure a department is working well and satisfies the needs of the other departments within the organization. Business liaisons are the intermediaries that translate business needs between departments. In larger companies, common business liaison titles are "business analyst," "project manager," "delivery," "facilitator," and "technical consultant." In smaller companies, the role of liaison usually is filled by departmental managers.

In one sense, every department within a company is a customer of every other department. And every department has very sophisticated users of the services of other departments. For example, the sales department has sales operations staff members who depend upon information from the finance department. The manufacturing department has technical personnel who use information from research and development.

The employees who fill the positions described above are called "power users." To accomplish their departmental roles, power users are required to have an intimate knowledge of their department as well as other departments. They must use the systems, information, equipment, or resources from another department to complete their jobs. Typical power users might have titles that include "specialist," "technician," "support," "administrator," or "leader."

> At the end of the day, a project will or won't get approved depending upon who is pushing it.
> —*President*

17. Internal Use IT Organizational Buyer Type

Most high technology products are sold directly into or are approved by the IT department of a company. While many high technology companies create products that require their sales efforts to focus on business line managers or end users, usually the IT department will have to bless the selection somewhere during the purchase process. At the very least, the selection of the product will have to conform to the standards set previously by the IT department. For example, most companies have standards regarding which desktop or laptop computers can be purchased.

The IT department's size is usually in proportion to the size of the company. The department's structure and organization will most likely reflect the complexity of the business and the complexity of the products it produces. For example, the IT organization of one of the "Big Three" automakers will reflect the nature and intricacy of the business. However, even a small IT organization can be very sophisticated in using technology.

Regardless of the size and complexity of the IT organization, you can classify people within the IT department into three basic categories of responsibility: product, management, and executive. Most likely, your solution is targeted at one of these categories. Your initial contact with the account and most frequent interactions with the customer will also be within one of these categories. Let's take a moment to define and understand the nuances of these categories.

Product Category

The product category includes individuals who work hands-on with technology. This includes programmers, systems administrators, networking analysts, security engineers, and specialists of all kinds. Typically, people within this category will have "administrator," "analyst," or "engineer" in their title. People within the product category have titles that explain exactly what they do, such as "computer programmer" and "application developer."

These people use a vendor's products to create a new product for their company. For example, the programmer is creating an application (product) by using programming tools and products provided by a vendor. The system operator is creating system availability (product) by managing the department's systems using hardware and software products provided by vendors. The security analyst safeguards IT assets (product) by using products from vendors.

Management Category

The management category provides direction to each of the various departments of the IT organization. The departments may include applications, systems, programming, networking, security, or Internet business. Departments also may be organized around initiatives or business practices. Typically, people at this level may have "director," "manager," or "leader" somewhere in their title.

While many different management styles exist, there are two fundamental types of IT department managers, the "domain expert" and the "business expert." The domain expert managers achieved their position by being the most knowledgeable person within their department. For example, a network manager may have been promoted to a management position because of his troubleshooting expertise. Domain experts are the "alpha," or dominant resource, that all the other members of the group consult for technical advice.

Meanwhile, business expert managers are responsible for representing their department to the other departments within the company. While they are still technical, they rely heavily on the technical opinions of a few key members of their team to make decisions.

Executive Category

In larger companies, the executive category is composed of people who have the word "president" or "chief" in their titles such as vice president, chief information officer (CIO), chief technology officer (CTO), and chief information security officer (CISO). In smaller companies, the category also includes individuals with "director" or even "manager" in their title.

Each category of responsibility has a different orientation toward the operation of the department. The executive category ensures the IT department is coordinated with the business strategy and major initiatives. The management category leads ongoing projects, day-to-day operation of the departments, and the supervision of the people responsible for products. Meanwhile, the product category is focused on the microcosm of the IT department.

Different areas of responsibilities with the IT department require different technical aptitudes, and this impacts who leads the organization and manages the individual departments. For example, the most technically astute network engineer is very likely to be promoted to manage the networking department. He is classified as a domain expert manager. However, it is unlikely he will become the CIO, as it requires business and political acumen to reach the top. In general, more of the executive level leaders have business expert manager backgrounds. However, certain departments require deep technical expertise, such as the security and risk management department. In this case, a domain expert manager who was an information security specialist may become the chief information security officer. Figure 17.1 illustrates this concept.

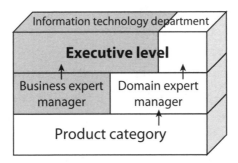

Figure 17.1 Evolution of IT leadership by domain or business expertise

Each vendor made their pitch to a panel of twenty people. Vendor A's sales guys did a good job of presenting to the senior executive types in attendance. However, there were people from IT and operations present who wanted to better understand specifics. In addition, people have different agendas and this project was going to be owned by IT. Vendor B had existing relationships and a track record with the IT organization. Vendor A needed to explain how and why they were better qualified from both the business AND technical standpoints. There were a lot of different points of view among the selection committee and overall their presentation was poorly received. In the end, we compromised and stayed with existing vendor B.

   —*IT Director*

The background of midlevel managers and senior executives also influences their orientation during the stages of the sales cycle. The technology sales cycle has four stages:

- *Customer research stage.* The customer conducts independent research about the various vendors, technologies, and methodologies he is considering via the Internet, analyst reports, product reviews, industry news, member associations, and so on.

- *Product stage.* Based upon his research the customer will contact a select number of vendors and meet with their salespeople to learn more about the products. The customer is validating his initial research and augmenting his knowledge of the respective products through interactions with each of the salespeople competing for the business.

- *Business stage.* As the sales process progresses, the evaluators will assess which vendors offer the best business value and are a philosophical fit to their business.

- *Political stage.* The last stage is making a final decision from the top two or three vendors. The final decision is typically influenced by many political factors beyond the attributes evaluated in the product and business stages.

Sales Stage Influencers

There are different types of influencers at each stage that determine which vendor is in the lead. Customer research is most influential at the beginning of the sales cycle, and then its importance tapers off. Conversely, the influence of internal politics and the group dynamics of the evaluation committee making the selection become more important as the sales cycle progresses. The attributes of the products and merits of each of the competing vendors remain relatively the same throughout the sales stages as shown in figure 17.2.

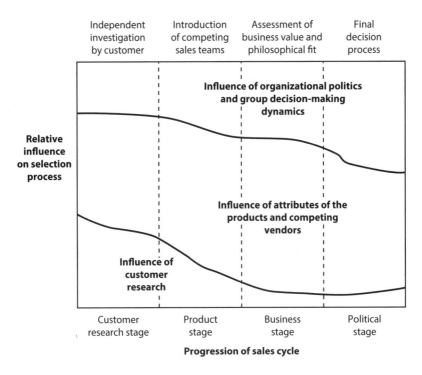

Figure 17.2 Sales stage influencers as the sales cycle progresses

The executive, management, and product buyer categories place a different emphasis on different stages. The product category tends to decide left to right and is primarily concerned with the product stage. The executive category tends to make decisions from the right to left, thinking about the political implications far more than the product attributes. Domain expert managers buy like the product category, and business expert managers behave more like the executive category.

> Our IT department is split between application and technology sides. I have the technology side and report to the CIO. I try to keep up my relationships with vendors so I know what the current offerings are. But I also have a manager of network

services and his role is to give me vendor recommendations on throughput and reliability of the system. But then I make the decision. I work with the CIO ahead of time during the budgeting process and to preapprove the purchase. He lets me select the vendor. That's my role. To set direction.

—*Chief Technology Officer*

Complex IT Organizations

Fortune 1000 organizations have complex IT organization structures, and IT departments can be organized by division, line of business, or geography under the oversight of a global corporate IT group. The interrelationship of the various IT organizations will influence which solutions are purchased and deployed. The "corporate control" environment is where the corporate IT group sets guidelines and standards that ultimately determine which products will be used at the subsidiary IT organizations. For example, the IT department at the headquarters in the United States may overrule the purchase decision being made at the IT department in the United Kingdom. "Independent IT" organizations are able to use their discretion and buy the products they prefer. "Interdependent IT" organizations are more integrated. They promote and cross-pollinate technologies among the IT organizations as shown in figure 17.3.

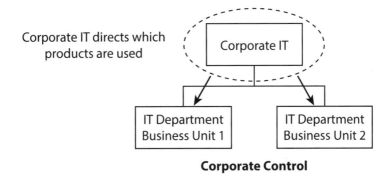

Corporate IT directs which products are used

Corporate Control

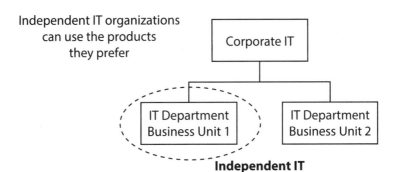

Independent IT organizations can use the products they prefer

Independent IT

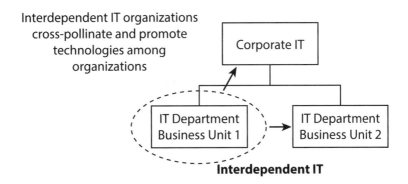

Interdependent IT organizations cross-pollinate and promote technologies among organizations

Interdependent IT

Figure 17.3 Influence of corporate control, independent IT, and interdependent IT organizations

The sales effort focus must be concentrated at different locations depending on the structure. Corporate control accounts must have a concerted effort at headquarters. All IT operations should be called on at interdependent accounts. Meanwhile, independent accounts can be sold individually.

18. Consolidator IT Buyer Type

Consolidators are departments that have C-level executives who seek to increase their power, authority, or control within their organization. To grow their sphere of influence, they launch grand initiatives, major company-wide projects that affect the operations of other departments.

The planning and creation of a grand initiative are at the direction of the department's executive leadership. This type of project does not typically percolate up from lower-level personnel through the chain of command; it is driven down from the top and out to the rest of the company.

Figure 18.1 illustrates the consolidator's flow of power. In this example, the vice president of the information technology department has decided to drive an initiative to move all applications and programs off the company's aging mainframe computers onto new, less expensive computer systems. After making this executive decision, he mandates that his direct managers fulfill his wishes. These direct reports assemble teams to plan the project and evaluate the vendors. The business liaisons who report back to the information technology department gather information from the various departments, schedule vendor demonstrations with departmental power users, and serve as intermediaries between the various departments during project implementation.

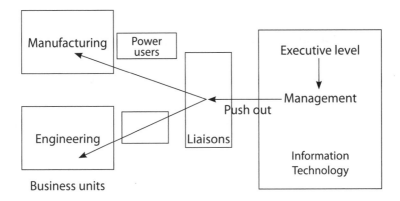

Figure 18.1 Consolidator buyer type

Notice that the boxes representing manufacturing and engineering are smaller than the information technology box and that the business liaisons box is larger than the power users boxes. This indicates who is more dominant and has superior power. The sizes of the boxes are different in the illustrations of the other types of departmental buyers.

> The objectives for this project were passed down from the senior-most level of our company. This project was fast-tracked with an aggressive completion date so we selected a vendor who we knew could get the job done based on our previous experiences with them.
>
> —*Director of Information Technology*

The underlying motivation behind grand initiatives like this one is usually power, whether it's to gain more, consolidate it, or decrease that of other leaders and their departments within the organization. In the example above, the information technology department is exercising its power over manufacturing and engineering. Sometimes a grand initiative is an executive-level coup, an internal revolution intended to change the way the company operates. For example, a business leader takes the initiative to buy a turnkey SaaS (software as a service) cloud solution to avoid being at the mercy of IT. Many times, this is a well-orchestrated conspiracy in the guise of a logical business project. Other times, this is an act of revenge against an intercompany archenemy.

Consolidators are typically a salesperson's dream because they have a propensity to make things happen. "Big-bang consolidators" tend to buy all the equipment and services they need to complete a grand initiative all at once. "Cautious consolidators," on the other hand, purchase the products and services they need piecemeal, taking one small step at a time in order to prove their project's success. Be forewarned, you should be tracking key executives when they switch jobs because they are definitely leaders who want to consolidate their power during their first six months on the new job.

> Like any other organization, we have a list of projects. We have near-term, keep the lights running projects, and bigger, more strategic projects. We go through an annual and thirty-six-month planning cycle. We have projects that fall in the next twelve months and ones that have longer time frames. We have a decentralized structure, so each division line has their own project budgets and manages them independently. However, strategic projects are consolidated at an enterprise project office where enterprise-wide capital expenditure decisions are made and the resources to support them are engaged to fulfill. So I have my own budget and projects come from my side, and each business has their projects, and the annual capital expenditure of budget is determined at that level. Now, there are those that I sponsor directly and there are others that come in from the business.
>
> —*Senior Vice President of Information Technology*

19. Consulter IT Buyer Type

Consulters are IT departments who have the characteristics and attributes of a consultant to their organization. They seek to understand the problems of other departments and offer recommendations on how those problems can be solved using their services.

They proactively share their proprietary knowledge and departmental expertise or offer unsolicited advice to other departments in an attempt to show how they can improve efficiency. Therefore, they are continually polling the other departments, seeking opportunities to promote their services, and pushing out their ideas, philosophies, and opinions. Liaisons are vitally important to consulters because they are gatherers and disseminators of information. As a result, liaisons have more power and influence with consulters than they do with consolidators.

Consulters are more prevalent in massive multibillion-dollar companies than in smaller organizations. The C-level executives are less powerful than their counterparts in the consolidator model, so they have to achieve their desired outcomes through finesse rather than brute force. Since consulters are constantly seeking customers for their services, the power users are more likely to be within the consulter's department than in another business unit.

> We quite often find ourselves in the position of being the functional champion, proactively showing solutions to the business it can help. We're always saying "Hey, could this help you?" We want their people to see something so we can get some champions behind it.
>
> —*Vice President of Information Technology*

Figure 19.1 shows the information flow of a consulter department. In this example, the information technology department liaisons are constantly polling the business units for their needs and pushing out information they believe is beneficial.

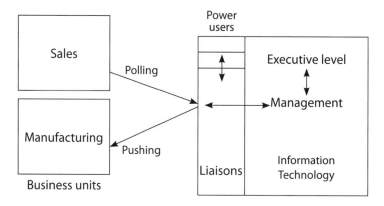

Figure 19.1 Consulter buyer type

For example, a liaison may seek out and meet with the vice president of sales, who expresses his dissatisfaction with the timeliness of the sales forecasting system. The liaison takes this information back to his department, and it travels up the chain of command to where a decision is made to investigate new sales forecasting solutions. Conversely, a liaison may hear about an exciting new technology from the chief technology officer. The liaison schedules a meeting with the technology vendor to learn more information. He then sets meetings with his constituents (power users of his department's services) in manufacturing to explain how the new technology may improve their operations.

> I report through the project management group straddling IT and the project management group. I work predominantly on IT projects so I am more of a liaison between the business and the project completion group. Vendors are constantly approaching us and we continually test the waters with other

vendors to see how they compare. Sometimes they perform well and other times they don't live up to their hype.

—IT Project Coordinator

Like a consultant hired on an hourly basis, consulters seek to continually validate their benefits and justify their existence to their customers. Selling to consulters differs from selling to consolidators because consulters enjoy the company of other consultants. They need vendors who will represent them professionally to their business user community.

20. Responder IT Buyer Type

Responders are weaker IT departments that operate under the direction of other departments. This is because the business unit is the primary decision maker on which the solution will be used and IT serves in an advisory role. Usually, the purchase is being funded from the business unit's budget. Therefore, it is critical that the sales strategy and customer interactions focus on the business unit impact and the user experience, as opposed to pure IT-related selling points.

> Vendor A understood our needs and came to us with ideas and suggestions, "What about this? What if? Next year you will be this size and here is what you'll need." They were telling us what we should be doing instead of what we thought we should. The other two vendors were very technical and described their solutions using technical jargon. The IT guys liked it, but the business guys were like, "What are you talking about?" We selected the company that did a much better job getting to the nontechnical guys.
>
> *—Director of Supply Chain*

Many times, responders are literally under attack from the business units because their needs are being unmet. In some cases, the business units have been disappointed by the responders' past blunders. As a result, responders tend to be treated disrespectfully and suffer from a lack of departmental esteem. Whereas consolidators seek to gain power and consulters seek to proliferate their services, responders are just trying to minimize the risk associated with a business unit's purchase and survive.

> Vendor A is well connected into the financial organization. They tend to sell to the CFO. Probably 90 percent of Vendor A's sales have been driven by the CFO. You have to learn who makes decisions in the organizations you serve and how you connect to them. Vendor B focuses on the IT people. While Vendor B hires good salespeople, they don't think about hiring salespeople who can connect with CFOs and business leaders.
> —*Executive Director Supply Chain Systems*

Figure 20.1 illustrates the power flow of a responder when the finance department is unhappy with some IT applications. Once again, the sizes of the boxes reflect the departments' dominance and control. The power users can be very influential in the responder model. In this example, IT is the whipping boy of finance, constantly enduring the department's criticisms. Important power users in the finance organization complain to management that their needs aren't being met. In turn, senior executives dictate their needs to midlevel managers, who relay the message to IT liaisons.

In this instance, the liaisons' main goal is to run interference on behalf of their department, sorting out the most important requests while trying to maintain a semblance of departmental decorum. For issues of extreme importance and urgency, senior executives of a business unit will contact their counterparts in IT directly and tell them to get something done. The power is clearly on the business unit side.

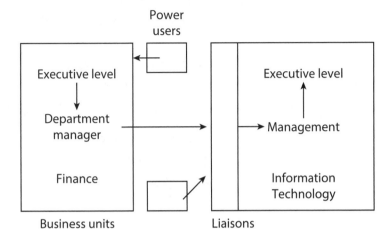

Figure 20.1 Responder buyer type

When selling to a responder, you must sell to the business unit, power users, and all levels of the department as well as IT, whereas with consolidators, your main sales effort should be directed inside their IT departments.

> IT doesn't have any other priorities that are different from the business. My IT strategy is really the business strategy with a slightly different lens on it. Our agenda is based directly on the business plan. There is no such thing as an IT project. It's a business project with a sponsor. In terms of prioritizing projects, IT does not prioritize projects. We facilitate the process by which the business prioritizes the projects and their execution. We are only an enabler. Now as a CIO, I use my influence to ensure we get things in the right sequence. But at the end of the day, the business determines its future.
>
> —*Chief Information Officer*

21. Bureaucrat IT Buyer Type

The final category of IT buyer type is the bureaucrat whose priority is to maintain the status quo through rules, regulations, and delaying tactics. The features of a bureaucrat are secretiveness, a response system that reflexively rebuffs demands made upon the department, and administrative centralization around the senior leader, the archbureaucrat.

> The usual disaster is the IT department gets railroaded into doing twelve projects and only has resources for eight. My role is to prevent that from happening, which can make you rather unpopular.
> —*Vice President of Information Technology*

The environment is structured similar to a military command-and-control hierarchy that stamps out innovative thinking from lower levels of the department and hinders the free flow of information. The bureaucratic monarchy considers other departments outsiders and issues edicts that must be complied with for fear of consequences.

> We are not doing any projects and management wouldn't spend ten cents to save twenty cents. We're doing nothing new.
> —*Chief Information Officer*

Figure 21.1 illustrates the shield that bureaucratic buyers erect around their department. In this example, IT dictates to the manufacturing department what products it will use. Meanwhile, the engineering department's recommendation is rejected, even though it is in the best interest of the company. One point to note is the lack of liaisons; the bureaucrat buyer is inwardly focused and less concerned about sensing the needs of other departments.

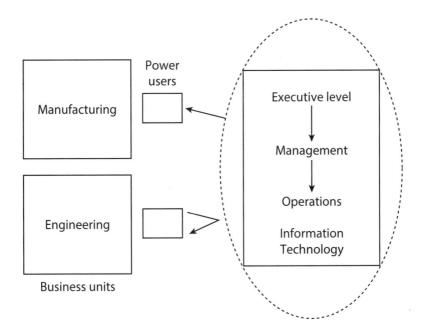

Figure 21.1 Bureaucrat buyer type

The five IT departmental types (internal use, consolidator, consulter, responder, and bureaucrat) have different orientations toward the operation of their departments. They buy products in different ways and for completely different purposes. It also is important to understand that an IT department can be different types of buyers depending upon the project. An IT department may be a consolidator for one project it is championing and a consulter on another. For example, the finance department may be driving a project to complete Sarbanes-Oxley compliance and the IT department is a responder. Conversely, the IT department could be the consolidator when driving new electronic data interchange technology that the finance department will use.

22. IT Leadership and Organizational Power

You must determine a project's wellspring to know to whom and how to sell your solution. For example, at one company, every employee had to undergo ergonomics training on the proper way to use computers. Based on this information, you might assume that the driver behind this company-wide initiative was the human resources department and its vice president of human resources. However, the CFO instigated this project so the company would qualify for reduced insurance premium rates.

The power of C-level executives and departmental leaders follows a pattern of behavior. When they join a new company, they are typically consolidators who are on a mission to establish authority by laying out their agenda of changes and the projects that are necessary to implement that change (which involves making purchases). This is one of the major reasons why you should keep track of executives on the move in your industry and be the first to call on them.

> Our previous CIO was not well liked. He fought some unpopular battles he couldn't win and burned bridges in the process.
> —*IT Director*

A leader who has been at a company for many years has an entirely different motivation for becoming a consolidator. He wants to leave his mark on the organization. He wants to be remembered by his employees and colleagues in his industry.

Over time, a consolidator will lose power. The projects and initiatives he championed will have less-than-spectacular results and fail to live up to their hype. As a result, he has to change his style and demeanor within the organization to accomplish his goals and becomes a consulter. As he continues to lose organizational power he becomes a responder. In an effort to get some power back he becomes a bureaucrat C-level executive, as figure 22.1 illustrates.

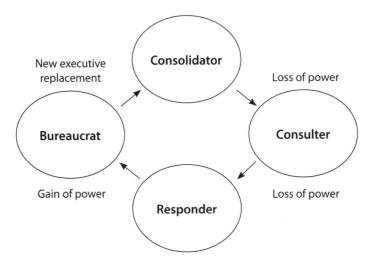

Figure 22.1 Evolution of C-level executive power

Finally, the executive team tires of working with the difficult bureaucrat and the members make a decision to change the departmental leader. They hire a new C-level executive who has a vision, a plan, and the power to change the department. The new executive is a consolidator, and the whole process repeats itself. In one sense, you can attribute the rise of "shadow IT," a term used to describe IT solutions purchased or built by business departments of organization without explicit IT approval, to ineffective responders and nonperforming bureaucrats.

I came to this company when they had to replace the old CIO. The new one came in and said to the senior management team that IT was not a group that was there to code based upon direction, it was supposed to partner with the business and lead. As companies including ours have shifted their staffing and downsized over time, that has given our company a competitive advantage.

—*Director of Information Technology*

Here's a quick exercise to help you understand where you win and why you lose. Write down the company names of your last five wins and note whether the buyer type was internal use, consolidator, consulter, responder, or bureaucrat. Then write down the same information for five major losses or no-decision deals. Quite often, you will find the losses were with completely different organizational buyer types than the wins. For example, if most of your wins were with consolidators, most of your losses were probably with another type, such as consulters or responders.

23. Identifying the Bully with the Juice and the Emperor

Four different characteristics of the people involved in the product selection process can be measured as displayed in figure 23.1. The vertical axis shows a person's insistence that things be done his way. This is called being a "bully." A bully will get his way at any and all costs.

> Even though IT may feel it was a good investment, it still comes down to dollars and cents. As a company, we're driven by the buying and selling departments. They pretty much call the IT projects here, and unless they see benefit to them, the project won't move forward.
>
> —*IT Manager*

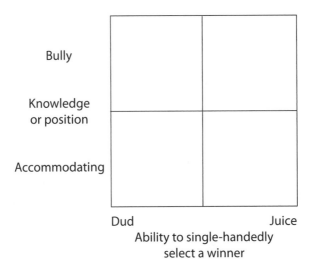

Figure 23.1. Characteristics of evaluators

"Bully" is not necessarily a negative term, nor does it mean that the person is physically intimidating. It is simply a description of a person who will tenaciously fight for his cause in order to get his way. People are more likely to be bullies when they have an elevated status within the evaluation team. The status could be the result of their domain expertise or their title and the authority it commands.

At the other end of the spectrum are people who are accommodating. They are apathetic about whatever solution is purchased. The degree to which people are bullies or accommodating depends on the effect the purchase decision has on them personally, their span of control, their position in the company, or their ability to perform their jobs.

On the horizontal axis are the concepts of "juice" and the "dud." Simply put, juice is charisma. But even this definition is too simple. Some people are natural-born leaders. They have an aura that can motivate and instill confidence. That's juice. Juice is fairly hard to describe, but you know it when you see it.

People who have juice do not necessarily act like superheroes, nor are they always the highest-ranking people involved in an evaluation. Instead, they are the ones who always seem to be on the winning side. Only one member of the customer's evaluation team has the juice. Single-handedly, he imparts his own will on the selection process by choosing the vendor and pushing the purchase through the procurement process. He can either finalize the purchase terms or instruct the procurement team on the terms that are considered acceptable. With large enterprise purchases, the bully with the juice is usually at the senior management level. To succeed, you will need sponsorship at this level.

Duds are named after the ineffective fireworks they represent. Sometimes the fuse of a firework will burn down, but nothing will happen. Other fireworks may be very big but produce disappointing results. Duds talk big but take little action. "Accommodating duds" are people who do not take an active role in the sales process. Even worse are "dud bullies," who pretend they have juice but don't. You may not realize who they are until it's too late.

> We evaluated them for over a year. I had project managers, vice presidents, operations, and business people involved but I drove the decision. What it came down to was do we build it ourselves or buy an off the shelf package. At the end of the day, the argument was more than compelling to buy. We selected a new vendor over our incumbent vendor. From their perspective, it was a shambles of a sales cycle and when they found out they lost it they were stunned. From the president on down, they thought they won it. I'm not sure they ever understood I was making the decision.
>
> —*Vice President of Merchandising*

For all the people involved in the sales selection process, you need to calculate their amount of juice and their propensity to be bullies. For example, John, Jim, Karl, and Rich are plotted by a salesperson who sells large-scale computer data storage equipment in figure 23.2. John is the senior purchasing agent. Jim is a network administrator. Karl is the director of information technology, and Rich is the CIO. They are going to make a $350,000 purchase.

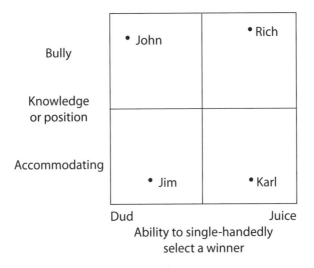

Figure 23.2 Plotting individual assessments

As shown in the figure, John is a dud bully, Jim is an accommodating dud, Rich has the juice, and Karl is accommodating to him. Even though Jim and Karl might conduct the vendor evaluations, their decision can be overridden by Rich. While they might have a vested interest in ensuring that their favorite vendor wins, you can assume their recommendation will match Rich's preference. His will may be imposed on the evaluation process through brute force or by finesse. Either way, his preference is "bullied" into the decision.

However, Rich, the CIO who has the juice, probably doesn't care which toner cartridges are purchased for the company's laser printers. He will be accommodating and support the decision of the people who make that decision. Someone else has the juice for the procurement of toner cartridges.

> We tried to build consensus, but it was my money. That's what it came down to. I wanted to consider everyone's needs, but at the end of the day, it was my decision.
> —*Vice President of Marketing*

Now let's assume Rich is making a $3.5 million software purchase. Once again, he is the bully with the juice and the evaluation team's recommendation matches the vendor he wants. However, he can't make a purchase of this magnitude by himself. It must be blessed by the "emperor."

In ancient Rome, the emperor would decide whether or not a beaten gladiator would live by gesturing with a thumb up or down. Today, the life or death of enterprise purchases is decided in much the same way by a company president, CEO, chairman, board of directors, or capital expenditure committee that has no personal attachments or vested interests in the purchase. This individual or group will decide whether the funds should actually be spent. This emperor will give a thumb up or down to release the funds to make the purchase, even though an exhausting evaluation of many months or even years may have been conducted by lower-level personnel.

> The initial decision was no. The leadership committee didn't believe the contribution margin was high enough. I went back three months later and had it approved after talking with a number of their customers and building a better business case.
> —*Vice President of Customer Care*

Two of the most important people in every sales cycle are the bully with the juice and the emperor. These people will ultimately make and approve the decision. Therefore, it is imperative that you truly understand the decision-making process. Who is the bully with the juice? Will an emperor have to ultimately approve the decision? Whether you are selling a product in only one or two sales calls or two dozen or more, you must always validate who the bully with the juice and the emperor are.

> The decision was made in a vacuum at the highest levels of our organization. The CEO had previous experience with a vendor who worked very well for him. He said that's what he needs here and we're going forward with it.
> —*IT Director*

24. Developing an Internal Coach

Salespeople know they need a constant, accurate source of information that reveals the internal machinations of the customer's selection process. For many years, the term "coach" has been used by all types of salespeople, selling every conceivable product, to define the person who provides this inside information. Coaches are individuals who provide accurate information about the sales cycle and competition to you.

Salespeople sometimes believe they have a coach when in reality they don't. Heavy Hitters know they have a coach when the person not only provides them with accurate information but also helps them by fighting for their cause. A true coach will represent and promote a salesperson's solution to his colleagues and, even better, to senior executive leadership. Finally, the information coaches provide is accurate. Figure 24.1 shows the five different types of coaches and their respective value to a salesperson.

Figure 24.1 Types of coaches

A frenemy is someone who befriends you so that you think he is a supporter. In reality, the frenemy is only acting the part and is truly an enemy who is against you. Frenemies are extremely dangerous because they lull you into a false sense of security that you are winning when they are really coordinating a plan to defeat you.

A well-wisher talks to you on an intimate, friendly basis. He provides information that you consider proprietary. However, the well-wisher is an extremely amiable person and is providing the same information to all the salespeople competing for the business.

Coaches can be either weak or strong spies. Weak spies are observers who provide you information about the internal machinations of the selection process. They report the thoughts of the various selection team members and the movements of other vendors.

Strong spies are not only observers but disseminators of information as well. Strong spies have a deeper, more personal connection to you than weak spies do. They're more akin to confidants than acquaintances.

Guides are trusted friends who will courageously defend you and your solution when you are not around to do so yourself. Guides are considered your best friends. Not only are they confidants who provide all the inside details about the internal politics of decision making, but they also help you plan and execute your strategy to win the business. Guides are usually seasoned employees. They've worked at the company for quite some time and understand how to get things done. They have the business acumen and the experience to provide adept advice on how to win the deal and get the contract signed. Most importantly, after helping devise the winning game plan, they play an integral part in executing it.

The ideal coach is the person with the highest authority or influence involved in the selection process. When this person becomes the coach, you will enjoy a unique advantage. For example, let's assume Rich, the CIO who is making the $350,000 purchase of storage technology, is your coach. Since he is the bully with the juice, you win. The next best scenario is when your coach can influence the bully with the juice.

> If the salesperson doesn't have strong business sponsorship at
> the right level, he is dead in the water.
> —*Vice President of Administration*

However, the coach could be anybody inside the customer's company or even outside the company, such as a consultant working on the project or channel partner who has established relationships. All of these advisors share a common characteristic. They have a selfish reason for wanting you or your company to win. This reason may range from the simple fact that they like you to the belief that your solution will help them gain power, prestige, or authority because of the complicated nature of internal politics.

Here are some interesting metrics that prove the importance of having an internal coach. Figure 24.2 shows an analysis of the type of coach the winning salesperson had developed by persuasion and creation sales cycles.

	Persuasion sales cycles	Creation sales cycles
Guide	55%	75%
Strong spy	30%	23%
Weak spy	12%	2%
No coach	3%	

Figure 24.2 Types of coach for persuasion and creation sales cycle wins

Quite often, salespeople mistake someone for a coach when in fact the person isn't a loyal compatriot. You should always have a certain level of paranoia about your coach. Is he secretly coaching the competition? Is he acting as your eyes and ears when you are not around? Is he truthfully telling you about what the other vendors are up to and about the preferences of the various selection committee members? Is he providing privileged and proprietary information to you that the other vendors aren't receiving?

One of the most important sales cycle goals is to develop a trusted coach—hopefully, a guide. Obviously, the more coaches you have inside an account, the better the quality and quantity of information you will receive. The information you receive from these coaches can be used to determine your standing in an account and help determine your course of action. Being at the mercy of a single person is a risky position to be in. What if your coach is wrong?

25. Positional Tactics

All technology sales is war. It is an intense, high stakes, very personal battle between two individuals or two groups of people: you and your competition. The victor will savor the spoils of winning while the loser experiences humiliation and sometimes much worse.

A variety of positional tactics can be employed to establish and maintain account control. These tactics are either directed at a vendor to lessen his leadership position or executed to improve the salesperson's position in the account. You'll find explanations for each of the following positional tactics.

Ambush	*Camouflage*	*Interrogate*	*Parting shot*	*Shield*	*Sniping*	*Unload the bus*
AWOL	*Crossfire*	*Land mine*	*Pincer attack*	*Smoke screen*	*Stalking*	*Wedge*
Bombard-ment	*Deep battle*	*Left flank*	*Right flank*	*Scorched earth*	*Tempo*	

- *Ambush.* Perhaps the most effective sales example of ambushing the competition is telling a prospect about the competition's customers who have dumped their products and switched to yours. Even a competitor who is way ahead in the lead can lose his position by these enormously destructive stories.

- *AWOL.* "Absent without leave" is a military term for soldiers who are away from their posts or military duties without permission. In sales, it quite often makes sense for salespeople who suspect they are losing to go AWOL and disappear. Doing so forces an interested customer to pursue the salesperson. For example, when the customer asks for information, the salesperson will not provide it until he gets the information or commitments he wants in return. Doing nothing sometimes frustrates the members of the selection team who are working against the salesperson as it forces them to spend additional time dealing with this disruptive person. Other times, it is exactly what they would like to have happen as they want the salesperson and his solution to quietly disappear.

- *Bombardment.* In the sales vernacular, "bombardment" refers to the tactic of sending a constant stream of technical information, business justification material, and company marketing propaganda to the various levels of personnel within the account you are trying to win. Senior executives should receive short, high-level summary information, such as press articles or one-page industry analyst reviews. Midlevel managers should be sent more detailed case studies from other successful customers and case-use white papers. Low-level, hands-on product evaluators should receive data sheets and detailed implementation guides. Bombardment is an excellent "beachhead tactic" to use when you are trying to develop some recognition and credibility with particular individuals you have yet to meet during the sales cycle.

- *Camouflage.* Salespeople employ the camouflage tactic by enlisting a member of the selection team or other key influencer to disseminate positive information about their solution and negative information about competitors while they remain hidden in the background. A very simple example of a camouflage is asking an internal champion or coach to casually endorse your product to the CIO over lunch.

- *Crossfire.* The crossfire tactic involves using other people that are part of your sales team to help you win a deal. It may include other members of your company, such as your presales system engineer, implementation consultants, or business partners, who have a vested interest in your winning. You fire away at the competition together. It's a logic-based sales tactic designed to cause doubt in the customer's mind about another vendor's capabilities while bolstering your position.

- *Deep battle.* Deep battle is an appropriate sales tactic when you sense a selection committee is aligned against you and fear its recommendation to senior management. The goal of deep battle is to use a coach—a friend on the inside—to introduce you to the ultimate and final decision makers, the bully with the juice and emperor who exist in every account. You want a chance to plead your case in person. A salesperson may also ask the president, vice president of sales, and other senior executives from within his company to blindly call their counterparts at the customer's company. If the tactic is successful, you will have neutralized the selection committee's power and have a chance to win the deal. If the tactic fails (which is often the case), you will have alienated the committee and therefore lost.

- *Interrogate.* The interrogate tactic seeks to force adversaries to answer uncomfortable questions about their products, companies, and reputations. You want the customer to interrogate them about their faults on your behalf. At other times, you want to influence the sales cycle such that the customer creates unnecessary and unimportant steps that keep the other vendors busy responding to minutiae.

- *Land mine.* A land mine is a premeditated action that is intended to stop a competitor as he tries to engage with the customer. What type of land mine will you execute? Will you lie in wait until that competitor makes a statement you know you can clearly contradict and ruin his reputation in the process? Will you demonstrate functionality that your opponents can't match? Are you going to tell the customer about a new, unreleased product; provide third-party objective opinions; or disclose negative information about a competitor based upon your own experiences? When will the land mine be set? Will it be during the big sales presentation on the third PowerPoint slide or in an informal meeting with the customer?

- *Left flank (logic).* Flanking is a battlefield movement that consists of changing one's position to gain an advantage. The left-flank tactic is based upon logic and information. Flanking to the left refers to the tactic of changing the customer's selection criteria or raising a critical issue the customer is unaware of. It is named after the left side of the brain, the part that is analytical and invokes rational reasoning and deductive logic.

- *Parting shot.* A parting shot is a sharp, telling remark or critical communication made by a salesperson to strike a blow at the decision makers' confidence. Examples include warnings about failed customer installations, critical memorandums sent to executives about the selection team members' competence, or predictions about the future failure of the project.

- *Pincer attack.* In sales, the two pincers that crush your opponents are relationships and information. When customers like you personally and believe your product to be best (whether real or imagined), you are placed in the advantageous position of being able to control and edit the information flowing to and from the other vendors. This lopsided combination of personal friendships and information superiority are pincers that crush the competition.

- *Right flank (people).* The right-flank sales tactic is associated with the people involved in the decision process. It is named after the right hemisphere of the brain, which is dominant for facial recognition, spatial abilities, and visual imagery. A right-flank movement is focused on finding coaches within an account. Coaches are individuals who seem to like you, are receptive to your position, and appreciate your company. For example, you might make a right-flank maneuver and go around your main contact within an account in order to set up a meeting and establish a relationship with a more powerful decision maker.

- *Shield.* The shield tactic involves developing advocates (guides and strong spies) within an account who shield and protect you from the slings and arrows of your competitors and from naysayers within the company. The strongest of these shields is provided by a senior executive—president, CIO, CTO, or vice president—who is backing your solution. Regardless of your advocates' direct involvement in the selection process, the private opinions of these powerful people work behind the scenes to ward off known rivals and unseen internal detractors.

- *Smoke screen.* The smoke screen tactic is based upon an indirect strategy. For example, salespeople schedule meetings to discuss product functionality when in reality they are using these meetings to discern the personal biases of decision makers. Salespeople may change the topic of conversation during a sales call to a strong point in order to avoid a discussion about a deficiency. They provide customers with detailed information or technical specifications about their products' strengths in order to divert attention from the products' known weaknesses.

- *Scorched earth.* This tactic involves using any means necessary to stop the deal from happening. At this point, you are only trying to prevent the other vendors from winning. This is an extreme measure of last resort. Examples include calling the customer's senior management and explaining that the selection process was biased because decision makers had improper relationships with the winning vendor, complaining to interested outside parties (regulatory boards, media outlets, financial investors, and the general public) about misconduct during the selection process, seeking legal action to stop the purchase, and offering to provide your product at a greatly reduced price or even for free.

- *Sniping.* Not everyone on the customer's selection committee will be enamored with you and your solution. Occasionally an individual may be so ardently opposed to you and your company that that person must be taken out of the selection process altogether. Sniping involves lying in wait for the perfect moment to discredit and take out a detractor. For example, a lower-level employee who is voicing opinions against you must be removed from the sales process. You instill fear in the senior executives that the project will be unsuccessful with this person on the team. Sniping is very uncomfortable to do, but there are times when you must silence your opposition.

- *Stalking.* Contrary to common sense, some salespeople are actually able to hound the customer into purchasing their solution. They will not abandon the account or leave the decision makers alone until the customer buys from them. The relentless, unapologetic hounding and stalking of the customer is a very risky approach as it can backfire as well.

- *Tempo.* The tempo tactic involves using the element of time to gain an advantage. In some sales situations a rapid full force response with your best resources in the quickest possible time is best. "'Rapid" means the ability to move quickly before an adversary can react. "Full force" can be defined as the ability to dominate an adversary both physically and psychologically. In other situations, it is necessary to spread out and lengthen the selection process. Offering to complete a detailed on-site study of the customer's business, inviting the customer to make site visits to other installations, and taking the customer on a tour of your corporate headquarters are great examples of tempo tactics. These events allow you to demonstrate your expertise, and they give you additional time to build the personal relationships you need to win.

- *Unload the bus.* This involves applying as many personnel resources as you can to an account. Sales calls are an opportunity to demonstrate company strength and the salesperson may ask his support team (system engineers, consultants, product managers, sales management, and so on) to attend.

- *Wedge.* The wedge tactic is based on the repetition of key differentiating information. Let's say you have advantageous benchmark information that shows your product is faster than your opponent's solution, which happens to be in the lead. At every possible opportunity, you harangue the customer about the implications of poor performance, the technical differences between the products that cause poor performance, how much unnecessary equipment would need to be purchased to rectify the performance problem, and the business impact of poor performance. You continually hammer on performance in order to create an opening, a wedge or gap between the leader and the customer, where you can begin to spread your company's story and your product's benefits to the decision makers.

Tactics can be employed together to drive a successful outcome. The right- and left-flank tactics work together. For instance, a meeting can be set up under the guise of one topic using the smoke screen tactic when the goal is really to gain access to a specific person (right flank) and influence that person to change the logical selection criteria (left flank).

26. Sales Cycle Turning Points

Every type of sales cycle (renewal, creation, or persuasion) has a critical moment, or "turning point," where it is won or lost. In some cases, the turning point is easy to spot. For example, a salesperson may be presenting his solution and encounters a dealbreaking objection that he is unable to overcome. Even though the customer remains cordial for the rest of the meeting, a turning point has occurred and the deal is lost. In most cases, the turning point occurs when the salesperson isn't present. It's in casual hallway conversations or internal e-mails that selection team members share opinions that influence vendors' futures. The only outward sign that a turning point has occurred is the perceptible change in deal momentum as evidenced in figure 26.1.

> When a salesperson sits across from me and tells me he has been selling for twenty-five years and has worked for Oracle and SAP, the first thing that comes to my mind is "Congratulations, you have been fired from some of the best companies in the business." That's not what I want to hear.
> —*Vice President of Merchandising*

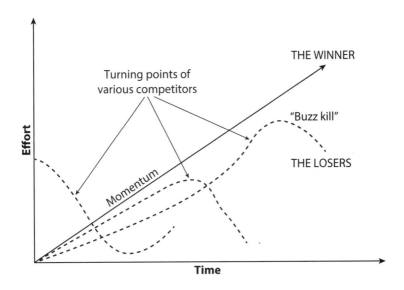

Figure 26.1 Turning points of various competitors

You probably noticed the term "buzz kill" on the graph. This represents the person, business reason, political issue, or technical obstacle that causes momentum to turn downward. Ninety-nine out of one hundred times you will not recover from a buzz kill.

However, some companies won't let salespeople stop working deals. You may even be familiar with the following drill, which I call the "walk of shame." All the various sales managers meet with the rep and theorize about all the possible ways to win. Then they mandate that the selling continue even though the salesperson knows working on a deal past a buzz kill is a waste of time.

> There was a company that I liked at the beginning, and we were just not going to give it to them. So we went through the whole procedure, making sure all the boxes were checked off by a panel of people.
> —*Chief Financial Officer*

Sometimes salespeople will decide on their own to continue the walk of shame. Since they have invested so much time, energy, and emotion into the deal, they find it impossible to let it go. This is particularly true for salespeople who have neglected to build up a pipeline of future business opportunities.

Time takes on an additional dimension of meaning during the sales cycle. Usually, we think of time as a continuum. We spend most of our mental energy thinking about the immediate tasks before us. We typically don't consider time to be a finite resource. There's always tomorrow, next week, next month, or next year. During the sales process, time is not just minutes and days; it is actually a measure of deal momentum. Therefore, increasing momentum in a deal represents good or positive time, and backward momentum is bad or negative time. Heavy Hitters keep the negative time they spend on deals to a minimum.

Time is a salesperson's enemy because time is finite. On average, there are thirty days in a month and ninety days in a quarter. Time is the governor that determines how many deals can be worked and where effort should be focused. The relentless march of time creates artificial deadlines by which deals must be won. Time is a precious resource that must be conserved, respected, and above all, used to your advantage.

Your most valuable asset is your time. First, in order to protect your time you must be able to recognize when a buzz kill occurs during sales calls. Second, if you are unsure why you are losing momentum during sales calls, bring along your manager or someone else and ask that person to help you identify buzz kill moments. Finally, write down the buzz kill moments of five deals you recently lost and prepare a counteractive strategy for each so history doesn't repeat itself again in the future.

Based on a number of factors, yes, we had a favorite vendor going in, and they won.
—*Chief Executive Officer*

Unfortunately, I have some very frightening news to share with you. Approximately 30 percent of the time the winner of the persuasion sales cycle was determined before the "official" selection process started. Another 45 percent of the time, customers had already made up their minds about whom they were going to buy from about halfway through the process. That means, 75 percent of the time, customers had made their decision by halfway through the process. Only 25 percent of the time did customers make their final decision at the end of the selection process. Therefore, if you are not clearly in the lead at the midpoint of the selection process, the odds are that you are going to lose. These numbers are even worse for certain technology segments. For example, 55 percent of on-premises enterprise-type software application decisions are made before the selection process starts. Figure 26.2 illustrates this point.

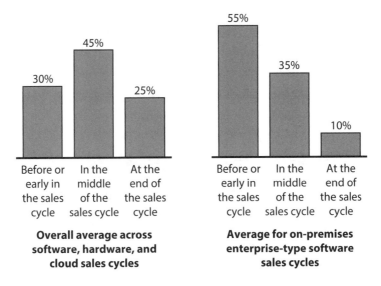

Figure 26.2 When customers make up their minds

Here's another frightening fact. In the overwhelming majority of cases, the decision wasn't even close between the top two choices. Even though customers had made up their minds, they still caused all the other salespeople to jump through a series of hoops for nothing, wasting their valuable time, resources, and mental and emotional energy.

> When we do an evaluation, it is definitely a numbers-driven evaluation. We build a matrix of needs and requirements and compare the vendors. We try to pick the highest-ranking vendor in most cases. But when the scores are close between vendors, other factors come into play such as whether one vendor is the incumbent and some are more esoteric like the quality of the existing relationship. But the vendors need to be closely ranked. Otherwise, it makes it difficult to justify the decision. I'll be honest, IT always has a favored vendor. They may have worked with them before and are used to them. So they always have some preference in their mind. At the end of the day, the evaluation process and RFP gives the opportunity to look at other vendors to see if they have any additional advantages. But the way it works out is usually driven by what IT really wanted in the first place.
>
> —*Procurement Director*

27. Psychological, Political, Operational, and Strategic Value

Establishing rapport is the only way to learn the true inner workings of a customer's selection process. In order to build customer rapport, you must demonstrate the value of your products, your company, and yourself. You must be able to convince the customer of the unique psychological value, political value, operational value, and strategic value you provide.

> Great technology companies are consumed with value add. It's not just selling the technology but helping you understand what is happening in the industry, having regular touchpoint meetings with the team, reviewing the road map, and sharing your knowledge of what your organization can do to help us execute our strategy. For me, strong technology companies have this engrained in their culture. They share information, don't ask for orders. In a lot of cases it doesn't lead to business. But what it creates is a stronger relationship where the organization you are working with becomes an advocate.
>
> —*Senior Vice President of IT Operations*

Psychological Value

At the root of every decision is one of four psychological values. People buy products they believe will help them fulfill deep-seated psychological needs: satisfying the ego, being accepted as part of a group, avoiding pain, and ensuring survival. All the other outward appearances of a customer's decision-making process—the analysis, return-on-investment calculations, and other internal studies—are the means to achieving an overriding psychological goal. Therefore, the psychological value is the most important value when it comes to purchasing decisions.

I have interviewed more than a thousand customers as part of the win-loss studies I conduct for my clients. The most important finding from these studies is that human nature is the ultimate decision maker for every major decision. While the customer may have publicly recited a laundry list of rational reasons to justify the decision he made, he truthfully revealed in private that politics, self-interests and personal emotions were responsible for the selection in the end.

Customers do not establish vendor relationships based upon the best business judgment; rather, they judge vendors based upon who establishes the best business relationships. A CIO I interviewed said it best: "We made it clear that we weren't buying a brochure or data sheet. For that matter, we weren't even buying a product. We were buying a long-term relationship with another company and, equally important, the team of people from that company whom we would have to work with on a day-in, day-out basis."

Customers purchase products that increase their happiness, esteem, power, or wealth. They rationalize these psychological decisions with logic and facts. For example, a vice president of a manufacturing company may explain that he wants to buy supply chain software because it will save a million dollars a year when, in reality, he is making the purchase to show the CEO that he is a prudent businessman. The desire to impress the CEO (the benefit) drives the software purchase (the action). The term "benefaction" refers to the psychological benefits that determine a person's actions.

Four core psychological drives determine selection behavior. These four benefactions are well-being, pain avoidance, self-preservation, and self-gratification. Physical well-being, the will to survive, is one of our strongest desires. It weighs heavily in the minds of both customers and competitors. Making customers feel their jobs are safe in your hands is a top priority during sales calls. Ideally, you would like them to believe (whether it is true or not) that the competitive solutions are actually threats to their livelihood. Customers are equally concerned with maintaining their mental and emotional well-being.

When something is hurting you badly, the desire to eliminate the source of pain can be all-consuming. Pain is one of the best purchase motivators because customers are forced to act quickly and decisively to eliminate it.

Companies experience different kinds of pain all the time. Nuisances can create dull aching pains in every department, such as a temperamental copy machine. Throbbing pains may reappear occasionally, like Internet service providers that go down momentarily every few months. Stabbing pains require immediate attention, for example, when the order-entry system is down and products can't be shipped and sales cannot be made. Companies can live with dull aches and cope with throbbing pains as necessary. But the stabbing pains receive immediate attention and dictate budgeting.

Self-preservation, the third core psychological drive, is the desire to be recognized for our unique talents while still belonging to a group. Customers and salespeople alike naturally seek the approval of others. Customers purchase items that they believe will enhance their stature and protect their group position. They not only want to be respected by their peers but also want to become group leaders. Naturally, salespeople want to be pack leaders too.

Self-gratification is our desire to put our own needs before everyone else's. Customers will go to great lengths to purchase something that makes them feel better about themselves and superior to others. Egos drive the business world.

Political Value

The second most important value, political value, involves organizational power. Many people think that power is dependent upon title and that the way work gets done in organizations is through hierarchical authority. However, this is not usually the case. Power is the ability to influence the environment for your own benefit. It is often used to get your way when diplomacy, consensus building, and negotiation fail. For example, while I have parental authority over my children, they have their own types of powers and associated strategies to get their way. Sometimes they will band together and recruit their mother to support their cause in order to override my authority. Companies operate in much the same way.

Your product provides customers the opportunity to achieve political power. It may enable them to increase their authority, help them become indispensable to the company, allow them to satisfy an internal powerbroker, or enable them to maintain authority. Interdepartmental coordination always involves the use of power. Your product can make someone more powerful, or for those seeking to become more influential, it can provide much-needed visibility that enables them to be in contact with the company's powerbrokers.

Operational Value

The third most important value is operational value. People's success in an organization is dependent upon the success of their department's operations. Therefore, every department has inherent pressure to accomplish projects that successfully add operational value.

The ways that operational value is determined are quite diverse. An ambitious manager might consider your product's operational value to be the ability to successfully complete the department's project that enables his department to proliferate its services throughout the company. Another customer might prize satisfying internal customers in other departments, and operational value to some might be found in products that enable them to resist change. For example, a bureaucratic IT department might add a new Internet interface to its existing mainframe rather than replace the entire system.

You can also think of operational value in terms of the customer's résumé—a list of all his successful projects and accomplishments. After the customer purchases your solution, what accomplishment or milestones would he add to his résumé?

Strategic Value

Strategic value, the fourth value, is based upon the appearance of rationality and impartiality. However, customers do not seek information that will help them make an objective strategic decision; they amass information that helps them justify their preconceived ideas of strategic value. In other words, your product's strategic value comprises the reasons and arguments evaluators give to senior management and others in the company as to why the product should be purchased, regardless of whether the reasons are real or imagined.

The seven basic types of strategic value enable customers to

- Gain a competitive advantage (increase market share, enter new markets, defeat competition)
- Increase revenues
- Decrease costs
- Increase productivity and efficiency
- Improve customer satisfaction
- Improve quality
- Standardize operations (increase ease of business and mitigate risk)

Some customers will say that a purchase provides a competitive advantage or will enable them to increase revenues. Others might argue internally that a purchase will save money in the long run. Some will show how customer satisfaction will be improved or detail improvements in operational efficiency.

The IT organizational buyer types perceive value differently. Consolidators will say that a purchase provides a competitive advantage or will enable them to increase revenues. Consulters might argue that a purchase will save money in the long run. Responders will show how customer satisfaction will be improved, and bureaucrats will detail improvements in operational efficiency. Figure 27.1 summarizes how consolidators, consulters, responders, and bureaucrats view each of the four different types of value.

	Consolidators	Consulters	Responders	Bureaucrats
Psychological value	Self-gratification Fulfill desire to achieve	Physical well-being Satisfy will to survive	Self-preservation Gain approval of others	Pain avoidance Avoid painful change
Political value	Consolidate power	Become indispensable	Draft off the powerful	Maintain authority
Operational value	Enable the grand initiative	Proliferate service offerings through organization	Reactively accommodate internal customers	Do as little as possible
Strategic value	Gain competitive advantage Increase revenues	Improve quality Decrease costs	Improve customer satisfaction Improve productivity and efficiency	Standardize operations Maintain ease of business

Figure 27.1 Different values based on IT organizational buyer type

Write down your psychological, political, operational, and strategic value to the customer. During customer interactions, present your solution to the potential buyer based upon these four values. You must communicate that *you* and *your solution* can help solve critical department problems, help the customer become an expert and an internal source of knowledge, and help him become successful and more powerful, and that you are providing a safe, long-term solution.

28. Why Customers Don't Buy

The real enemy of salespeople today isn't their archrivals; it's no decision. What is it that prevents a prospective customer from making a purchase even after he had conducted a lengthy evaluation process? The reasons may surprise you.

Regardless of the prospective customer's confident demeanor, on the inside he is experiencing fear, uncertainty, and doubt while making his selection. The stress this creates serves as the key factor in determining whether or not a purchase will be made. Therefore, all salespeople need to understand this lowest common denominator of human decision making—they need to understand the nature of stress.

From a psychological perspective, stress shortens attention spans, escalates mental exhaustion, and encourages poor decision making. From an organizational perspective, when anxious evaluators experience too much stress it typically results in analysis-paralysis. They are too overwhelmed with information and contradictory evidence to make a decision. It's the salesperson's responsibility to anticipate and diffuse the main sources of customer stress during the selection process: budgetary stress, corporate citizenship stress, organizational stress, vendor selection stress, informational stress, and evaluation committee stress.

Budgetary Stress: Is the Money Available and Justified to Be Spent?

Whether a purchase is actually made is directly related to the perceived risk versus the anticipated reward. A company's budgeting process is not only designed to prioritize where money is to be spent but also to remove the fear of spending it. Here's a quote from a senior executive IT decision maker I interviewed that explains this point:

> There are two main criteria for deciding on whether or not to make the purchase. One is value to the company as measured by return on investment and how it compares to other projects being considered. Then there are strategic projects that are critical to our long-term success such as protection of our brand or improving customer satisfaction. While projects may be approved initially for further evaluation, a cross-functional team of senior executives reviews the final recommendation and whether the money should be actually allocated and released.

Every initiative and its associated expenditure is competing against all the other projects that are requesting funds. Purchases are continually reprioritized based upon emergencies and in response to changing conditions. For example, when new executive leaders join organizations, one of their first acts may be to freeze major expenditures and reevaluate all requests. The bad news is that a salesperson may have worked on a deal for most of the year only to find out that it was never truly budgeted.

Corporate Citizenship Stress: Is It in the Best Interest of the Company?

While customers inherently want to do what's in the best interest of their company and to be good corporate citizens, the fundamental dynamic of corporate-employee loyalty has changed. Today, business is a "survival of the fittest" world where employment is never guaranteed and loyalty frequently goes unrewarded. In some situations, prospective buyers can feel continual pressure to put their individual needs before the company's.

> There's no such thing as picking the wrong solution so long as it helps you land your next job.
> —*Director of Information Technology*

Even after a formal evaluation process, the likelihood that a purchase will not be made jumps tenfold when the solution recommended is not aligned to a company's goals and direction. This is frequently the case with projects and purchases that are instigated by lower levels of an organization as they bubble up the chain of command for review. There is not a compelling business case to drive the purchase forward so it never garners senior level support. Similarly, technology solutions that are sold to the business face the hurdle of gaining the approval of skeptical IT departments that want to control their infrastructure landscape and applications.

Organizational Stress: How Do My Colleagues Perceive Me?

Peer pressure is a powerful influencer of group dynamics and evaluators are constantly worried about how the purchase decision will reflect on them. Senior executives are worried about what investors, the board of directors, and members of the leadership team think about them. And of course, they want their employees to respect them as well. Midlevel managers suffer competitive pressure because all are striving to advance in their careers and move upward in the organization. Lower-level personnel are continually seeking to prove themselves to their managers.

We did a blind RFP because we were considering an outsourcing arrangement that would impact our employees. After five months, we finished the selection process and had to build a business case and present it to our board because of the significant dollar value of the contract. They had only given an initial approval to complete the study. At the time, it felt like they were putting us through a meat grinder. We had to show pricing for the vendors, explain why we selected the more expensive solution, detail the implementation risks, and what the world would look like afterward. I was unsure the project would be approved after all the time and effort.

—*Chief Information Officer*

Whether from above, below, or the same level in an organization, coworkers are continually evaluating the behavior, success, and failures of those tasked with the decision-making process. Obviously, this exerts pressure on the evaluators to make the right decision and not to make a decision if there isn't an obvious choice or clear-cut direction.

Vendor Selection Stress: Is the Tug of War between Vendors Equal?

One of the biggest problems during the sales cycle is that the difference between most products is extremely small. Compounding this problem is that everyone is presenting the same basic messages to the customer. Take a moment and visit the home page of your company's website and those of your two biggest competitors. You'll see that the words and claims are basically interchangeable.

There tends to be a higher no-decision rate where product differentiation is extremely small. Since all the competing products share the same basic features, functions, and benefits, evaluation team members may take longer to make their decision or postpone them indefinitely.

Informational Stress: Is the Information Being Presented Truthful?

We live in very skeptical times in which information presented by the media and experts is continually challenged and constantly debunked. In addition to being subject to the general cynicism of our society, most customers have had negative experiences with some salespeople sometime in the past. Therefore, customers are always in the stressful position of separating fact from fiction. Meanwhile, even the most ethical salesperson carries the burden of proving he's telling the truth.

Worse yet, as the sales cycle progresses, competing vendors may try to escalate FUD (fear, uncertainty, and doubt) in the customer's mind about the wherewithal of the competitors and the capabilities of their products. For example, competitors will try to sabotage one another with facts such as unfavorable performance metrics, missing functionality, and tales of unhappy customers. In turn, the attacked competitors will provide the customer with believable information that contradicts the original attacks. Therefore, the sales cycle naturally disintegrates into a quarrel between salespeople and this scenario helps set the stage for no decision to be made.

Evaluation Committee Stress: Why Can't We Agree?

Whenever a company makes a purchase decision that involves groups of people, self-interests, politics, and group dynamics will influence the final decision. Tension, drama, and conflict are normal parts of group dynamics because decisions are not typically made unanimously. As members promote their own personal agendas, the interpersonal conflicts can cause the decision-making process to stagnate and stop. Other selection team members may not be 100 percent certain they are picking the right solution. All of this uncertainty encourages no decision.

> If I don't believe the business case, then I reserve the right to exercise my veto. Even though another executive wants to do it, I have to believe the business case or I will resist it. It's not like I have an ax to grind with IT, R&D, marketing, or sales, but I have to remain independent and wear my corporate hat. I also have the duty to say no when the level of change represents an unacceptable level of risk.
> —*Vice President of Finance*

Customers are stressed out. They don't know whom or what to believe. They are under immense peer pressure, and they are torn between doing the right thing for the greater good of the company and acting in their best personal interest. To make matters worse, the vendors increase the pressure by injecting claims of their superiority and accusations about their competitors' inferiority. For all these reasons it's no surprise that no decision is the top competitor today.

29. Human Nature and Decision Making

To understand the impact of the subconscious mind on decision making, let's study Bob, a college-educated professional with a doctorate in computer science. Successful in his career, he has become the CIO of a Fortune 500 company. Bob is a smart businessman who employs sound business practices and possesses the acumen to get to the top of the corporate ladder.

Let's say Bob is facing two very important decisions. The first decision involves making a multimillion-dollar technology purchase for the division he runs. The second decision involves proposing marriage to Maggie, his girlfriend of nine months. Bob approaches each of these decisions in a very different way.

For the business decision, he first conducts an in-depth study of the inefficiencies of his current infrastructure. Next, he presents his findings with an internal rate-of-return study for replacing the old equipment with state-of-the-art machinery to the senior management team of the parent company. Then he performs a detailed analysis of the various equipment vendors and makes a final selection.

Getting married is one of life's most important decisions. Bob has fallen in love with Maggie. He feels good being with her, thinks about her often, and looks forward to their time together. She has the qualities he admires, and when compared to girlfriends of the past, she is the best. Bob decides he will ask her to marry him.

However, as he moves forward in his decision-making process, an unexpected change in Bob's thought process occurs. The subconscious mind, the self-regulating system designed to prevent us from making unwise choices, is on vigilant watch. It drives Bob to perform a "gut-check" of the rational, logical information regarding the equipment purchase. Beyond the facts and figures, does the decision feel right? He second-guesses himself and asks whether the move will help or hurt his career.

> I wasn't completely sure their solution would work, and my job hung on the success of the project. I took a leap of faith and believed what they had told me.
> —*Chief Information Officer*

Conversely, the emotional high associated with the idea of marriage is tempered by reality. He now evaluates Maggie's little habits that he once thought were cute with a more rational eye. He studies other aspects of their relationship with equal intensity. Figure 29.1 illustrates the changing nature of the decision-making process.

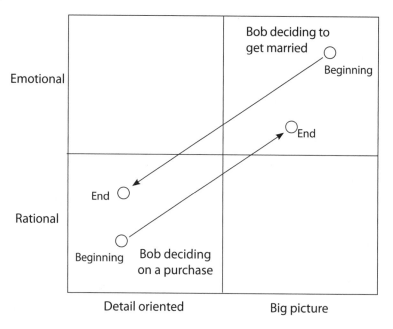

Figure 29.1 The changing nature of decision making

We were most impressed with Vendor A's sales team, but their product wasn't up to par. There was something about their salesperson that made me feel like they absolutely understood all of our concerns and what we were trying to accomplish. It was interesting, because if I was basing it solely on a human relationship factor they probably would have won.
        —*Senior IT Analyst*

Anticipate the impact of the subconscious mind during the sales cycle and take it into account during sales calls. The customer with whom you had a "red-hot" initial sales call will suddenly turn cold and fail to respond to your follow-up calls. The prospect who has established an elaborate selection process will ultimately be influenced by emotions. Knowing this ahead of time, you can plan to use different types of words that correspond to a logical, emotional, and psychological appeal in interactions with your customers.

> They were completely unwilling to think outside the box with us. We consider ourselves unique, so we like the people we work with to treat us differently. I don't know whether it was because the salesperson was so bad or the fact that their company is so rigid that they wouldn't even entertain the idea. After I told them we weren't moving forward with them, I almost got this autoresponse: "We're sorry to hear that; keep us in mind; blah, blah, blah." I thought, "Don't you want to know why, you idiot?"
>
> —*Chief Financial Officer*

PART III

New Account Penetration Strategy

30. Dead Words

We connect with people through the words we speak, the way in which we say them, and the congruence of the words to our demeanor. However, the words we use are complex objects that don't mean the same to everyone. To understand this, let's do this word association exercise. What is the first thought that comes to mind when you read the words "dog," "sports," "church," "marriage," and "children?"

If you have a dog, you probably thought of your dog. A picture of your dog may have come to mind, and you may have said your dog's name to yourself. The word "sports" may have caused you to think about the sport you played in school because words are anchored to our memories. The word "church" could elicit many different responses, ranging from a sense of purpose to a resistance to authority, depending upon your orientation. Meanwhile, marriage is to some a blessing; to others, a dream; and to the unlucky, a nightmare. So your reaction to the word "marriage" is likely based on your experience.

All of these words have something in common. In order to be understood, they must be interpreted into something meaningful: familiar thoughts and terms. This process occurs in three steps: determining the lexical meaning of a word, translating the word into personal meaning, and finally, forming a psychological impression determined by how the word is cataloged.

The first step is comprehension, checking whether or not the word can be found in the personal dictionary you keep inside your mind. Your lexical dictionary determines your word comprehension. The average person's dictionary contains about fifty thousand words.

After your lexical dictionary has defined a word, personal meaning is associated with it. For example, your lexical definition of the word "children" might be "kids between two and twelve." In your mind, children are not teenagers or babies. Your mind then tries to derive personal meaning from the word "children." If you have children, you might immediately think of your son, your daughter, or all your children. You might think of a child playing or even a schoolroom. Thus, another level of personal interpretation occurs. The deepest level of meaning occurs inside the mind's word catalog, where the word is associated with psychological meaning. While your lexical dictionary defines the basic meaning of words, your word catalog links that meaning to your past experiences. For example, you may have felt a sense of pride when you thought about your children and a specific memory, such as a school graduation ceremony or sporting event they competed in.

New words are continually introduced into the English language. They pass through periods of introduction, adoption, and then widespread use when they are universally known and called "general words." Then they are subject to "linguistic inflation" from overuse. For example, the word "green" as it refers to environmental friendliness is in a period of linguistic hyperinflation and is quickly losing its value. At the end of an overused word's life cycle, its meaning is deadened from the word's excessive use. This is what has happened to the words "powerful," "reliable," and "scalable." Overused words that have lost impactful meaning are called "dead words."

Sometimes the terms your marketing department believes are so important and persuasive actually detract from your credibility. I have reviewed hundreds of corporate PowerPoint presentations. Not only do they all look the same, but they all use the same general words to describe their company's unique advantages. Open your corporate presentation and see how many of these terms and phrases you can find:

World leader	Increase revenues	Scalable
Market leader	Reduce costs	Manageable
Best-in-class	Competitive advantage	Reliable
Best-of-breed	Greater productivity	Powerful
Cost effective	Improve customer satisfaction	Easy to use
End-to-end solution	Better visibility	Dynamic

These dead words have been so overused that they actually have a negative impact or no impact at all. As opposed to dead words, "rich words" evoke a deeper personal meaning, importance, and even cachet. For example, a "salesperson" can also be called a "solution specialist." Rich words can be used to describe product qualities like "intelligently" designed, "straightforward" operation, or "ingenious" craftsmanship.

Whether you are trying to connect with a CEO or a computer programmer, the first step of communication is to check comprehension—whether or not your spoken words can be found in the personal dictionary that is kept inside his mind. Don't assume the customer understands the lexical meaning of the words you're using just because everyone in your own company does. Avoid using dead words that detract from your credibility and actually decrease rapport. Instead, use distinguishing rich words that impart significance.

31. General Words

Suppose you go to a pizza parlor and when you are asked for your order, you say, "pizza." The server will give you a blank stare. Do you want small, medium, or large? Do you want toppings? Unless the restaurant has only one pizza on the menu, "pizza" is a general word. A general word requires the use of additional words for the message to be received accurately. These additional words, called "operators," are used in conjunction with the general word to change the meaning. For example, adding the words "large," "deep dish," and "pepperoni" add meaning to the word "pizza."

If you tell a customer your solution is "fast and reliable," what have you communicated? It's through the use of operators that specific meanings are added and meaningful communication is completed. If you tell a customer your solution is "fast and reliable, will print two hundred pages per minute, and has a 99.99 percent uptime rate," you have communicated something meaningful.

It's important to recognize the difference between general and specific words. In sales, general words are used predominantly to describe and market product advantages. Probably three of the most regularly used terms are "performance," "reliability," and "scalability."

The phrases below were taken from the website home pages of three prominent high-technology companies:

- "ABC Company enables organizations to exceed performance and reliability expectations."
- "DEF Company combines power and scalability to meet your business needs."
- "XYZ Solutions automatically and intelligently delivers the best possible performance and availability."

Other popular general terms include "new and improved," "flexibility," "manageability," "powerful," and "price performance." Little meaning can be derived from these product claims unless operators are added. Here's the point: when speaking with buyers, always validate the general claims about your products with specific features or specific examples to give credence and meaning to your statements.

Not all words are equally persuasive. General words such as "performance," "reliability," and "quality" by themselves are not influential. Operator words, words that improve the persuasiveness of general words, must be added to influence a customer's mind. Adding "nine hundred pages per hour" to define "performance" adds a comparison-point meaning. Adding "one hundred thousand hours mean time between failures" to specify "reliability" helps makes the general word more convincing. Believability is improved when "lifetime guaranteed replacement" is associated with "quality."

32. Pattern Interruption

Put yourself in the position of the customer for a moment. You've met hundreds of salespeople and have found many of them to be friendly, courteous, and professional. Each of them also wants to build a personal relationship with you. You can't let this happen. You aren't going to build a friendship with everyone when you know you are going to select only one person to do business with. That wouldn't be practical or comfortable. Therefore, you are reserved and on guard and you keep your distance.

You also have met your share of salespeople who were pushy, arrogant, or just plain incompetent. Some salespeople lied straight to your face and broke their promises. They overcommitted what their products could do and misled you about what they couldn't. As a result, you initially treat every salesperson you meet with extreme wariness.

Now if you're the salesperson meeting this customer, the first step of your call should be to perform a pattern interruption to break the customer's mode of thinking and stand out from the competition. A pattern interruption consists of a cowcatcher and a hook. Let me explain with the following analogy. A smartphone can store thousands of songs. If you thumb a playlist each song has just a few seconds to capture your attention. If the introduction isn't interesting, different, or exciting, you move on to the next song. The term I use to describe this critical lead-in is "cowcatcher." The catchy part of the song is called the "hook." It can be the melody, phrase or the chorus that you remember and in some cases, can't get out of your mind.

Most people associate the term "cowcatcher" with the metal grill on the front of a locomotive. However, "cowcatcher" had an entirely different meaning in the early days of the entertainment industry. It was a radio or television show's opening moments in which the performers tried to grab your attention and caused you to stop and look.

A great cowcatcher engages the mind, appeals to the imagination, and helps the presenter gain credibility. One technology company I worked for was the top-rated NASDAQ stock for a period of five years. In fact, during one two-year time frame, $32,000 worth of this company's stock grew to be worth $1,000,000. I always opened my presentations with a chart of the stock price as the cowcatcher and then explained the facts behind the stock's appreciation as the hook. The customers would be more than intrigued; they were downright fascinated and eager to learn more. Many would buy my company's stock that very day.

I worked at another company whose core technology was originally developed by the California Institute of Technology and funded by a grant from NASA. Explaining the origins of the company during presentations—not with one simple slide with a few bullet points but using highlights of the project and its results set against a backdrop of the space shuttle in outer space—was a great cowcatcher and hook. We differentiated ourselves and gained instant credibility.

Customers are not only skeptical, they're nervous. Meeting someone new is a stressful experience, and the customer's internal dialogue is on high alert. One of the biggest challenges you face is establishing a sufficient level of customer rapport to ensure your message is received in an open and honest manner. This is why you must interrupt customers' patterns of negative thinking and lower their natural defenses. From this point forward, think how you can begin every telephone call, sales call, and presentation with a pattern interruption.

33. The Perfect Elevator Pitch

Even senior salespeople may find this exercise to be very challenging. What makes it difficult is that you already think you can do it easily. The exercise requires you to time yourself because it must be completed in no more than forty-five seconds. Ideally, you want to be in a private place where you can say your answer aloud.

I would like you to pretend that you are in an elevator at one of your industry's trade shows. You are heading down to the lobby when the doors open on the thirtieth floor. You instantly recognize the executive who walks in and quickly glance at his name badge to confirm he is the CIO of the most important account you would like to start working with. You have never met him before nor have you been able to generate any interest from his organization. You have forty-five seconds to introduce yourself, explain what your company does in a way the CIO would find interesting and applicable, and motivate him to take the action you suggest. Ready? Go! So, how did you do? You are to be commended for completing this exercise. Even the most successful salespeople find this pressure-packed exercise difficult. At sales meetings, I will ask salespeople to perform this exercise with me in front of their peers. Many times they become flustered or quit halfway through and they ask me if they can start over again. My answer is always no because you have only one chance to make a great first impression. Here are the six most common mistakes salespeople make with their elevator pitch:

- *They use truisms.* They believe their company's own marketing pitch, which makes claims that are not considered entirely true by the listener. As a result, they instantly lose credibility.
- *They describe themselves using buzzwords.* They repeat industry buzzwords or, worse yet, use technical buzzwords that are known only within their company.
- *They use fillers.* They make too much small talk or ask frivolous questions that reduce their stature and make them even more submissive to the customer.
- *They demean themselves or the listener.* Their statements make them into mere salespeople, not business problem solvers. They unintentionally demean the listener by asking impertinent questions or assuming the listener knows exactly what they are talking about.
- *They present an unreasonable close.* They don't take into account that they are talking to a senior company leader and use a close that is unrealistic or demands too much of the customer.

- *They are incongruent.* Their tone, pitch, and tempo of speech don't match. They speak too fast and their quivering tone broadcasts that they're nervous and submissive.

Here's an example of a poor elevator pitch. The problems are identified in brackets. Luke Skywalker, a salesperson for XYZ Technologies, is attending a trade show and happens to be in the elevator with Norman Bates, chief information officer at Wonderful Telecommunications.

> Hello, Norman. How are you today [filler]? Do you have a moment to talk [filler]? My name is Luke Skywalker and I work for [demeans salesperson] XYZ Technologies. Have you heard of XYZ Technologies [demeans listener]? Umm . . . [filler] Well, we are the leading provider [truism] of business transformational outsourcing [industry buzzword]. We have a unique extended-hybrid implementation methodology [technical buzzword]. Do you have time for me to buy you a cup of coffee and hear more about it [unreasonable close]?

A successful elevator pitch will incorporate the following linguistic structures:

- *Softeners.* A softener eases listeners into the next thought or is used to set expectations. When you say, "I'm sorry to bother you," you are using the preapologizing softener technique.
- *Facts.* A fact is the undisputed truth. Facts are recognized instantaneously.
- *Logic.* Logic is inferred by the listener to be true. Two main types of logic are used in sales situations: linear and geometric. The formula for linear logic is A plus B equals C, meaning when A and B are true statements, then the C statement or idea is also true. For example, "Our solution is 10 percent faster" and "We are 25 percent cheaper"; therefore, "We are the better solution."

The formula for geometric logic is if X is true, and X equals Y, then any statement that is true for X also applies to Y. For example, "We are helping Allstate Insurance reduce costs 10 percent" and "You are an insurance company like Allstate Insurance"; therefore, "We can help you reduce your costs 10 percent."

- *Metaphors.* Metaphors are educational, personal, and action-based stories. The purpose of each of these metaphors is to tell, teach, and enlighten the listener, with the ultimate goal of changing his or her opinion or behavior. While educational metaphors appeal to the conscious intellect, personal and action-based metaphors can be tailored to the subconscious mind. Also, all three types can be connected, interwoven, and mixed together in any combination.

- *Suggestions.* Foreground suggestions are direct and explicit ("*Informationweek* magazine gave our product the highest rating"). Background suggestions are indirect and their meaning is inferred ("One of their customers recently switched to our product").

- *Fallback position.* Every customer conversation is actually a negotiation between verbal dominance and submissive silence. Instead of giving ultimatums that force the customer to accept or reject your close, provide options from which customers can select. Always have alternate suggestions prepared in advance.

- *Silence.* Silence is an important and useful linguistic structure. It indicates you are listening and waiting for a response. Silence can actually be used to gain dominance during conversations.

Here's an elevator pitch that incorporates these linguistic structures:

Norman, hi, I'm Luke Skywalker with XYZ Technologies [fact]. It's a pleasure to meet you [softener]. I'm not sure if you are familiar with us [softener], but we work with AT&T [fact]. They've had to reduce their IT costs during these tough times [geometric logic]. I'm here because James Bond, the CIO of AT&T, is presenting a case study on how he cut his IT costs by 20 percent using our outsourcing solution [metaphor, background suggestion]. There'll be CIOs from some of our other customers, including General Electric and Johnson & Johnson, speaking as well [fact, background suggestion]. The session is tomorrow at 1:00 p.m. if you can make it [foreground suggestion, softener]. [Pause—silence, waiting for response.] That's too bad [softener]. I'd be delighted to send you his presentation [fallback position, foreground suggestion]. Great. Just to confirm your e-mail address, that's Norman.bates@wonderful.com. Is there anyone else I should send it to [fallback position]? [Pause—silence]. Okay, that's Ferris Bueller, your vice president of infrastructure. Thanks, Norman. You'll be hearing from me shortly.

The most important linguistic structure used in this elevator pitch are the metaphors. Ideally, a metaphor will cause the mind to immediately recognize the importance of the information, accept the message, and follow the suggestion. The proof of a metaphor's success is evidenced by a change in the verbal and physical language the listener emits. This could range from an enthusiastic verbal response to a subtle readjustment to an open posture indicating the person is receptive to your ideas.

Your words are your most important competitive weapons. In this regard, your ability to deliver a compelling elevator pitch is your biggest and most reliable armament. There are many sales situations where you have only a minute or two to conduct an entire sales call. For example, you could be walking down the customer's hallway and bump into the CIO or meeting with a lower-level contact when the vice president drops in. You must be able to deliver a compelling and memorable message during this pressure-packed time sensitive encounter. Write down your elevator pitch and analyze its structure for the use of buzzwords, fillers, and truisms.

> I used to be a reporter in a previous life so it's natural that I use an investigative approach. My goal is always to talk to the highest-level individuals. I don't give them an elevator pitch of feeds and speeds. I'm crafting a personal story that draws the listener in.
>
> —*Top Technology Salesperson*

34. Cold Calls, Letters, and E-mails

If selling is about speaking the language of the customer, then there are as many varieties of languages as there are customers. However, you have only three basic communication vehicles at your disposal to reach new customers: cold calls, letters, and e-mail. While you can use any of these three communication vehicles to secure initial meetings with customers, let's take a moment to review the pluses and minuses of each method.

Cold Calls

Here are some observations about cold calling. First, the odds of connecting with the person you are trying to reach are around 5 percent so you will most likely go to voice mail. Most of the time salespeople talk too fast when they leave their message. In particular, the phone number at the end of a long-winded speech is said the fastest. Is someone really going to replay the voice mail three times to get your phone number right? Some salespeople assume the listener knows exactly what they do when the opposite is true. Many salespeople are either nervous, bored, or both. They ramble on in a dreary, unexciting way. Why should they expect me to have any enthusiasm for what they're selling when they don't show any?

You must be able to leave a succinct message. In no more than twenty-five seconds you must identify who you are and why the customer should call you back. Your message must be delivered in a clear, commanding, yet approachable tone. Therefore, every time you plan on making cold calls you should rehearse leaving the voice mail. I suggest that you call your own voice mail three to five times and practice leaving the message you plan to use. Listen to your voice mail, put yourself in the customer's place, and ask if you would call yourself back.

> The number of cold calls that I get from IT vendors is phe-
> nomenal to the point that I don't even answer my phone.
> There are so many cold calls per day. I know what my problem
> is and I know where to look. I don't want to interact with
> everybody. So I'll start with the vendors who I have a relation-
> ship with; they understand and appreciate my needs.
> —*Director of Systems and Process*

I have some more bad news to share with you regarding the effectiveness of cold calls. Almost all of the C-level executives I have spoken to have never returned a cold call. Should you cold call senior executives? Yes, cold calling does have a specific purpose during the new account penetration process: it should be used mainly as a follow-up device after an e-mail or letter has been sent. However, I have a totally different attitude toward cold calling lower-level and midlevel personnel. I have heard so many stories over the years about large deals that started with a cold call that I can't recall them all.

The way we found out about them was from a cold call. We haven't seen them at the conferences we go to or in our industry periodicals. Maybe they should think about how they are marketing themselves. Had they not called we never would have looked at them.

—*Programmer*

Salespeople who relentlessly cold call someone are making a mistake. I guess they think their persistence will win that person over. Conversely, these salespeople are infringing on personal time and space. They will grow to be despised. I have a very different opinion about e-mail because it is a cafeteria-type communication channel. Voice mail is a serial communication channel. A person has to go through messages in order, one at a time. E-mail is different; someone can pick and choose which e-mails to open and do so in whatever order he wants. Therefore, it's not so bothersome when someone sends an occasional unsolicited e-mail as you can block the sender if the frequency gets too intrusive.

They are doing a lot of cold calling and known for being very persistent. I get feedback from people here that they are a little tired of the calls. He may be a great guy, but to have this level of persistence over something of such a low level of importance is distracting for the folks here. If you're not getting somewhere pretty quickly, you shouldn't persist.

—*IT Director*

Letters

Letters sent by snail mail must meet one important condition: the letter and associated marketing collateral that is sent to the customer must be totally unique. The material and message you send should vary according to the level of personnel in the account you are trying to penetrate. Senior executives should receive short, high-level summary information, such as press articles, one-page reviews, and case studies about their competitors whom you are doing business with. Save the company brochure, white papers, data sheets, and other detailed information for the midlevel and lower-level personnel.

Think about all the different types of items you can send to a potential customer other than a standard letter of introduction. You can send interesting news clippings and serious-sounding industry updates that help validate your marketing claims. You can send company tchotchkes such as T-shirts, baseball caps, and mouse pads that carry your company's name and logo. Most of the time these items are taken home and given away to family and friends, and it's great advertising when Junior parades around the house wearing your company's T-shirt. Remember, whatever you send should be as unique as possible while still promoting a professional image.

E-mails

One of the first lessons every new salesperson learns is to "call high," to try to reach the most senior-level executive. Therefore, it's not surprising that senior-level executives are continually harassed by salespeople. When you try to call the CEO or vice president of a company, you face a monumental challenge because the entire organization is designed to protect him from you. Most likely, you will be screened by an assistant or directed to an underling. The letters you send to executives tend to suffer the same fate. Given this reality, the preferred vehicle of communication is e-mail.

> I received an e-mail. I usually never bother with them. But this one caught my attention and I actually read the entire e-mail. I forwarded it to one of my managers and asked him to bring them in for a meeting.
> —*Vice President of Engineering*

The subject line is the single most important part of the e-mail. Its sole purpose is to catch someone's attention and motivate the person to open the e-mail. The best e-mails start with a great cowcatcher (see chapter 32). Here are some actual examples of bad subject lines from e-mails I have received.

- *Subject: Increase Revenues 1000%!* This overpromising subject line means the e-mail will immediately be considered spam and deleted before it has a chance to be read.
- *Subject: Business Proposal Information.* This subject line incorrectly sets readers' expectations. They'll feel deceived when they open the e-mail and see it is from a stranger trying to sell them something.
- *Free White Paper.* A C-level executive doesn't want to waste time reading this.
- *Would you be interested in XYZ Product?* The answer is no when the question is presented this way.
- *Don't Break the Bank! Product of the year saves money and eliminates network bottlenecks.* It's just too long to bother with.

The hook is the catchy part of the e-mail. It's the first few sentences that deliver a punch and motivate you to keep reading. The cowcatcher and the hook work together synergistically. Great e-mails have an interesting cowcatcher and a provocative hook. Here's an example of a terrible e-mail exactly as I received it with my critique immediately following.

Subject: Please advise

The pressure is on to grow revenue faster. How will you adapt business to reach goals?

XXXX can help you gain a strong competitive edge. Let me show you can use XXXX to:

- Drive better results.
- Increase customer satisfaction and loyalty
- Expand your market share.

Do you have time this week or next for a brief discussion about your business needs? Please reply with the best time for me to contact you.

Best regards,
XXX XXXXXX

This e-mail has the wrong subject line. It is titled "Please advise," which gives the reader the impression it is from someone the reader knows about a business issue the sender needs advice on. When the reader opens the e-mail and sees that it is spam, it creates a "negative receptive state" because the reader feels deceived. If this e-mail was intended for a vice president of sales, a better title would have been "Increase revenues by increasing sales calls." If intended for a CFO, "Five tips to decrease your cost of operations" could have been used. These titles set the readers' expectations and create a "positive receptive state."

The e-mail suggests the sender is a simpleton. It also has typos and grammatical mistakes. We'll discuss the roles of dominance and submission during communication in chapter 65. This submissive e-mail is written at the level of a fifth grader when scored by the Flesch-Kincaid test. Is a senior-level executive really going to want to meet with an elementary school student?

The e-mail is also too generic to grab the reader's attention. It uses strategic terms like "grow revenue," "competitive edge," and "increase customer satisfaction" generically without any explanation. These terms are so overused by everyone in sales that they are "dead words"—they have no meaningful impact. The sender didn't conduct any background research so that he could craft a message that would appeal to the recipient. The best way to tap into these values is by tailoring your message directly to the intended recipient based upon the person's role within the company. A one-size-fits-all e-mail is less effective because the vice presidents of marketing, sales, and finance face very different day-to-day challenges.

The Internet has fundamentally changed the way people communicate. You must master how to use e-mail to penetrate new accounts. Your success will increasingly depend upon it in the future. You'll never get an initial face-to-face meeting if your introductory message doesn't connect with its intended target.

> E-mail is always the best way to make initial contact with me. Then I'll check out your website to see what you have and who your customers are. I'll either respond to the e-mail or it's the best time to call me after that.
>
> —*Director of Application Development*

35. The "1, 2, 3, Rest, Repeat" Campaign

The strategy to penetrate new accounts is called the "1, 2, 3, Rest, Repeat" campaign. It requires adopting a new philosophy about contacting senior executives and other employees within organizations based upon three principles.

First, you must believe that every company will become a customer of yours because you honestly believe that you can help the business. Essentially, it's just a matter of time before you connect and work together. You must believe in what you're doing. Your efforts cannot be based upon half-hearted motivations. You must have a conviction that you, your products, and your company are the only true solution for the customer. When you have this mind-set it is impossible to consider yourself an obnoxious telemarketer or discourteous e-mail spammer. Rather, you are on an urgent mission to save the customer from making an ill-advised decision that will create a less-than-perfect workplace.

> What resonates with a CIO? I come back to the most funda-mental activities of a salesperson. First, don't give up! If I am not interested in something, don't give up and move on. Do what you need to do to establish the relationship because a lot of times it is about timing. I always say the best salespeople, and I probably only count them on one hand in my twenty-five years of IT, never give up. The really good salespeople can establish a relationship with you over voice mail. They leave a voice mail every month or so or drop me a note and over the course of time, I actually know who they are and they have a relationship even though we've never met in person. When a deal isn't going to land in the short term, look longer term and take the time to understand my business and invest the energy to find out what my needs are.
>
> —*Chief Information Officer*

Second, your attempts to contact a customer will take time. In essence, you are running a political campaign that will take several months and in many cases over a year. While you obviously want to generate immediate interest, you need to set your own expectations so you don't get frustrated by a lack of results and stop campaigning. The campaign ends only when the customer buys your solution or specifically tells you to stop contacting him.

Third, the reason why the customer doesn't respond to your message is not that he's disinterested or too busy. Rather, consider it your fault because you didn't send him the right message. While you didn't get the message right this time, you should also know that you will get it right over time. Therefore, you should never be bashful about contacting the customer again.

The 1, 2, 3, Rest, Repeat campaign is based upon sending a series of three unique messages that have different structures and intentions. These actions are followed by a period when you go quiet and do not make any attempts whatsoever to contact the customer. Once this time frame is over, you start another campaign with a series of different messages. Here's how the campaign works:

> *Step 1—Send an initial credibility message.* This introductory message identifies in an interesting way who you are and what you do.
>
> *Step 2—Send a tactical offer message.* This message is centered upon a business problem or industry theme.
>
> *Step 3—Send a final message.* This message is the culmination of the campaign.
>
> *Step 4—Rest.* During this period, you do not contact the customer.
>
> *Step 5—Repeat.* After the rest period has ended, you start another campaign with a series of three entirely new messages.

Most companies and salespeople make two critical mistakes when they try to reach customers. They either contact them once and stop if they don't get a response or contact them way too much. They mistakenly believe they are gaining mind share and acceptance by sending a newsletter or announcement every other week or once a month. The exact opposite is true. They are devaluing and diluting their message.

> They're too aggressive in their sales tactics, and this is upsetting. Big organizations like us have a process you must go through. It's good they don't take an initial no for an answer,

but they're kind of relentless in contacting us. Once they reach the ultimate decision maker who says "not at this time," they are looking for different people and angles to work. But it eventually goes from "not at this time" to "I don't want to work with those guys!"

—*General Manager*

Your strategy to penetrate a new account should not be a one-time action. Instead, it requires an ongoing campaign that can utilize all three communication vehicles at your disposal: e-mail, telephone cold calls, and letters (direct mail). Ideally, you should coordinate the order in which you send the communiqués. For example, you could send a letter in step 1, follow up with an e-mail in step 2, and phone call the customer a few days later.

Typically, the time frame to accomplish the first three steps should be between sixty and ninety days. If you try to shorten the contact period, your messages will run the risk of being considered a nuisance. The rest period should be at least two to three times the time it takes to execute steps 1 through 3. For example, if you are messaging to someone on a once-a-month basis over a three-month time frame, the rest period should be six to nine months.

What is your philosophy to penetrate new accounts? If you're like most salespeople you probably don't have one. Rather, you reflexively increase your prospecting activity when your pipeline is empty. The 1, 2, 3, Rest, Repeat campaign leverages sales linguistics to secure initial meetings. Follow the steps explicitly and you will achieve even greater sales success.

Structuring Messages for the 1, 2, 3, Rest, Repeat Campaign

Because people have different motivations, they have different perceptions of a product's value. The perceived value depends on the psychological, political, operational, and strategic value it provides the evaluator (see chapter 27).

Psychological value is one of the most important values in terms of motivating purchasing action. At the root of every decision is a desire to fulfill one of four deep-seated psychological needs: satisfying the ego, being accepted as part of a group, avoiding pain, and ensuring survival. Therefore, you should understand your product's psychological value and how it applies to the person you are trying to reach.

Political value involves organizational power. Your product can make someone more powerful outright, or it can provide much-needed visibility that enables a person to be in contact with the company's powerbrokers.

People's success in an organization is dependent upon the success of their department's operations. You can think of operational power in terms of how your solution impacts a person's résumé.

Finally, strategic value is the reason evaluators give to others in the company as to why they are purchasing a product. Strategic value includes gaining a competitive advantage, increasing revenues, decreasing costs, increasing productivity, improving customer satisfaction, improving quality, and standardizing operations.

The message you send to customers should be based upon these four product values. You must communicate to potential buyers that you can help them solve critical department problems and help them become experts and an internal source of knowledge, thereby making them powerful. To see how this can be done, let's look at an example of a generic e-mail for a marketing campaign targeted at senior executives in the automobile industry.

Subject: Increase Profitability and Maintain Dealer Partnership Loyalty!

Dear Mr. Smith,

My name is John Johnson from XYZ Corporation. We are the leader in providing solutions that help accelerate time to market and improve customer communications. We're helping customers such as Ford, Toyota, and Honda automate their relationships with their distributors, dealers, and parts suppliers.

In a recent strategic implementation, we were able to deliver Ford a robust solution that allowed them to communicate more effectively with their worldwide dealer distribution channel, drastically increasing customer service and loyalty. XYZ Corporation can help you

- Improve communications with critical partners
- Speed time to market and increase dealer retention
- Implement a "best practices" approach for all enterprise communications

For a free evaluation of our robust solutions, please call or e-mail me at your earliest convenience.

Best regards,
John Johnson

Here's another version of the same e-mail. While the main message isn't changed significantly, the goal is to employ a better cowcatcher and hook and to tap into all the different types of customer value.

Subject: How Toyota Maintains Critical Dealer Relationships

Mark,

Q. How do Toyota, Ford, and Honda maintain near-perfect dealer relationships?

A. XYZ Corporation has helped them automate and streamline all aspects of partner communications.

For example, Toyota distributes thousands of unique messages and memorandums to its worldwide dealer distribution channel on a daily basis. Toyota has drastically reduced turnaround times while increasing customer service using XYZ's solution. As a result, they have cut costs and accelerated time to market.

If you would like to learn how you can improve relationships with all your important business partners, contact me at your earliest convenience. Finally, please expect my call next week to discuss our free dealer communication analysis program.

Thank you,

John Johnson
(123) 456-7890
John.johnson@XYZcorporation.com
www.xyzcorporation.com

The most important aspect of the e-mail is not the bullet points of benefits; rather, it is the psychological impression it creates on the reader. When salespeople try to penetrate a new account, they are considered enemies, so they are met with disdain and fear. Salespeople must turn negative resisters into positive accomplices. In the above example, I was trying to make the e-mail recipient become psychologically attached to the sender. One recipient might envision starting a grand project like Toyota's for his own personal gain. Another might want more information so he could impress others with his expertise. Someone else might have criticized his company's dealer communications in the past and thought, "If it is good enough for Toyota, it should work for us." He just wants this painful problem solved.

Before you attempt to send an e-mail or letter or make a cold call to penetrate a new account, you need to research the business and the person whom you are trying to gain an initial meeting with. Old-fashioned detective work is still vitally important today. Study every page of information on the customer's website. Read the annual report, press releases, and product information, and scan all the various financial documents. From these documents you can derive your initial thoughts about your product's strategic, operational, political, and psychological value.

The purpose of your investigative research is to enable you to tailor your subject line so the reader feels compelled to open it. Another key reason for conducting research is to help you determine the different values your solution offers. Reading the CEO's letter to the stockholders in the company's annual report will help you understand the state of the business and the major initiatives planned for the new year. Reviewing the 10-K financial report will provide you with details about the business challenges the company faces. Press releases announce new programs and company crusades that are being undertaken. Meanwhile, industry analyst reports explain how the company is faring compared to the competition. Notice how the e-mail doesn't recite a list of product features and benefits. It explains real-world results in a plain-spoken way without buzzwords.

Take a look at the last sentence of the closing paragraph, "Finally, please expect my call next week to discuss our free dealer communication analysis program." This sentence employs two linguistic strategies. First, the sender *grants* himself permission to contact the recipient next week. Let's examine the e-mail from the recipient's perspective to understand this concept. This e-mail was written respectfully. It created a positive receptive state when the reader opened it, provided valuable information, and at 125 total words didn't take too much of the reader's time. It also established credibility via customer metaphors and employed an interesting cowcatcher and hook. It was well written from a grammatical perspective, which confirmed the sender's professionalism. As a result, the recipient would not be offended if the sender followed up next week with an introductory phone call. However, the call must be made. If not, the momentum and credibility of the e-mail established are lost.

The second linguistic strategy is to purposely use general words. What is a "dealer communication analysis program"? Frankly, the prospective customer wouldn't know what it is, and that's the idea. We spoke about general words and their interpretation in chapter 31. In this instance, the e-mail is building credibility, momentum, and rapport. The original e-mail was self-centered and closed with "For a free evaluation of our robust solutions." In the revised version we are purposely using a general word structure (dealer communication analysis program) because we want the customer to interpret these terms in the way that is most important to the customer and relevant to his problems and aspirations. One final point: while this example is of an e-mail, this message structure applies to letters as well.

Finally, timing can be everything. While emergency and interrupt-driven purchases can be made at any time during the fiscal year, planned spending occurs in the fourth quarter when budgets are approved. Therefore, it is imperative to introduce your solution to new prospects no later than the third quarter time frame, as shown in figure 35.1.

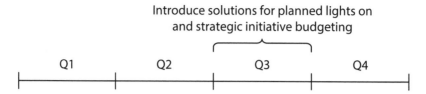

Figure 35.1 When to contact the customer for planned spending in the next fiscal year

The following comment from a director of IT shows the importance of timing.

> There is a delicate balance in trying to contact me because you don't want to waste my time, but it is good to check in with me once in a while. If someone is continually hounding me they get turned off pretty quickly. Let's say once a week for three weeks. If you send me an e-mail once every two weeks for months you will automatically go to delete without being read. We go through an annual budgeting process and capital expenditure request. The first step in the process is a real rough benefit cost analysis. My submission process has got to be completed around September. Usually, around June, July, and August I start putting my ducks in a row and coming up with cost justifications. From my point of view, if you don't let me know about your product until January or February then you have missed my cycle. It really behooves you around June or July to remind me of your product so that I can decide whether or not I want to do the analysis for the next capital expenditure routine. I'll have a very short list of products I know will work, what they cost, and I have a comfort level the vendor can deliver. It's a very personal decision. Next I will sit down with the CIO to talk about the request. Then he will take it to the President and the rest of the executive group and they figure out whether to move forward or not. Money is released at the

beginning of the year. But that doesn't mean I go out and start buying stuff.

  —Director of eCommerce

Put yourself in the customer's position and theorize on the psychological, political, operational, and strategic value you and your solutions provide. Control your destiny. Don't send e-mails that are mini-infomercials that give away the power of responding solely to the customer. Study the message structure and fight the urge to explain too much. Instead, structure the e-mail so the customer finds it enticing and awaits your follow-up action with anticipation.

36. Step 1–The Credibility Message

The purpose of the first message of the 1, 2, 3, Rest, Repeat campaign is to establish credibility and develop some level of recognition with the customer you are trying to reach. In the example below, Michael Corleone, a salesperson for Acme Advertising Solutions, is trying to reach Vincent Vega, the chief marketing officer of ABC Technology Company, a multibillion-dollar technology giant. Pay particular attention to the tone of the e-mail. It's not too personal. Since the two men have never met, the message is intentionally more formal. However, Michael doesn't want to be overly formal with the use of language and the salutation, or the recipient will discount the letter as a sales pitch.

To: Vincent Vega, CMO@ABC Technology Company
From: Michael Corleone@Acme Advertising
Subject: Vincent, Marketing Campaign Meeting Request

Hello Vincent,

Acme Advertising Solutions has provided online marketing solutions for many leading technology companies including:

Apple	IBM	NEC
Cisco	Intel	Oracle
EMC	McAfee	SAP
Hewlett-Packard	Microsoft	Symantec

Our clients have cost-effectively improved their brand recognition while increasing new sales opportunities.

"Acme Advertising's targeted online marketing campaign increased our lead generation activities by 300%."
　—Jack Sparrow, CMO, Oracle Corporation

"Acme's 'One World, One System' commercial series has improved our name recognition across all our key market segments."
　—James T. Davis, CMO, Hewlett-Packard Corporation

"We were thrilled to win the prestigious Zippy Award for our innovative online advertising campaigns."
　—David Bowman, CMO, Intel Corporation

I'd be delighted to meet with you and share some thoughts and ideas we have for ABC Technology Company. Please expect my introductory call next Tuesday at 3 pm.

I look forward to speaking with you,
Michael Corleone
(123) 456-7890
Michael.corleone@acme.com
www.acme.com

The subject line is the cowcatcher, solely intended to encourage Vincent to open the e-mail. His name is part of the subject, so the inference is that the message is from a real person asking for a meeting, not from an automated spambot. As he opens the e-mail, the first thing his eyes will focus on is the list of recognizable company names. This is due to the e-mail's "heat map."

A heat map is a representation of where the eyes look first and gravitate toward next when initially viewing a website page, PowerPoint slide, letter, or e-mail. Figure 36.1 shows an example of a heat map for a PowerPoint slide of someone who reads left to right. Areas are colored according to the instinctual tendency to look at them from hot (high) to cold (low).

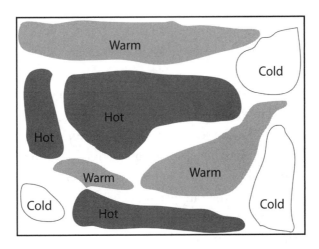

Figure 36.1 Sample heat map for a PowerPoint slide

This hook makes him go back and read the entire message. Notice how this e-mail avoids making outrageous claims like "Acme is the world's leading advertising firm." Rather, it is completely factual: these are our clients, and this is what they have to say about us. Nor does the e-mail go into a detailed explanation of what Acme Advertising does.

The subject line uses the term "marketing campaign." To a CMO like Vincent, the term can mean a wide variety of things: advertising campaigns, lead-generation programs, online marketing, customer research, competitive research, brand development, and so on. Intentionally, the e-mail does not point out what it's referring to. This is an example of a broadcast-unicast messaging technique. It's intended to let the recipient derive his own personal meaning from an ambiguous term.

While researching the business, Michael found out that ABC Technology's sales are down from last year. Therefore, he theorizes that the sales department is haranguing marketing about needing more qualified leads. If this is the case, Vincent might interpret the e-mail from the standpoint of lead generation, and Michael has a higher likelihood of securing a meeting. The first customer quote reinforces this interpretation. This is an example of a background suggestion.

The list of companies provided in this e-mail is extremely important. Examples of customers that are successfully using a company's products and services are the most important metaphors a salesperson can use. The personal connection between a customer example and its relevancy to the prospect's experiences will determine to what extent the salesperson's claims are accepted. Therefore, the pertinence of the examples chosen is critical. Presenting a company that closely mirrors the prospect's business environment will make the salesperson's statements more powerful.

Specific customer quotes were selected for this e-mail. Since Michael has never met Vincent, he really doesn't know what's on the CMO's mind. He doesn't know if he thinks his job is in jeopardy or he's next in line to become the president of the company. So Michael wants quotes that will connect to the different psychological benefits. The first customer quote focuses upon pain avoidance. Based upon Michael's past experience working with CMOs, he knows that lead generation is always a source of pain. Maybe Vincent feels inferior to his peers at the other companies listed in the e-mail. He might hire Acme so he can be part of the group. This is self-preservation. Or since he's worked with his current ad agency for seven straight years, he might feel it's time for a refreshing change. This is related to mental and emotional well-being. The third quote is based upon self-gratification and the ego. What CMO wouldn't want to win a prestigious Zippy Award and prominently display the award in his office?

The three customer quotes in the e-mail could also be replaced with case-use examples. They are examples showing how customers are using the products and the benefits they are receiving. The three bullet point examples below would replace the comments.

- *Oracle increased lead generation by 300 percent using ABC Advertising Solutions.*
- *Hewlett-Packard generated $16.7 million of validated leads with a $100,000 investment.*
- *Intel reached 300,000+ key technology buyers as a result of targeted online advertising.*

The credibility message you send to a prospective customer is a critical communication event. Creating a message that earns you an initial meeting is both an art and a science. Over the past year alone, I have reviewed hundreds of credibility messages for my clients, and more than three quarters of them actually do more harm than good. Now it is time to conduct a very important exercise. I would like you to close this book and review the standard introduction e-mail or letter you send to customers. Put yourself in their position. How would you respond to it?

It's always tough to find out why someone is talking to you. Why would I schedule an hour or two with my staff? Sometimes you can be too smart and you have to dumb it down. Tell me what it does and how it is going to help me in a simplistic way. There are a lot of buzzwords out there. Pull me in with some business benefits and let me know about your customers.

—*Senior Vice President Product Management*

37. Step 2–The Tactical-Offer Message

Assuming the customer didn't respond to your first e-mail, you send him a second, tactical-offer e-mail. In the example below, Luke Skywalker, a salesperson for XYZ Technologies, is trying to secure a meeting with Norman Bates, chief information officer at Wonderful Telecommunications.

To: Norman Bates, CIO@Wonderful Telecommunications
From: Luke Skywalker@XYZ Technologies
Subject: Norman, Recession Strategies for CIOs

Norman,

During today's tough times, IT organizations are required to maintain round-the-clock uptime with smaller budgets and fewer resources than ever. Below, you will find links to articles that address this critical issue.

7 CIO Strategies to Maintain Application Availability with Fewer Resources

Gartner Group Study of the Recession's Impact on Long-Term IT Planning

How to Reduce Operational IT Costs by Outsourcing

When and Where Outsourcing Makes Sense

XYZ Technologies has helped hundreds of CIOs maximize their IT budgets through application outsourcing.

"We were surprised by the cost savings. It has been 20 percent more than we expected."
—Charles Foster Kane, CIO, AT&T

"We started small by outsourcing non-mission-critical applications three years ago. Today, 70 percent of our applications are outsourced."
—Forrest Gump, CIO, Johnson & Johnson

"We've achieved our primary goal of reducing costs while maintaining our service levels. Now we've freed up valuable resources to work on critical new business projects."
—Stanley Kowalski, CIO, General Electric

Norman, please let me know if you are interested in our complimentary outsourcing cost-savings analysis. The complimentary study takes approximately two days to complete and will provide you with a detailed savings assessment, key risk factors, and completion timelines. I will follow up with you next week to answer any questions you may have about our analysis program.

Luke Skywalker
(123) 456-7890
Luke.skywalker@xyz.com
www.xyz.com

Based upon Luke's research and experience, he knows that one of the main challenges CIOs face during tough economic times is providing high levels of service with less money and fewer resources. "Norman, Recession Strategies for CIOs" is a topical cowcatcher. It's quite different from "Norman, Meeting Request."

The subject line also indicates that the e-mail is not from a salesperson asking for a meeting but from an important source of independent information that could potentially help the CIO.

Obviously, Luke wants to secure a meeting so that he can begin the cost-savings study. However, any forward progress in starting a relationship with the CIO should be considered positive. For instance, if Norman clicks on a link to one of the articles, this is a positive step and the e-mail was a success.

This e-mail has three major parts. The first part is the offer. This fulfills the e-mail's requirement that it provide independent information. Four links are provided to articles that most CIOs would find relevant and interesting. Although they may have been written by XYZ Technologies, they are informational as opposed to vendor-centric promotional collateral. (It's important to note that e-mails with attached documents are more likely to be caught by spam filters.) The articles are the e-mail's hook.

The second part is composed of customer metaphors, stories from customers confirming the salesperson's solution or company. Since most CIOs are extremely risk averse, all of the quotes are intended to make Norman feel more comfortable that outsourcing is mainstream. Included are quotes from CIOs of another telecommunications company and traditionally conservative companies General Electric and Johnson & Johnson.

These customer quotes are also examples of the simulation persuasion technique. Simulation is structuring language to provoke a particular emotional or physical response. For example, salespeople want the customer to simulate the benefits and feelings of owning their products during a sales cycle. Car salespeople are experts at using simulation. The test drive is a way to get the buyer to simulate the fantasy of owning the car. They want the test driver to enjoy the smoothness of the ride, experience the "new car" aroma, and feel the power of the acceleration. They know that a person who successfully simulates ownership during the test drive is a good prospect for a sale.

The same principle applies to the CIO. If Luke can get Norman to envision being a happy customer while reading the e-mail, he is well on the road to securing a meeting. Simulation exercises the senses and engages the personality. Luke wants Norman to ask himself, Why aren't we outsourcing?

The third part of the e-mail is the tactic to get the initial meeting. This is the call to action. In the e-mail Luke is asking Norman to participate in a cost-savings analysis project. A tactical e-mail needs to have a much stronger closing statement than a credibility e-mail because you are specifically asking the executive to take action to fulfill one of his fantasies. Therefore, an operator is added that explains what the analysis entails.

All sales involve selling a fantasy. The fantasy is that the product you are selling is going to make the customer's life easier, make the customer more powerful, save money, or enable the customer to make more money. The feature set of your product validates the fantasy elements of your story.

38. Step 3–The Final Message

At this point, you may have attempted to contact the customer twice without success. You can either send another credibility message, a follow-up tactical-offer message, or the "final" message of the campaign. In the example below, Willy Loman, a salesperson for Interstar Networks, is trying to reach John Blutarsky, the chief technology officer of Freedom Financial Investments. Through his research, Willy knows that Freedom Financial Investments is using his archrival's product, Slowmo Networks. Please note that it is more important to pay attention to the more aggressive tone and structure of the language in this example than to understand the technical terms being used.

> To: John Blutarsky, CTO@Freedom Financial Investments
> From: Willy Loman@Interstar Networks
> Subject: John, Slowmo Networks Performance Comparison
>
> John,
>
> I've sent you e-mails to explain Interstar Networks' advantage over Slowmo Networks. We offer superior performance because our architecture is based upon virtual processes. This is more efficient than Slowmo Networks' architecture, which uses a single-machine address. While the single-machine address solution redundantly broadcasts all messages, our solution sends specific information packets to the applicable computer. This results in up to 75 percent less network traffic.
>
> For example, Goldman Sachs recently switched from Slowmo Networks and improved its network performance by over 60 percent. I would be delighted to set up a conference call for you to talk with John Smith, CTO at Goldman Sachs. Could we schedule a time?
>
> Willy Loman
> (123) 456-7890
> Willy.Loman@Interstarnetworks.com
> www.interstarnetworks.com

The above e-mail shows several examples of how operators can be used. Operators are required to take the generic claims and translate them into proof points the customer understands and believes (see chapter 31). For example, in the e-mail to the CTO, the general word "performance" is being operated on by the descriptor "architecture is based upon virtual processes." The term "more efficient than" is being operated on by the phrase "uses a single-machine address." The salesperson then details the differentiation between the two architectures, which is less traffic and faster performance.

To further validate his argument, Willy offers a specific customer example to illustrate his claims. Equally important, to have his claim accepted as the truth, he offers to introduce the prospect to the existing customer. In other words, he says, "Don't take only my word on this; talk to my customers."

Here's another example of the final message that is structured from a business perspective using client proof points as opposed to the previous technical example. Notice the reference to the financial investment firms in the subject line and throughout the e-mail to entice the CTO to open the e-mail and read it.

To: John Blutarsky, CTO@Freedom Financial Investments
From: Willy Loman@Interstar Networks
Subject: John, Goldman Sachs & Schwab Network Advantage

John,

I sent you a couple of e-mails because I wanted to share with you how leading investment companies including Goldman Sachs, Schwab, Morgan Stanley, and JP Morgan are solving their toughest network performance issues. For example, Goldman Sachs will have more than 250,000 online users on an average day with zero network latency using Interstar Networks. Could we schedule a meeting to discuss how Interstar Networks can help you resolve your most difficult network challenges?

Willy Loman
(123) 456-7890
Willy.Loman@Interstarnetworks.com
www.interstarnetworks.com

The last in the series of messages of the 1, 2, 3, Rest, Repeat campaign is called the "final message." After sending this message you will not contact the customer for weeks or even months in some cases. Therefore, you need to structure the final message more aggressively than the credibility and tactical messages. The final message should have a harder close than the credibility and tactical messages. Penetrating new accounts requires a concerted and concentrated campaign that is conducted within a psychologically compelling linguistic framework such as the 1, 2, 3, Rest, Repeat campaign.

39. How Top Technology Salespeople Use LinkedIn

I recently conducted a study on how top technology salespeople use LinkedIn to research accounts, prospect for leads, and generate sales. All of the study participants sold technology-based products to mid- to large-size companies.

The study included three types of salespeople: 33 percent were inside salespeople who sold exclusively over the phone, 41 percent were outside field reps responsible for acquiring new accounts, and 26 percent were outside field reps who managed existing client accounts. The results suggest there are four basic LinkedIn user classifications:

- *Enthusiast.* Twenty-five percent of the study participants were classified as enthusiast users. Enthusiasts have fully developed LinkedIn accounts and use LinkedIn continuously during the day. They believe it is an important tool for generating product interest and promoting their company to potential customers. Enthusiasts were more likely to be outside salespeople responsible for acquiring new accounts. The average enthusiast has around 700 contacts, and one had over 1200.

- *Casual user.* Forty percent of participants were classified as casual users who access their account on a regular basis. They consider LinkedIn a useful tool to research and learn more about prospective clients. Casual users have about 250 contacts on average, and all use a free LinkedIn subscription.

- *Personal user.* Fifteen percent of participants would be classified as personal users. Their LinkedIn accounts have ample information about their job history and past accomplishments. Their main purpose for having a LinkedIn account is for job-related networking and they rarely, if ever, use LinkedIn for work-related purposes. Personal users averaged around 300 contacts.

- *Nonparticipant.* Twenty percent are nonparticipants. Nonparticipants don't have a LinkedIn account or their profile contains very little personal information and fewer than twenty contacts. They don't consider LinkedIn a priority and seldom access their account. These salespeople were more likely to be older than enthusiasts, and the majority worked in the same position or at the same company for many years.

Contact Types

The composition of contacts varied greatly between enthusiasts and casual users. About 30 percent of enthusiasts' contacts were with existing clients, compared to only 5 percent for casual users. Over 85 percent of enthusiasts indicated they use their LinkedIn account to engage prospective customers during the sales process, while only 20 percent of casual users did. Twenty percent of enthusiasts' contacts were prospective customers, whereas it was less than 4 percent for casual users. Partners (resellers, consultants, industry influencers, and so on) who affect customer purchasing decisions account for about 28 percent of contacts for enthusiasts and roughly 17 percent of casual users.

Customer Research

Every enthusiast and nearly half of casual users use LinkedIn to find out whom they should contact in order to secure customer meetings. Over 90 percent of enthusiasts and 65 percent of casual users use LinkedIn prior to customer meetings to find out more about the people they will meet. Specifically, they are interested in where the customers have worked in the past and whom they might know in common. Both groups also use LinkedIn extensively to verify a person's title. About 55 percent of enthusiasts and 10 percent of casual users use LinkedIn to research their competition. In addition, enthusiasts mentioned they will monitor a prospective customer's connections to find out which competitors and salespeople are working on the account. Overall, LinkedIn was rated as a research tool (on a scale of one to five, with five being highest) by enthusiasts at 4.1 and 2.5 by casual users.

Account Prospecting

Less than 15 percent of enthusiasts and none of the casual users ever reported making an unsolicited initial customer contact directly through a LinkedIn invitation. Nearly all salespeople commented they were fearful this would be perceived negatively by the prospective client. Instead, over 85 percent of enthusiasts and 50 percent of casual users indicated they would use LinkedIn to ensure they were contacting the right person but make first contact via e-mail. The majority of both enthusiasts and casual users indicated their companies supplied better prospecting tools than LinkedIn. Overall, LinkedIn was rated as a prospecting tool by enthusiasts at 3.8 and 2.1 by casual users.

Use of Groups

On average, enthusiasts belong to twelve groups and casual users to four. Both enthusiasts and casual users indicated their main purposes for joining groups was to keep in touch with colleagues they had worked with in the past, follow companies of interest, and improve industry-related knowledge or sales skills. About 40 percent of enthusiasts and less than 20 percent of casual users responded that they belonged to groups their prospective customers were part of. No one indicated he had generated an initial customer meeting based upon a group membership.

Existing Client Communication

Seventy percent of enthusiasts and 18 percent of casual users reported they used LinkedIn to keep existing customers informed about their company's offerings. Those who did used LinkedIn to send short messages that contained links to press releases, white papers, analyst reports, product announcements, and company-produced videos. However, both groups overwhelmingly preferred to use e-mail to stay in touch with existing clients. LinkedIn was rated as an existing client communication tool by enthusiasts at 2.1 and 1.5 by casual users.

LinkedIn Generated Revenue

Over 40 percent of enthusiasts indicated they have successfully generated revenue based upon LinkedIn-related efforts. Less than 20 percent of casual users successfully generated revenue directly attributed to LinkedIn.

Overall, 18 percent of all survey respondents indicated they have generated additional sales as a direct result of their LinkedIn activities. However, this number is deceiving. In order to truly measure LinkedIn's effectiveness you must take into account how many salespeople are enthusiasts, casual users, personal users, or nonparticipants.

The research suggests that LinkedIn is most valuable to outside field salespeople and inside salespeople responsible for winning new accounts. LinkedIn is also a valuable networking tool for channel salespeople. LinkedIn is least valuable for install-base salespeople who manage a small number of accounts.

PART IV

Sales Call Strategy

40. Sales Call Strategy Using Sales Linguistics

Customers today are smarter. Information is not only easier to find but available in greater detail than ever before. In addition, technology has become a way of life. Via the Internet, customers can research products, prices, and opinions. Our cars, appliances, and toys have become computerized tools. Collectively, this has raised the level of sophistication (and skepticism) of the customers we must converse with and sell to. Power is definitely in the hands of today's buyers and the situation will only continue to get worse.

Your competitors have not sat idly by either. They've educated themselves about your products and sales tactics, and they're more focused on defeating you than ever. Fortunately, they usually believe the best way to defeat you is by frontal attack based upon their product features, when in reality, using language to build customer relationships is the winning strategy.

This strategy requires differentiating yourself from the competition by building a stronger relationship with the customer than the competition through the words you speak. Customers can think of you as a salesperson who is trying to sell something, a supplier with whom they do business, a strategic partner who is of significant importance to their business, or a trusted advisor whose opinions on business and personal matters are sought out and listened to. Obviously, a trusted advisor enjoys significant advantages over a salesperson.

> I look at vendors by measuring three important aspects. One, the relationship and that starts with the point-person who owns the account. Two, what they do for our day-to-day business. Do they deliver on their value proposition? Three, what kind of innovation can they bring to the table? It's not about keeping the lights on because that is what all the vendors can do. When I think about a partner as opposed to a vendor, I think about those three things.
>
> —*Chief Information Officer*

Language is studied in many well-established fields. Sociolinguistics is the study of language use in society and social networks. Psycholinguistics is the study of how the mind acquires, uses, and represents language. Neurolinguistics is the study of how brain structures process language. Today, an exciting new area of study called "sales linguistics" applies aspects from these fields to the conversations salespeople have with customers. The goal of sales linguistics is to understand how salespeople and their prospective customers use and interpret different languages during the decision-making process. There are seven different types of sales call languages shown below:

1. *Word catalog language.* The mind's method for receiving and interpreting information based upon the three sensory channels—visual, auditory, and kinesthetic.
2. *Internal dialogue language.* The never-ending stream of communication inside the mind that represents honest, unedited, and deep feelings.
3. *Physical language.* Also known as body language, the nonverbal communication that is constantly being emitted by the customer's body posture.

4. *Intersecting activity language.* Interests, hobbies, and personal pursuits by which the executive displays his personality, beliefs, and values.
5. *Technical specification language.* The androgynous, nonpersonal, and technical communication that is based upon the nomenclature and technical terms of the executive's industry.
6. *Business operations language.* The language that is specific to the daily running of the executive's business and his role in the organization.
7. *Confidential language.* The most powerful trust-based language by which the customer explains his personal needs, desires, and plans along with the strategy by which he hopes to fulfill them.

While we'll talk about these languages in more detail, let's spend a moment to review the internal dialogue language. Your internal dialogue is the never-ending conversation you have with yourself. It's repeating the words of this sentence to you now. It is very dominating. It's always on, always engaged, and always talking to you. It drives the language you speak to prospective customers during sales calls as well as your actions. Your customer's internal dialogue is equally active.

When you make a sales call, you are not talking to people. You are actually talking to their internal dialogues. Understanding this will help you conduct successful sales calls because your main concern is a customer's state of mind. Remember that the words customers actually say represent only a fraction of their true feelings.

There are three pillars of persuasion: the logic and reason of what you are saying, the personal connection you establish, and the psychological appeal of you and your solution. These pillars impact customers differently. Logic and reason appeals to the conscious or "controllable" mind while your psychological appeal impacts the subconscious or "uncontrollable" mind.

The nature of conversational themes depends upon the nature of your relationship. Salespeople engage the customer in friendly conversation, suppliers talk about their products' capabilities and attributes, strategic partners discuss business matters, and trusted advisors talk about future plans along with the people and politics behind them.

In addition to conversational themes, you need to master the seven different languages used by salespeople and customers during sales calls. These languages can be divided into two categories. The lower-level languages are responsible for the personal connection between people and consist of the word catalog language, internal dialogue language, and physical language. The higher-level languages are logic and psychological appeal languages. They consist of the intersecting activity language, technical specification language, business operations language, and confidential language. Figure 40.1 represents these languages and their associated conversational themes.

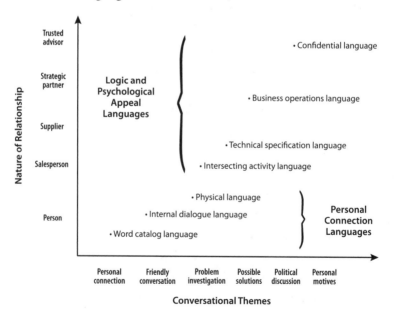

Figure 40.1 Ideal progression of languages during sales calls

When you strike up a conversation with customers you probably believe that everyone is speaking a common language. However, no universal language exists because everyone's mind is so distinct. People actually talk in many diverse languages. Therefore, if you want to communicate more persuasively and learn how to make lasting impressions, you should learn to speak each of the different languages listed in figure 40.2.

Confidential language	The most powerful trust-based language by which the customer explains his personal needs, desires, and plans along with the strategy by which he hopes to fulfill them
Business operations language	The language that is specific to the daily running of the customer's business and his role in the organization
Technical specification language	The androgynous, nonpersonal, and technical communication that is based on the nomenclature and technical terms of the customer's industry
Intersecting activity language	Interests, hobbies, and personal pursuits by which the customer displays his personality, beliefs, and values
Physical language	Also known as body language, the nonverbal communication that is constantly being emitted by the customer's body posture
Internal dialogue language	The never-ending stream of communication inside the mind that represents honest, unedited, and deep feelings
Word catalog language	The mind's method for receiving, interpreting, and transmitting information based on the three sensory channels—visual, auditory, and kinesthetic

Figure 40.2 The seven sales call languages

To differentiate yourself from the competition, you must speak more impactful languages with your customers. The ideal progression during sales calls is to quickly establish a personal connection with the customer and then progress through the higher-level logic and psychological appeal languages with the ultimate goal of having the customer speak the confidential language with you.

> Are you talking generically or specifically? Tell me how you are going to help our business. Tell me how you are going to help our factories. Tell me how you are going to help our employees. I've had salespeople come rolling in my office with some bright idea and say that it is really great. But until I understand you and until you understand me, I'm not going to buy.
> —*Chief Executive Officer*

41. Sales Call Goal and Personal Outcome

The first step toward conducting a successful sales call is to determine your goal and outcome for the meeting. The ultimate goal for the sales call is simple: you want the customer to expose his internal dialogue to you. You want him to honestly explain what he is trying to accomplish and why he is doing it from a business and, more importantly, personal standpoint. You want him to tell you about his personal needs and career desires along with how he plans to fulfill them. You want him to speak the confidential language with you.

You are not there to sell anything. Your goal is to become a trusted advisor by asking questions and intently listening to the answers so that you can apply your expertise to solve the customer's business problems or complete his initiatives. As figure 41.1 shows, the conversational theme starts with establishing a personal connection, and is followed by investigating the problem and discussing possible solutions. Ideally, the conversation flows into an off-the-record talk about the politics of his organization and his ulterior motives.

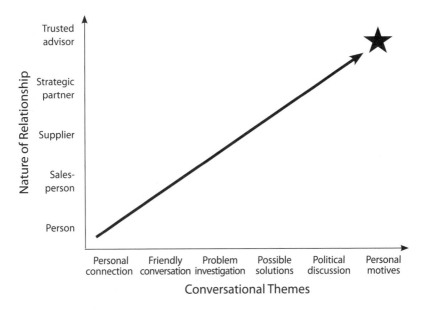

Figure 41.1 Trusted advisor goal

You might be worried that this important sales call may be your only chance to meet with the customer; therefore, you feel you *must* explain to him how wonderful your company and products are. However, if you go into this meeting with the intention of selling something, you'll be proven right: it will be the last time you get on his busy calendar.

Never forget that although you are excited about the meeting, the customer isn't that excited about your products and not all that interested in your marketing pitch. He's seen them and heard them before, and they all seem the same. You will be granted continual access if you can demonstrate how you can help solve his business problems and help him achieve his personal ambitions.

Unfortunately, the majority of sales call conversations never reach the confidential language. The discussion gets stuck at the technical specification language or the business operations language. Usually, this is because the salesperson is too busy talking about his products and what they do instead of what the customer wants to change. At other times, this is by design because the customer doesn't trust and believe in the salesperson enough to speak frankly and share his thoughts with him.

Moreover, too many meetings end without any definitive results. First meetings are short and the time passes quickly. Therefore, it is important to identify a specific personal outcome of the meeting beforehand so you can judge whether you have achieved your goal.

Professional athletes understand personal outcomes. Sprinters will visualize an entire race and see themselves on the winner's stand receiving the gold medal. College basketball coaches will ask their teams to mentally rehearse cutting down the net after they win the national championship.

Your personal outcome may be to have the customer tell you at the end of the meeting "It sounds great. Send me your proposal." In this example, you create a mental picture of the person and hear those words being said as he shakes your hand. You can measure the success of the call based upon what actually happens and how closely that matches this visualization.

The tactical objectives for the meeting can be quite diverse. The objective could be to *gather* information and find out how you are perceived versus the competition or other details about the selection process. It could be to *impart* information about your products or make a special pricing offer. It could be to *create* relationships or *influence* opinions. It could be to *negotiate* terms and conditions.

Whatever the tactical objectives for your meeting may be, you should define the words the customer must say to know that they have been achieved. You want to hear the customer say something definitive like "You are our preferred solution" or "Yes, we have a deal," not "We are still evaluating options" or "We'll consider that." Only when you hear the customer say the words that validate your meeting's outcome have you actually achieved it.

The most important difference between you and your competitors is not your products, your company, or the services and support you offer. It's you and your ability to build a deeper relationship with prospective customers. The proof of a successful sales call comes when the customer speaks the confidential language with you and shares the unedited thoughts of his internal dialogue.

Prior to every sales call, think about the exact words you would like the customer to say that proves he respects you. What would he say to show he trusts you more than the competition? What commitments would he make to you at the close of the meeting? Most importantly, how would he communicate the sales call was a success and he likes you and wants to see you again?

42. Technical Specification Language

Every industry has developed its own language to facilitate mutual understanding of terminology and an exact meaning of the words used throughout the business. The technical specification language consists of these abbreviations, acronyms, business nomenclature, and specialized terms. Since it is one of the primary languages your customers speak, you must be able to speak it fluidly. For example a semiconductor salesperson might tell a design engineer that his, "1575.42 MHz SAW filter has a usable bandwidth of 35 MHz."

Technical specification languages have three major characteristics. First, unlike normal day-to-day language, words within a technical specification language have very narrow meanings. The language is precise and exact. For example, "100 Mbps" means "100 megabits per second," not 99 or 101. Second, the meaning of general words can be completely changed by the addition of operators. Third, the language is completely androgynous. In general, no reference is made to feminine or masculine characteristics. Finally, the language is usually nonpersonal. After all, it's referring to products, not people.

> I don't have the time to educate salespeople. I expect them to
> walk in the door knowing everything that I do.
> —*Director of Information Technology*

Unfortunately for salespeople, the technical specification language usually is adopted by customers as the default standard for all of their communication. This presents salespeople with a significant problem. They are trying to create a personal relationship with the buyer. However, the buyer is communicating in an androgynous, nonpersonal, technical language. More importantly, given the use of this unusual language, salespeople must somehow decipher the underlying meaning and intent of the customer's words.

In addition, the technical content of the language is the yardstick by which a customer's technical peer group (the team selecting a product) measures a person's relevant knowledge. Outside of formal titles, it's another way members of the peer group will establish a hierarchy. It's also how they will validate the sales team's value to them. Conversely, it is how the sales team members will present their product's features and the technical reasons for selecting their product.

When you are speaking to a pure technologist, you have to be a pure technologist. Every sentence becomes a cat and mouse game where they are testing what you know.
—*Top Technology Salesperson*

It's the language C-level executives use to communicate with their subordinates and instruct them what to do. For example, the CIO may instruct the vice president of infrastructure that he would like to "Replicate the SAP IBM server data in New York to the NOC in Los Angeles." Obviously, a computer salesperson who doesn't understand these terms will have a difficult time winning the company's business.

The technical specification language is one of the primary languages that is used during sales calls. Therefore, you must know the technical specification language of your products and industry. You cannot expect to conduct successful sales calls and drive account strategy if you don't understand one of the fundamental languages your customers speak.

You must internalize the technical specification language and speak it fluently. Role-playing with your company's technical experts can help you practice and test your knowledge. Stay on top of the latest industry news. Start your own blog to demonstrate to prospective customers that you know their industry. Include the blog's URL on your business cards and in the signature line of every e-mail you send.

43. Business Operations Language

The business operations language is the language executives and managers use to run their organizations. Some salespeople have the misconception that you must have an advanced degree in order to speak effectively with a C-level executive. For instance, you require a master's of business administration before a CFO will value your opinion. You need an engineering degree to hold a truly meaningful conversation with a vice president of engineering because of his advanced technical background.

> Our IT organization is broken into two basic divisions: infrastructure or keep the lights on and innovation or application development. If I am looking to develop a partnership with an IT solutions provider, I'm looking for them to help me in the innovative space and bring on new innovative applications. But I am also looking for them to help me optimize my lights-on activities so I can allocate the savings for more innovation. I am not measured by keeping the lights on, I am measured on business value. The definition of innovation can be simplified into two important elements: process and information. My mandate calls for me to help my company be more efficient by process improvement and help the business make better decisions based upon information delivery. For example, how can I make it easier for our customers and partners to do business with us? How can I get our customers and partners the information that helps them measure us on the delivery of our value proposition? That's where IT contributes business value. Process improvements result in better customer experience and lower cost. Information results in better decision making and being more proactive as a business.
> —*Chief Information Officer*

While having a deep domain-area expertise is the ideal situation, in reality, all C-level executives, midlevel managers, and lower-level managers perform the same basic duties associated with running a company. They are either creating something new and providing business innovation or controlling an ongoing process in order to control costs. These duties fall into "create" and "control" categories. The business operations language consists of these create and control descriptions:

CEO:
: Creates corporate direction through top-level business goals.
Controls which departmental initiatives will be undertaken to accomplish these goals.

VP of Sales:
: Creates revenue through customer relationship strategies.
Controls sales force behavior through compensation plans and sales forecasts.

CFO:
: Creates the financial plans to run the business.
Controls money through budgets, accounting practices, and company policies.

Figure 43.1 Understanding the customer's business orientation

The orientation of the business operations language varies by the level of the organization you are selling into. First, the higher levels of the organization are responsible for short- and long-term organizational planning. Next, the lower levels of the organization are responsible for the execution of the plan as defined by management. Finally, the higher levels of the organization are responsible for the measurement of the execution of the plan by the lower levels as well as the plan's overall success. As a result, the create and control languages are spoken differently. People in the lower levels will tend to talk about their specific jobs and what they are trying to create, while people in the higher levels will speak about department goals. Successful customer communication is based upon providing relevant information, and the language you use to send your message must be tailored to the person's organizational role and responsibility. Figure 43.2 illustrates these differences.

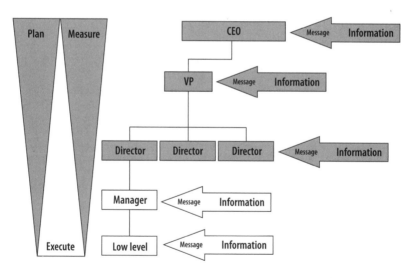

Figure 43.2 Business operations language differences by organization level

Think about the senior most executive you met during a very important recent sales call. Check each of the following create and control functions that are applicable to that person's role in the organization.

Create
__ Prepare and present the fiscal budget.
__ Provide forecasts.
__ Implement new programs and policies, and provide their general administrative direction.
__ Develop and execute departmental best practices.
__ Sign financial agreements and long-term contractual agreements.
__ Provide justification for all recommendations and decisions on capital expenditures.
__ Conduct new business development activities to promote growth or decrease costs.
__ Foster departmental and company communication.
__ Build positive relationships with customers, the press, trade associations, and industry organizations.
__ Develop and maintain relations with employees, customers, and the community.
__ Maintain responsibility for the selection, appointment, and retention of key management personnel.

Control
__ Administer the management of daily operations. _
   Analyze operating results versus established objectives.
__ Take appropriate steps to reverse unsatisfactory results.
__ Work closely with other departmental executives to ensure the company is functioning smoothly.
__ Supervise budget performance throughout the year.

___ Ensure that the growth of the company is in accordance with identified goals.

___ Maintain the desired quality of products, customer service, and professionalism.

___ Ensure that the company is in compliance with federal laws and local regulations.

___ Operate the organization in a profitable manner.

___ Provide oversight of and make recommendations for business initiatives.

___ Resolve all departmental business and human relations problems.

___ Ensure that the company's policies are uniformly understood and administered by subordinates.

___ Establish standards for managerial performance.

___ Recommend staffing and compensation changes within the organization.

___ Approve all personnel promotions and staff reductions, and oversee the hiring/firing processes.

___ Conduct periodic performance and salary reviews of personnel.

Let's assume that you sell network performance management software and are meeting with the chief information officer at a new account you are trying to close. Before the call, you write down five create and control attributes of your solution that you plan to discuss using the business operations language.

Create
1. Improve the perception of the information technology organization within the company.
2. Improve responsiveness to the company's changing business needs.
3. Improve systems uptime and availability.

4. Maximize the existing infrastructure's life span.
5. Use staff more effectively, focusing on highly visible company projects.

Control

1. Reduce departmental staffing costs.
2. Control unexpected capital outlays.
3. Eliminate crisis situations that defocus daily operations.
4. Reduce IT project delays.
5. Control the demands of remote device support (smartphones and tablets) on IT.

Ideally, you should prepare product positioning statements (see chapter 49) for each of the create and control points above. The product positioning statements explain how you accomplish the create or control objective using meaningful terms, specific benefits, and proof points.

Since a sales call is based upon the exchange of information, it is critical to tailor your message and deliver it according to the person's level in the organization. Let's assume you are meeting with a low-level network engineer at the same account as the CIO above. The create and control points you discuss will be focused on the engineer's ability to better execute his daily job duties:

Create

1. Improve daily effectiveness by quickly identifying the source of performance issues.
2. Make troubleshooting of network problems easier.
3. Proactively test and audit network performance.
4. Create network readiness prior to new technology deployment.
5. Increase the speed of network performance and throughput.

Control

1. Reduce network downtime.
2. Reduce the number of open support tickets.
3. Reduce escalations.
4. Reduce travel time to remote sites.
5. Reduce the number of network analysis tools used.

The create and control discussion will vary depending upon the organizational level of the person you are speaking with. People in higher levels will be more interested in planning and measurement, while people in the lower levels will focus on tactical execution. Certain features and functions of your solution are associated with create and control tasks. Be sure to adjust your message and the manner in which you speak to mirror the business operations language of the customer you are meeting with.

Finally, one of the biggest differences between you and your prospective customer is perspective. While the average IT person will work at a dozen different companies over the course of a career, you are probably exposed to several times that amount of companies in any given year. Therefore, you have the opportunity to share your knowledge and expand the IT person's scope of create and control functions as shown in figure 43.3.

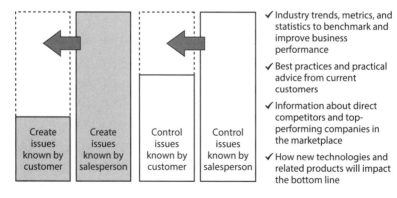

Figure 43.3 Expanding create and control issues

There is a conversation I have with vendors that have the potential to be partners. I will sit down with them and walk them through our business strategy. I'll ask them to take it away and come back with their ideas on how they can help us achieve our goals and their strategy. Some vendors don't know how to respond to this, or respond poorly. Other vendors will elevate themselves to that partnership level with their response. Smaller IT vendors have a difficult time securing that strategic meeting.

—*Chief Information Officer*

44. Confidential Language

The most important language spoken during sales calls is the confidential language. While the business operations language is a process-based language about what customers do on a daily basis, the confidential language is a personal language based upon what they want to do in the future. It's the language associated with the human nature of self-promotion and leading a group of people to accomplish a specific objective.

The confidential language is the most significant language spoken on sales calls. It's the language of strategic planning because it provides the customer's personal motivations for pursuing a project, the internal politics of the organization, and the unedited truth about the customer's real goals.

Statements in the confidential language are personal revelations that would not typically be shared with someone who wasn't trusted. They reveal the customer's off-the-record opinion, personal dilemma, and ulterior motives, as well as the stress he is under. They aren't statements that would be made in public for everyone to hear. They would be said only to a salesperson who was trusted. Conversely, generic statements that could have been said to all the salespeople are not examples of the confidential language because they aren't personally revealing.

Customers will speak the true confidential language to only one of the salespeople they are selecting from. Therefore, you should always assume they are speaking it with one of your competitors if they are not speaking it with you. Confidentiality is not freely granted by customers. It is earned through multiple interactions over time and requires you to prove you can be trusted.

> During the evaluation process each company put technical teams on site for a few weeks to work with our technical personnel. Vendor A had the better technical team. They asked the most insightful questions, and when you asked them to propose a solution, their answer was the most solid. Vendor A's salespeople were pushing for the sale and trying to wine and dine us. I mean it's nice when someone in a $150,000 dollar Mercedes tries to take you out to lunch, but that doesn't matter to me. I would rather someone sit down with me in my office and discuss business. Vendor B did that, talked straight to my level. It was a very close decision and we went with Vendor B. I'll be blunt; we took some of Vendor A's ideas and passed them along to Vendor B.
> —*Senior Vice President of IT*

45. Sales Call Themes

The objective of every sales call is to build deal momentum. You should always be gaining momentum with the account and need to have tangible evidence that the deal is moving in your direction. Evidence of this movement includes the elimination of other vendors, meetings with upper management or people involved in procurement, and other buying signs such as contract reviews. The three underlying sales call themes that enable you to build deal momentum are your personal demeanor, your communication style, and the messages you deliver, as shown in figure 45.1.

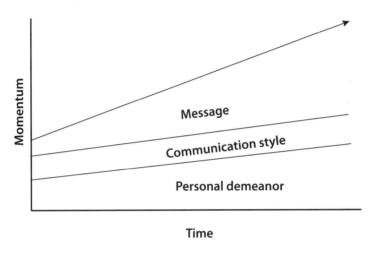

Figure 45.1 The three underlying sales call themes

You can think of personal demeanor as your physical presence. For example, some salespeople have such a lighthearted presence that customers will buy almost anything to keep them around—they're attracted to a humorous type of presence. Other customers want to associate with someone better than themselves, a person who has a character trait they feel they lack. For example, they may want to be around someone more outgoing, confident, charming, attractive, or worldly.

Our communication styles vary, depending upon whom we are presenting our arguments to. Giving long orations about your product will not win over the customer's heart and mind, whereas speaking passionately and knowledgeably will. Honest enthusiasm for your company and its products will permeate your customer's mind. The most persuasive salespeople are passionate about the company they work for and what they do for a living.

Through your communication style you establish situational dominance and customers are influenced to follow your recommendations. Depending upon whom you are meeting there are situations that require challenging them, while with others, aligning to their thoughts is the best course of action.

Tailor your message to individuals rather than using a one-size-fits-all approach, reciting the same pitch to every prospect. Instead, you want everyone you meet with to take away his own personal message from your presentation. You want each person to have a positive feeling about your solution and how it will impact his role in the company.

Regardless of how long you have been in sales and how accomplished you believe you are, you need to regularly evaluate your personal demeanor, your communication style, and the messages you are sending during sales calls. Therefore, I strongly suggest you make a video of yourself giving a fictitious sales presentation. In addition, use your smartphone to record your side of the conversation for the next five phone calls you make. Then while watching your video and listening to your calls, ask yourself this important question: If I were the customer, would I buy from yourself?

46. Sales Call Structure

From a sales linguistic perspective, each of the underlying sales call themes (personal demeanor, communication style, and message) has three stages, and each stage requires different linguistic strategies. The opening stage comprises the few minutes at the beginning of the call, the main stage is the longest period of interaction between the salesperson and customer, and the closing stage is time at the end of the call. Each of the stages has different linguistic components, as shown in figure 46.1.

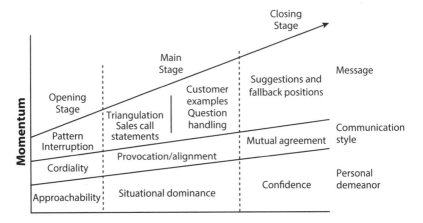

Figure 46.1 The stages and linguistic components of a sales call

Your personal demeanor should vary at each stage, moving from approachability (not overfriendliness) in the opening and then to establishing situational dominance when interacting with the customer in the main stage. At the closing stage of the call you want to exude confidence.

Your initial communication style should be cordial initially (courteous and genuine). The main stage of the call is where a provocation or alignment strategy is employed. In some sales situations it is absolutely necessary to be aligned with the customer's thought process in order to win. In other circumstances the customer's thought process must be transformed and gently shaped over the course of the sales cycle. Finally, it may be necessary to divert and separate the customer from his existing thought process and change his way of thinking to stand out from the competition. This can require a subtle or radical realignment of his beliefs through provocation and challenging his preconceived ideas, biases, or methodology.

The opening message you deliver at every sales call should be a pattern interruption, which differentiates you from the competition. The main stage consists of discovery and triangulation to ensure you are receiving accurate information, sales call statements, customer examples specifically selected for the customer, and an individualized question-handling strategy. This is when you present ideas that are tailored to the customer's needs. Your "reaction read" is how you gauge the verbal and nonverbal reactions (acceptance, rejection, or indifference) the customer transmits after hearing your call statements. It's also your overall opinion of the customer participants in the meeting. Who is for you? Who is against you? And who can be swayed? The closing stage communication style is based upon mutual agreement where both the customer and salesperson agree on the next steps going forward.

During the closing, offer the customer suggestions and have prepared fallback positions in case your suggestions are rejected. We'll cover each of these linguistic components in more detail in the following chapters.

47. Triangulation

While most salespeople operate in a world of incomplete or incorrect customer information, Heavy Hitters (top technology salespeople) have a different strategy, called "triangulation." Triangulation is the process of identifying your position by using three or more data points. Heavy Hitters constantly try to triangulate their position by answering these questions: Is there a deal? Am I winning? Whom do I have to watch out for, and what can ruin this deal?

> My top priority is to qualify whether the opportunity is winnable. The worst mistake is wasting precious time.
> —*Top Technology Salesperson*

The following discussion shows how you can carry out the triangulation process. It is based on the metaphor of a baseball diamond, shown in figure 47.1. (After all, Heavy Hitters are trying to score a home run.)

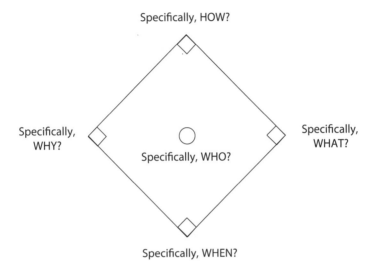

Figure 47.1 The triangulation diamond

First Base

On the triangulation diamond, first base is the "what" base. What are the content-level words being spoken by the prospects? What specifically do these words mean? You are trying to determine as specifically as possible what the customers mean when they speak. Questions asked on first base include the following:

- Specifically, what are you trying to accomplish?
- Specifically, what business problem are you trying to solve?
- Specifically, what technical problem are you trying to solve?

As the customers answer these questions, you're trying to decipher their high-level requirements into very specific targeted needs. For example, let's say you sell a financial application and are meeting with prospects who are unhappy with their company's accounting system. You need to help them define exactly what is making them unhappy. Is it functionality, performance, ease of use, support, or flexibility? Suppose it's functionality. Is it accounts payable, accounts receivable, human resources, or integration? Suppose it's accounts receivable. Is it customer creation, payment application, or delinquent accounts reporting?

Second Base

Second base is the "how" base. Use second base to understand how the customers will take action. Again, try to determine in as much detail as possible how the sales process will happen by asking specifically how the customers will accomplish a task. Questions asked on second base include the following:

- Specifically, how will you make a decision?
- Specifically, how will you implement the solution?
- Specifically, how will you determine if it is successful?

You will want to know the prospects' evaluation criteria, the steps of the evaluation, and how they will determine if the evaluation is successful. Members of your triangulation team will gather this information from their respective contacts. Together, they will compile and assimilate the results. From this exercise, you will identify areas of product strength, weakness, and information you don't know. Once again, don't assume anything. Rather, you want the customer to provide clear verbal answers to your questions.

Third Base

Now that you know specifically what customers are planning and how they intend to accomplish their goal, you need to understand why. Third base is the "why" base where you want to understand the following from the company's perspective.

- Specifically, why is the company evaluating a new financial system?
- Specifically, why is our product a better fit than our competitor's?
- Specifically, why would the company select our product?

The second element of "why" is the personal agendas of the individuals involved with the initiative. Items on these agendas are called "benefactions," personal benefits that come from taking a particular action. Our definition of "benefaction" is "an advantage that contributes to one's well-being, such as happiness, esteem, power, or wealth, and that results in influencing the way the person behaves during the sales cycle." At the personal level, ask the following questions about each participant in the customer's selection process:

- Specifically, why is this particular person on the evaluation team?
- Specifically, why would this person endorse our product?
- Specifically, why would this person oppose our product?

Home Plate

After rounding third base, you are headed for home plate. Home is the "when" base. Even if you reach third base every time you hit the ball, you don't score until you reach home. All the work the Heavy Hitter has done on the account is moot if the customer doesn't have a time frame to evaluate, decide, and purchase. On home plate, the questions include the following:

- Specifically, when will the evaluation start and finish?
- Specifically, when will a decision be made?
- Specifically, when will the customer buy?

The Pitcher's Mound

In baseball, the pitcher can throw the ball to any base at any time. The pitcher's position represents "who." "Who" can be applied to each base to determine who decided on the criteria, who will perform the evaluation, who will make the decision, and who will buy.

If you are a senior salesperson, you've probably participated in thousands of sales calls. After so many customer interactions, the mind tends to generalize the experience. Many times, you are actually going through the motions of account qualification. You assume information that isn't true, ignore important details, and misinterpret critical facts. Occasionally, you will be jolted back to reality when you are blindsided by a surprising loss. A quick review of the triangulation diamond before important sales calls will remind you that you must never take any sales situation for granted and that discovering reality is a main objective.

48. Questions to Discover Reality

One of the most important parts of the sales call is at the beginning of the main stage when you have the opportunity to ask questions. This is your "discovery" part of the sales call. The questions you ask also provide the opportunity to demonstrate your technical proficiency and show the customer that you understand how his business operates. Successful discovery is the first step toward building a foundation of trust and respect.

Suppose you sell enterprise software to banks and you have your first meeting with the CFO of Acme Bank, one of the world's largest banks. You are competing against Archrival Software. You assemble your sales team and make a list of all the possible questions you can ask the CFO. The five types of questions to ask customers are based upon the triangulation diamond (figure 47.1) and asking what, how, why, when, and who. Here are some of the questions you can ask:

> What would you say the top five most significant challenges are?
> What has prevented you from addressing these business challenges in the past?
> What metrics does your CEO tend to be most interested in?
> What is the toughest part of your job?
> What are the three most important qualities you look for in a business partner?
> Why are you looking for new software?
> Why wasn't this project started a year ago?
> Why are these problems getting attention now?
> Why is your budget $10 million for this project?
> Why are you in charge of this decision, as opposed to the CIO or COO?
> How long have you worked at Acme and did you work before?
> How familiar are you with us and the solutions that we offer?
> How do projects get prioritized, and where is this project in the priority?
> How do we stack up against the competition?
> When will the evaluation be complete?

When will the contract approval process start, and how long would it take to get the project approved?

When can we show you a demonstration and who do you think should attend?

Who prioritizes projects like this, and how are they prioritized?

Whom else are you looking at right now?

Who will be part of the evaluation team and why have they been selected?

Whom should we work with in each step of the evaluation process?

Are you aware that Big World Bank is now moving to our solution because of our superior service and track record?

What are the most important questions to ask? It depends. Aside from qualification questions, the best questions to ask are called "hypothetical questions" and "leading questions." Hypothetical questions enable you to gauge the strength of your personal relationship and include questions like those below:

Would you like to meet with our president next Thursday when he is in town?

We usually partner very closely with our customer executives and have regular advisory council meetings. Would you like to attend one?

Would you like to make site visits to other financial institutions that are using our solution?

Would you like to attend the Super Bowl with me next weekend?

Leading questions are planned in advance so that the customer's answer guides the discussion to your product's unique strategic and operational value. For example, you could ask, "What metrics does your CEO tend to be most interested in?" in order to provide the opportunity to explain the unique metrics your executive dashboard provides.

Obviously, you won't be able to ask a hundred questions during a brief sales call. Therefore, you must prioritize your list beforehand to ensure it includes your top ten most important qualification and leading questions. Even though you may have asked the same questions many times of low-level and midlevel personnel, you need to ascertain reality according to the C-level executive in charge. The C-level executive's perception of the pain, problem, and future plans may be vastly different than the reality that has been presented to you by his staff.

49. Product Positioning Statements

Your corporate sales presentation positions your company and products to potential clients. While you are well versed in presenting your slides, here are some steps you can take to make your delivery more compelling:

- Provide independent confirmation of your facts wherever possible.
- Provide quotes from authorities (customers, analysts, and media).
- Quantify beneficial claims with specific numbers.
- Use real-world examples, which are more powerful than hypothetical statements.
- Arrange your arguments from strongest to weakest.
- Keep it simple. Remember, the simpler explanation is usually preferred.
- Be prepared for contradictory facts from other vendors and have factual responses ready.

- Quantify results from adverse consequences (for example, loss of revenue due to system downtime).
- Present extremes and worst-case scenarios to make the other options to solve the problem look worse than they really are.
- Use the rule of three: whenever you make a claim, support it with three different facts.
- Understand that it is all right to draw big conclusions from small statistics. Sometimes the biggest points can be made from the smallest samples.

Become a storyteller, not a walking, talking data sheet. Use metaphors to explain concepts. Instead of saying "A poll showed customers prefer us three to one," say "Gartner Group surveyed four thousand senior IT leaders from across the country and found that three thousand, or 75 percent, thought our technology was far superior."

After the salesperson has been allotted a certain amount of time by the customer to ask introductory questions, the natural flow of the sale call shifts to the call statements phase. This is where you position your product and answer the customer's questions. The structure of call statements is very important because as listeners receive information, they check to verify a statement's accuracy.

As discussed earlier in chapter 31 on General Words, little meaning can be derived from standard product claims unless operators are added. Here's how to incorporate operators into call statements. Start with a high-level statement and then continue to define the statement into meaningful terms, specific benefits, and proof points:

We	help save you money
	increase your revenues
	provide better technology
	offer a more comprehensive solution
	provide better functionality or ease of use
Because of our	superior technology or functionality
	quality, people, customer service, or support
	ease of use or breakthrough paradigm
In comparison to	the way you conduct business today
	how the competitor's product operates
	how your existing process functions
As a benefit, you will	increase revenues by 30 percent
	save 25 percent
	improve your output by 3,000 units
	achieve 45 percent improvement
For example	ABC Company implemented our solution and has saved $750,000 in the first six months
	DEF Company increased revenues by $10 million in the first year
	XYZ Company improved production by 400 units per day
Final proof point	I would be delighted to introduce you to John Smith at ABC Company.
	If you like, I could arrange a visit to DEF Company.
	Here's the case study on XYZ Company for further reading.

Use product positioning statements to clearly articulate your competitive differences. The demeanor and communication style you use to deliver them should be based on confidence, not arrogance, and perhaps a sense of urgency. Using product positioning statements is a more sophisticated strategy for talking to your customer's mind. Instead of barraging the customer with point-by-point facts and figures, structure your arguments in a logical way using a story line that builds momentum while you deliver it.

50. Handling Questions

One of the hardest things to do in all of sales is handle tough questions from skeptical prospective customers. After interviewing more than a thousand prospective buyers, I can tell you with certainty that answering customer questions successfully is often the difference between winning and losing. Here are six points to consider when answering questions:

- *Clarify the question first.* Customers ask two basic types of questions. Some are very specific questions about a feature or issue, while others are more general about a broad topic or your opinion. In both instances, make sure you understand the question before answering it. Either rephrase the question in your own mind with your own words and repeat it to the questioner aloud or ask the questioner to further explain what he meant before answering. Many times, salespeople are too eager to give an answer to a question that wasn't even asked.
- *Show your domain expertise.* If you intimately know your industry, company, and products and how they compare against the competition, you need not fear even the toughest question.
- *Make sure everyone understands.* Since most sales calls are conducted with groups of people, you should give a little background information with your answers to ensure everyone understands the topic of conversation. Don't assume everyone understands your company's buzzwords or nomenclature.

- *Provide an expert point of view.* Never forget, your customer would rather do business with a trusted consultant who has intimate knowledge of the industry than an ordinary salesperson who simply understands how the product works.

- *Remember: demeanor speaks volumes.* The most powerful response to the most difficult question isn't solely the answer you give. It's also how you say it! Regardless of the question, keep a calm and confident demeanor. Most of all, do not get defensive. Stay positive. This is a critical lesson. When confronted by someone who disagrees with your opinion, it's okay to disagree without being disagreeable.

- *Redirect inane and unfair questions.* Don't get flustered when you are asked an inappropriate question. Simply redirect the question by saying something like, "The question you really should be asking is . . . "

Behind every question customers ask is an ulterior motive. They may want to validate a bias or throw you off track. That's why you shouldn't be too eager to answer or say yes to every question you are asked. The first step is to quickly theorize why the question was asked. Then formulate your response strategy to demonstrate your industry and business expertise in order to command respect. Sometimes, it is best to address inappropriate questions by providing an answer that guides the customer to a different topic. Most importantly, maintain your composure at all times.

> Always assume the customer is burned out. Proactively tell a story that captures their attention and makes them want to buy.
>
> —*Top Technology Salesperson*

51. Defensive Call Statements

Many times salespeople are asked underhanded questions by customers. This questioning is disguised as information gathering but in reality only serves the selfish motivations of the interrogators. Unfortunately, novice salespeople fall into the trap and try to respond to questions to which there are no correct answers. Anything that is said is used against them.

Defensive call statements are specifically structured responses to the toughest questions customers ask. You create them by writing two to four high-level talking points followed by a short written script. Since it's common to be nervous on important sales calls, talking points serve as mental tags to help you remember your script. Here's an example of one of my defensive call statements that I use with reporters and prospective customers.

"Steve, there are thousands of books about sales. Why is yours any different?"

Here are some talking points:

- It is written for senior salespeople with five, ten, or fifteen-plus years of experience.
- It is based on extensive research and more than one thousand interviews.
- It provides advanced real-world strategies that can be used immediately.
- Conclusion: its goal is to help salespeople influence the politics of decision making.

Here's the written script:

I think there are three major differences. First, it is written for senior technology salespeople who have been in the field for five, ten, or fifteen-plus years. The book is based upon extensive research and more than one thousand interviews with technology decision makers and top technology salespeople. Finally, it provides advanced real-world strategies that can be used immediately to close more business. The goal of *Heavy Hitter I.T. Sales Strategy* is to help salespeople influence the hidden organizational politics that impact every technology purchase.

The demeanor and communication style used to deliver defensive call statements is calm, collected, and matter-of-fact. However, you want to build momentum as you make the statement and finish on a high note. This is called a "buildup." When you speak to a customer, you want to confidently peak during the final sentence of your paragraph. You don't want your voice to trail off, signaling uncertainty or lack of conviction.

The talking points in the example above are sequenced according to whom the book is for, what it is about, and how the reader will benefit. The last talking point is to remind you about the buildup and to close on a high note. It summarizes the book's value in an interesting and assertive way.

A critical aspect of the sales call is not necessarily what you have planned to say. Rather, it is how you handle the tough questions the customer asks you. Your question-handling ability is what separates you from the pack. Prepare defensive call statements in advance to protect yourself as you answer uncomfortable questions about your products, company, customer, and competitors.

> In every deal someone is lying. I say X and my competitor says Y. One of us is lying. I have to defend myself and get that lie out fast to get the upper hand.
>
> —*Top Technology Salesperson*

52. Customer Success Stories

Salespeople love to tell stories. Of all the stories we tell, none are more important than the metaphors (or examples) about the customers that are successfully using our products and services. The personal connection between a customer example and its relevancy to the prospect's experiences will determine to what extent the salesperson's claims are accepted. Therefore, the pertinence of the example chosen is very important. Presenting a company that closely mirrors the prospect's business or technical environment will make the statements more powerful. Presenting a company that the prospect doesn't recognize will have less impact. In reality, it may actually hinder the argument because the prospect might think the product is not pervasive or popular.

At the lowest level of relevance, the example used could be a well-known organization, such as Coca-Cola or Shell Oil. Certainly, these are companies that would be known by the customer. The level of relevance improves when the example company is known for its past innovations, such as FedEx or Intel, or is well respected for its quality and brand, such as Mercedes-Benz or Nordstrom. By providing examples of customers that have a dominant position in an unrelated business, such as Google, Amazon, or Starbucks, you also receive implicit approval since it is highly likely the prospect has successfully used the services or products of these companies personally. Therefore, the prospect makes the logical assumption that the salesperson's product works successfully.

The company example could also include a technical environment similar to the customer's. In this case, the company's name or business is de-emphasized while its technical environment is highlighted. Let's assume the prospect is using Hewlett-Packard computers and Cisco network equipment. By providing a customer example that identically matches this combination, the salesperson is able to validate his technical claims that his product works in the prospect's exact technical environment.

Geographic proximity is a very compelling attribute of a reference. If the customer's company is based in New York, a reference to a company that is based in Los Angeles is not nearly as strong as a reference to one that is based in New York.

The ideal reference is a customer's direct competitor. This example provides the highest level of relevance and the most persuasive argument to use the salesperson's product. The best customer reference of all is a company in the same business, in close geographic proximity, and with the same business initiatives.

> Gartner and AMR are important to us for validating vendors. Much more important than trade rags. But the most important is peers in our industry. We want to talk to someone like ourself. If you don't have someone like us then you're probably not going to get the sale.
>
> —*General Manager*

Whenever you have an initial sales call, whether it is over the phone or in person, review your entire list of customers beforehand. Select five to ten customers from your list who share similar characteristics as the potential customer. The potential customer may be in the same industry, a user of these companies' products, or a direct competitor.

The power of customer success metaphors lies in their individual interpretation. While the conscious mind is listening to the content of the surface-level story, the subconscious mind is deciphering its own message. On the surface, explaining how a customer is successfully using a product is a story the conscious mind will follow logically. Underneath this story, a message can be sent to the customer's subconscious mind that it is in his personal interest to select your product.

An effective method of structuring customer success stories is to break them into four parts: history and situation, options, evaluation process, and decision reason and results. Below, you will find an example of each part and descriptions of ideally what message should be sent to the conscious mind and the connection to the subconscious.

Part 1 describes the history and situation.

- *Conscious message.* Describe the business problem or condition the customer was trying to solve or improve and the situation that created it.
- *Subconscious connection.* Specifically identify the people involved in the selection process, including their names, titles, and backgrounds. These are people the customer can identify with. When you provide these names, you are also offering them as references. Therefore, your examples should always be based upon happy, referable customers.
- *Example.* "I would like to take a moment to tell you about one of our most difficult customers, ABC Company. Their requirements were so complex that they were unsure whether any off-the-shelf product would work for them. Frankly, we had never seen a business that processed so many transactions. Their CIO, Bob Smith, was also one of the most meticulous and demanding customers I have ever met."

Part 2 presents the options.

- *Conscious message.* Describe the different products or methods that could have solved the problem or improved the customer's situation.

- *Subconscious connection.* Explain the impact of these circumstances in terms of the decision maker's job, career, or emotional state of being.
- *Example.* "Bob decided to bring in the top two products, ours and XYZ's, for intensive evaluations, even though he honestly believed that neither product would handle their requirements."

Part 3 delineates the evaluation process.

- *Conscious message.* Outline the process the customer undertook to determine the best solution.
- *Subconscious connection.* Describe the personality, preferences, and motivations of the evaluation team members.
- *Example.* "Bob tested every aspect of the solutions: installation, ease of use, performance, and technical support. One month into the pilot test, Bob stopped testing XYZ's product because it just wouldn't scale. He spent another two months verifying every feature of our product. He wanted to make sure everything worked precisely as advertised."

Part 4 describes the decision reason and results.

- *Conscious message.* Describe the final selection and its impact on the decision maker or company.
- *Subconscious connection.* Translate the outcome into personal terms.
- *Example.* "When Bob was completely sure of his decision, he finally purchased our solution. Today, Bob is one of our happiest customers and his project has been a complete success. I am sure he would be happy to host a site visit if you would like to tour his operation."

53. Sales Call Main Stage Strategy

Here's an important mantra to always keep in the back of your mind when meeting a new prospect: the purpose of the sales call is to talk about *his* problems, not *your* products. A successful sales call is not based upon how much product propaganda you impart. Rather it is about the quality of the information you collect about the customer's problems and then how you prescribe your cure to improve and correct the situation.

The conversation will be conducted mainly using the business operations language. It will typically take place in two phases during the main stage of the sales call. The first phase is your discovery of the problem: understanding the customer's specific problem, its cause, the goal that will be realized when the problem is solved, the possible options and vendors being considered to solve the problem, and the employees who will assist him in solving it.

After you conduct your discovery, you reach a critical decision point in formulating your sales strategy where you decide on the level of situational dominance to apply (see chapter 12). In every account you have an important choice to make. Will you provoke and challenge the customer to think differently about how he does business and uses technology? Will you try to align yourself to his current thought process and show him how you solve his problem in the manner he prefers? Or, will you remain adaptable and selectively challenge or align yourself depending upon individual topics of conversation?

The second phase is the customer's discovery of your solution. Once you have decided on your strategy, you then define how you might solve the problem by explaining how you have helped companies in similar situations. You accomplish this by providing real-world examples that equate your solution to the four different types of product value we reviewed in chapter 27. While these examples straightforwardly explain the strategic and operational values, the political and psychological values are suggestions that are inferred by the customer when listening to the stories. Finally, you will describe the unique features and functions by which your solution achieves the customer's strategic and operational values.

> The IT world is incredibly jumbled and most folks don't take the time to fully understand the needs of the organization. What they do is they generalize way too much, and they think from a quick conversation that they fully understand your situation. "Here, we can make our software meet the needs of whatever your needs are." The solutions that Vendor A was talking about had nothing to do with the business issues at hand. A lot of software guys are very generalist and very good salespeople, but they don't understand the uniqueness of doing business.
>
> —*Director of Supply Chain Systems*

Here's an example to help you understand and apply this concept. Let's assume you work for a software company that provides workforce productivity software—the Laborsaver 3000—and you are meeting with the COO of a large food-processing company. The sales call starts with your asking questions to discover the COO's problem. In this case, the CEO has mandated that all departments cut their budgets by 20 percent. The COO will comply with this request by cutting raw material, labor, and shipping costs. He determines that half of the cost savings will have to come from reduced labor costs. However, he dreads laying off people and wants to avoid across-the-board pay cuts and employee reassignments. He would rather drive the labor cost savings through less-intrusive methods that don't hurt employee morale.

Once you have understood his problem, you decide to employ a high level of situational dominance and specifically prescribe how he should solve his problem. You frame your solution based upon examples about how other large food-processor customers, Dole Food Company and Kraft Foods, have reduced labor costs 10 percent through more-efficient and more-accurate scheduling of skilled employees against actual demand. The customer examples to be used are important and should be chosen with care. These stories show the COO how he can accomplish his reduction goals and achieve strategic value (he can tell the CEO he's cut labor costs 10 percent) and operational value by improving his department's efficiency. Politically, he has satisfied the powerbroker CEO, and psychologically, he has gained the approval of his employees for preserving their livelihoods.

As the conversation progresses, the executive wants more details about how the solution works and is implemented. You then describe the relevant features and functions of the Laborsaver 3000 software that specifically explain how the strategic and operational values are achieved. The structure of the main stage of the sales call is represented in figure 53.1.

> Honestly, they didn't present well. Their sales engineer was great and I really liked their sales guy. But in front of our leadership, he tends not to read the room well and this didn't play well. He was too informal and way too casual. He was playing to me during the presentation instead of directing himself to our leaders. I kept looking at him, trying to give him clues to address them, not me. His competitor positioned themselves as much more peer-to-peer with our executives.
>
> —*Director of Technology*

Problem	Cause	Goal	Possible options
I have to reduce department costs that consist of raw materials, labor, and shipping	Sales are down and the CEO mandates 20% budget cuts	Realize a 10% labor cost savings with minimal impact on my employees' lives	1. More efficient workforce 2. Employee reassignment 3. Pay decreases 4. Layoffs

Executive converses in business operations language

Salesperson discovery: asking questions

Strategy decision

Provocation
Challenge the customer's thinking and prescribe recommendation

Adaptability
Decide to provoke or align based upon specific topic

Alignment
Dovetail to customer's thought process

Decision point
The degree to which prospective customer's existing thought process, business model, or technical environment is challenged

Applicable solution	Strategic and operational value	Political and psychological value	Product
Improved workforce planning and labor budgeting	A 10% labor reduction at Dole and Kraft	Satisfying CEO while maintaining department morale	Laborsaver 3000 features and functions that create the labor cost savings benefits

Salesperson converses in business operations language

Executive discovery: asking questions

Figure 53.1 Sales call main stage phases and strategy decision point

Know your strategy decision options ahead of time and prepare for the main stage of a sales call by dividing it into two parts. The first part is your discovery based upon asking questions that cause the customer to respond in the business operations language. The second part begins once all the possible options the customer is contemplating are discussed. This is the presentation of your solution, discussion of its value, and answering of the customer's questions in the business operations language. Be careful to avoid a mismatch of languages between you and the customer. Even the most experienced salespeople have a tendency to recite product features and specifications when nervous. A good rule of thumb is to only speak the technical specification language when the customer does.

> Their ROI model was way off, and the general perception within our company is that their sole concern is for them, not us. Frankly, it is to the point where our people don't even want to deal with them. They present recommendations as if they are in our best interest but are really solely in theirs.
> —*Vice President of Business Development*

54. Sales Call Closing Strategies

Remember the last time you were being pressured into doing something you didn't want to do? Whether the pressure came from a boss, colleague, spouse, or child, your natural response was to resist and push back. It's human nature to resist high-pressure tactics. So, how should the closing of the sales call be structured? The answer is to create a primary closing strategy, utilize fallback positions, and select an appropriate delivery technique as represented in figure 54.1.

Figure 54.1 Sales call closing strategies

Your primary closing strategy should be based upon securing the main objective for the meeting. The objective could be to be granted a follow-on meeting, have the customer start a product evaluation, receive approval to conduct a site survey, or negotiate final purchase terms. You also need fallback positions, alternatives you prepare ahead of time to present should the customer reject your primary closing strategy.

Your primary closing strategy and fallback positions are based on choosing to issue a command or present foreground and background suggestions. A command is an instructional statement that creates a binary type of yes or no response from the recipient. It is typically associated with a hard close and "take it or leave it" mentality. Foreground suggestions (medium close) are explicit, but they deflect the source of the request from the demander. Background suggestions (soft close) lead recipients to believe they are acting of their free will when in fact they have been directed to follow a message.

Let's pretend I am a passenger in your car and I feel you are driving too fast. A command would be "Slow down!" A foreground suggestion would be "You know the speed limit is forty-five miles per hour and police ticket a lot of speeders here." A background suggestion would be "A speeder was in a horrible accident last week in this exact spot." While the background suggestion may be more subtle in its delivery, it can trigger a more profound reaction.

In a sales situation, a command might be "We always recommend you benchmark the products you are evaluating." A foreground suggestion might be *"Consumer Reports* gave our product the highest rating and recommended it as the best buy." An example of a background suggestion is "One of my customers tried the other company's product and recently switched to ours."

After you have determined your primary closing strategy and fallback positions, select the delivery technique to be used during the meeting. Here are some examples, assuming the main sales call objective is to close the business deal:

- *Time-based technique.* This technique incorporates a time-based deadline.
  - *Command (hard close).* "This is the last time we'll be able to extend this offer and we need your answer now."
  - *Foreground suggestion (medium close).* "My boss told me that this pricing expires December 31 at midnight."
  - *Background suggestion (soft close).* "Think it over tonight and I will call you at 10 o'clock tomorrow morning."
- *Linkage.* This technique connects different events, subjects, or ideas.
  - *Command (hard close).* "If we give you those terms, then you must have our contract signed by the end of our quarter."
  - *Foreground suggestion (medium close).* "I'll talk with my boss and if he okays the terms, could we have the purchase order by month end?"
  - *Background suggestion (soft close).* "Our implementation team will be fully booked starting in September, so to

complete your project by year end, we'll need to have the contract signed in the next couple of weeks."

- *Power of print.* This technique leverages a document or printed company policy.
  - *Command (hard close).* "Our new price list is coming out in thirty days, and I can't hold these current prices for you after that."
  - *Foreground suggestion (medium close).* "Here's our volume discount schedule. If you spend another $100,000, you'll receive an additional 10 percent off the entire order."
  - *Background suggestion (soft close).* "Should I send you a formal quotation that details the purchase price and terms?"

Maintain control of the sales call so you can employ your primary closing strategy and be prepared with fallback positions should your primary closing strategy fail. You can sequence your primary closing strategy and fallback positions with commands (hard close), foreground suggestions (medium close), and background suggestions (soft close). For example, your primary closing strategy might be based upon a hard close; first fallback position, a medium close; and final fallback position, a soft close. Or, your strategy could be completely opposite depending upon the circumstances and the type of person you are meeting with.

> We had invested about a year on the account, and many of our technical and management team were involved. We had contacts at all levels of the business and IT executives. We were the front runners and proposed a deal with a price near seven figures. They approached us about cost concessions but we wouldn't budge on our numbers. We just thought they were taking a chunk of flesh. We did come back with a price in their range but it was too late. We had lost.
>
> —*Top Technology Salesperson*

55. IT Buyer Personas Roles

The marketing and sales operations departments of many technology companies create buyer personas for the various titles of the buyers their salespeople must call on. Buyer personas provide practical messaging and information on how the salespeople should interact with different people they meet with. Using the Laborsaver 3000 example from chapter 53, there might be buyer personas created for each executive level decision maker (CEO, COO, CIO, CFO and vice president of human resources), midlevel managers (director of operations, IT, finance, and HR), and lower-level technical evaluators such as HR analysts and IT project managers. The buyer persona is usually a single page or two in length and includes the following types of information:

- Elevator pitch to this type of person
- Challenges engaging this type of person
- Industry pain
- Cause of pain
- Questions to ask
- Key messages
- Solution to propose
- Possible objections

- Business decision-maker benefit
- Technical decision-maker benefit
- Competitive differentiators
- Expected financial/operational results
- Customer successes
- Industry analyst proof points

Unfortunately, these buyer personas typically don't address the self-interests, politics, and group dynamics that influence the final decision. Individuals will jockey for position to ensure their favorite vendor is selected, align themselves with more powerful coworkers for political gain, or stay out of the fray and refuse to take part in the decision. Buyer personas can be further detailed based upon the decision makers' attributes and their different roles within the organization. This segmentation will help you formulate your sales cycle strategy and better understand where you win and why you lose. Equally important, it provides a blueprint for sales call execution.

> The deals we win have certain similarities. You can spot them by the different types of people who are on the evaluation team.
> —*Top Technology Salesperson*

Tension, drama, and conflict are normal parts of group dynamics because typically any decision on what to do is not unanimous. Selection team members always feel an underlying tension because they are never 100 percent certain they are picking the right solution. Drama builds as the salespeople make their arguments and provide conflicting information to refute their competitors' claims. Interpersonal conflict between group members, as evidenced by disparaging remarks and criticisms, occurs whenever there is intense competition for a highly sought-after prize.

Beyond their formal titles and their positions on organization charts, people take on specific roles when they are part of a selection committee. Some assume roles they believe will enable them to take control of the group and steer the decision toward their preference. Others adopt new behavioral roles to deal with the tension, drama, and conflict. You may not have realized it, but even your presence as a salesperson influences how customers act.

Selection committee members, ranging from the CEO to the lowest-level evaluator, will adopt four different decision-making roles during sales calls and sales presentations. These roles are based upon information, character, authority, and company:

- *Information roles.* Information roles are based on the type of information people believe they should gather and the unique way in which they process and transmit information.
- *Character roles.* Character roles are based on the way people feel they should behave when they are part of a decision-making group.
- *Authority roles.* Authority roles are based on people's degree of command and their ability to dominate the group.
- *Company roles.* Company roles are based on the political power people wield and their personal disposition toward their company.

Figure 55.1 summarizes the four different categories of roles that prospects adopt during sales calls and presentations.

Information Roles	Character Roles	Authority Roles	Company Roles
Analytical	Class clown	Bureaucrat	Fifth columnist
Believer	Dreamer	Dictator	Hired gun
Intellectual	Hothead	Empty suit	Intern
Slacker	Maven	Old pro	Politician
Summary seeker	People pleaser	Proctor	Pollyanna
	Schadenfreuder	Pundit	Revolutionary
	Straight shooter	Soldier	Vigilante

Figure 55.1 The four group IT buyer persona roles

In chapters 56–59, we'll introduce each of these roles. While it makes sense to determine the role of every person during sales calls, it is crucial to understand the roles of the key decision makers. Ideally, you want to anticipate their behavior beforehand so you can use the right demeanor, create the right messages, and then deliver those messages in the way that they will be best received and understood.

In addition, you probably aren't going to attend all your sales calls alone. You might bring along your sales manager, vice president of sales, product marketing manager, professional services director, and even your CEO. Therefore, you need a common terminology to describe the customer to others. Segmenting sales calls by these roles will help you communicate your sales call strategy to colleagues and prepare them for the type of customer they are going to meet.

56. Information Roles

Everyone involved in the sales call and selection process has the responsibility to assess vendor information for accuracy and provide an opinion as to which solution is best. However, evaluators assume this duty with different levels of due diligence, ranging from focusing on minutiae to being big-picture oriented. Here are the most common information roles that evaluators assume.

Analytical

Analyticals are full of doubt and have the highest levels of skepticism. They verify every statement made by a salesperson, and they want to validate every piece of information. Therefore, analyticals immerse themselves in features, functions, and specifications. They take their role as information gatherer very seriously and do not want to be embarrassed by missed details.

Customers with advanced degrees in the sciences (computers, mathematics, engineering, etc.) are more likely to be analyticals. This should not be a surprise since they've had years of systematic education followed by a business career that was heavily focused on scientific methods and data analysis.

When meeting with an analytical, do not go on the call without someone on your side who has commensurate technical or industry knowledge. You have only one chance to make a great first impression, and being unable to satisfy the customer's analytical mind will be the death knell of the meeting.

However, your overriding objective should not be to let technology talk or deep discussions about minutiae dominate the entire meeting. Rather, you must keep the meeting on track and drive the agenda to reach your desired outcome for the call. Never let your own technical team hijack the meeting and take control. They should know in advance that they are there under your direction.

Believer

You will meet some believers who unquestioningly accept your information at face value. In some cases, this is because it requires a vendor's product to make the project that the person is so emotionally committed to become a reality. The project might be his brainchild or a determining factor in his career progression (or whether or not he keeps his job). Therefore, there is a tendency to believe vendors and promote them internally.

In other cases a customer is a believer because he is not well versed in working with salespeople or buying products. It might be early in his career, or he might be new to the management role or the company. Believers don't know what questions to ask or how to make a major procurement within their own company. If this is the case, you must adopt a different familial role with them than when working with an analytical. You need to mentor them through the process like a father explaining to his adult son how to fill out his tax forms or an older brother explaining to his younger sibling the criteria that should be used when selecting a college.

Believers have the propensity to be found in certain departments. For example, the vice president of human resources, chief talent officer, or chief learning officer are wired quite differently than the CFO, CEO, and CIO. They're usually not as adept at dealing with salespeople. Since they might not wield much organizational power, they often don't know how to make large purchases happen. When the senior-most leader in the deal is a believer, there is a higher likelihood that no purchase will ever be made. Therefore, the sales strategy has to take this into account and you must "help" the believer sell internally.

Intellectual

When it comes to details, an intellectual is the opposite of an analytical. Intellectuals are more interested in the general, theoretical, and philosophical aspects of products. Intellectuals approach the gathering of information in a cerebral, professorial way. They are open to learning and seek personal enlightenment. For example, an analytical might want a side-by-side checklist comparison of a product's features, whereas an intellectual would be more interested in the product's underlying architecture and why it was made in the first place.

Be forewarned about intellectuals. You're going to think a meeting with them went great because the topic of conversation was at the 30,000-foot level. Usually, meetings with intellectuals end on a positive note and with everyone involved feeling good. That's the style of intellectuals. They're not typically going to confront you and devalue your solution in person. For them, every meeting is a learning experience.

Later, intellectuals will let their department members sift through the details. You should anticipate that this team will find technical objections and a variety of other reasons why your solution won't work for them. Therefore, you must continually be selling at all levels of the organization if you suspect the C-level executive is an intellectual. Solely executing a top-down sales strategy will most likely fail.

Slacker

Slacker customers will conduct a low level of due diligence and a cursory verification of the information that is presented to them. Slackers don't know, don't care, or will mistakenly ignore important information. In addition, they will deny that they know anything when asked tough questions by salespeople.

Slackers are typically found in very large companies with immense bureaucracies where one department has no clue what another is doing. While slackers are rare, you might run into one in federal, state, and local government accounts or monolithic industries such as automobile and insurance.

The single most important question to ask yourself when you meet a slacker is, does this decision maker have the wherewithal to make a purchase? Nine times out of ten the answer will be no.

Summary Seeker

A summary seeker is a curious person who is more concerned with the big picture than small details. Summary seekers quickly grasp complex subjects and tend to make snap decisions about the relevance of information. They are typically more trusting than analyticals but less patient than intellectuals. Heavy Hitter salespeople love to sell to summary seekers.

It's not surprising that the majority of C-level executives are summary seekers because they are extremely busy. The nature of running a department or company means they have to manage down to employees, out to customers, and up to even more important executives and the board. Therefore, they don't have the time or mental bandwidth to process tons of detailed information. That's why important facts, risk assessments, value judgments, and the rewards of moving forward with the purchase should be summarized and presented to them in a succinct manner that is easily understood.

Identifying information roles helps you understand whether to present a high-level summary to a summary seeker or be prepared to dive into the details with an analytical. If the latter is the case, you know that you must bring along your colleagues who have a commensurate industry background and technical expertise.

The type of information gatherers you call on vary by industry. Analyticals are more common in the semiconductor business because of the technical nature of designing and manufacturing computer chips. There are far more summary seekers in the advertising industry, and this makes sense because people tend to make quick decisions on ads based upon first impressions. Over time, your goal should be to develop the specific breakdown of information role types for customers you call on for the industry you're in. For example, you should know that 55 percent of your sales calls are with analyticals, 25 percent with summary seekers, and 20 percent with intellectuals.

> I work with people; I do not work with companies. Everything I do is individually tailored to that unique person who is sitting across the table from me.
> —*Top Technology Salesperson*

57. Character Roles

Just as people change their behavior whenever they are in groups, evaluators adopt new character traits depending upon which of their colleagues are participating with them on the sales call. They will behave quite differently in front of fellow employees than when they are alone with you. Here are the most common character roles that evaluators assume.

Class Clown

Class-clown customers thrive on being the center of attention and always seem to have a smart remark or joke handy. While a psychiatrist might say the class clown's disruptions are driven by thoughts of inadequacy, this character role serves an important selection-process function: the class clown's silliness releases the evaluation team's pent-up stress.

Be careful when you meet with class clowns. Since they are so friendly and jovial, it is easy to be lulled into a false sense of security and take their word at face value. Moreover, when evaluators become class clowns, they are attempting to remove themselves from the stressful position of being the final selector and dissociate themselves from the decision.

Dreamer

Whether they have a momentary daydream about a vacation to a tropical destination or a fantasy about marriage that has been fostered since childhood, people love to dream about the future. Some dreamers are fixated on one goal, while others long for just about everything. During sales calls and the selection process, dreamers tend to fall in love quickly with a particular salesperson or the solution they believe will help them realize their fantasy soonest. However, they are impulsive buyers who suffer from immense mood swings, which can cause them to second-guess their initial selection and frequently change their minds.

As opposed to the class clown, dreamers are salespeople's dreams come true. Their main motivation is usually based upon satisfying their ego, and that's a powerful purchase driver. In a perfect world you want your dreamer to also be a powerful customer—someone who can make the grand initiative happen because he is the bully with the juice or the emperor (see chapter 23). However, you should be extremely skeptical of dreamers because they will talk the big talk but in reality are frequently duds.

Hothead

You definitely know when you meet with a hothead. They are impatient people with very short tempers. Sometimes hotheads explode during the sales call and publicly berate their own employees and colleagues. Worse is when they are combative and condescending to you. Hotheads don't like to meet with salespeople, so they verbally abuse them in front of their staffs! The best way to handle this intentional act of humiliation is to maintain your composure as best you can and not take the attack personally. I have found that many company founders happen to be hotheads. They are used to barking orders and getting their way through domination.

Maven

The goal of maven customers is to use the selection process to demonstrate their knowledge and intelligence to others. They're smart and they know it. Quite often, mavens are fascinated by electronic gadgets and own the latest technologies. They may adorn their bodies with these precious objects in an expression of prowess. They typically won't listen to the opinions of others or accept personal criticism because they already know exactly what's best. Therefore, you won't win arguments with mavens. Selling to them requires an indirect psychological sales strategy as they will not be swayed by any vendor's logic or reason.

> Our CIO was least excited about Vendor A. I think he personally didn't like their sales guy. My CIO is an über-geek. He wants to talk technical crap all the time. He just couldn't understand the benefits in our environment. While there was initial excitement about their solution, it diminished with every meeting, and we had fifteen conversations.
> —*Manager of System Operations*

You must sell to a maven's ego. At every opportunity elicit his feedback, not so much for its own merits but so your maven can hear himself talk about your solution. Bring the specialists within your company to your meeting—technical gurus, product managers, and various members of the executive staff. Invite mavens to participate on customer advisory boards or provide feedback on internal product specification reviews. If you treat the maven with the respect he deserves, you'll find out he isn't such a tough person to sell to after all.

People Pleaser

Some evaluators feel compelled to befriend everybody, including all the salespeople from the various companies who are calling on the account. People pleasers dislike confrontation and feel very uncomfortable knowing that someone is at odds with them. Therefore, the information they provide must always be discounted because it is being given for the sole purpose of pleasing the questioner and may not be the actual truth. People pleasers will be amenable to any decision because they always go along with the group.

Personally, I cannot stand people pleasers. I want to know where I stand in an account. I want to know the answer to the most important question in all of sales: "Will I win the deal?"

Tell me the truth as soon as possible so I don't waste my precious time. I don't want prospective customers to tell me what they think I want to hear. I want the truth, and so should you.

Schadenfreuder

Some people take delight in the failure and misfortune of others. This delight is called "schadenfreude." While a hothead wears his emotions on his sleeve and might explode in rage, a schadenfreuder plots quietly behind the scenes against you. While a hothead is searching for the best solution and actually plans on buying something, quite often the schadenfreuder never intended to buy from you in the first place. It is all a game to him and he delights in tormenting salespeople. The most extreme schadenfreuders are misanthropes—they hate people.

Schadenfreuders are truly evil, and at the end of your encounter you will have psychological scars to prove it. Sometimes they present just enough optimistic information to keep you engaged when they really have no intention of buying your product. They'll entice you with claims of big purchases that are just off in the horizon. I remember attending a meeting with one of my salespeople who called on a schadenfreuder CTO. At one point the CTO asked the junior salesperson how he was going to spend all the commission he was going to make off the sale, but the CTO never intended to buy. It was an obnoxious trick question and I wanted to punch him in the nose. You must exercise self-respect and walk away from the schadenfreuder's account.

Straight Shooter

Straight shooters have a strong sense of honor and integrity. They are not alarmists but usually even-keeled evaluators who will listen to what each salesperson has to say. Heavy Hitters love selling to straight shooters. Straight shooters are sincerely interested in finding the best solution for the people who will implement and use it. They work together with their colleagues toward a common goal and vision. They are open-minded, they listen to others' opinions, and they take pride that they are part of the team.

The best way to sell to a straight shooter is to become one yourself. While an aggressive, high-energy strategy might be appropriate in certain sales situations, mirroring the straight shooter's behavior is an equally effective strategy. Every communication with him should be structured and well documented. Don't fudge on the truth; give definitive truthful answers to his questions. Consciously slow down your speech, breathing, and mannerisms from your normal hyperactive pace.

The straight shooter's orientation is long-term, and you will probably not be able to accelerate the selection process. The evaluation process will be well thought out and lengthy. The winner will be the last vendor standing, the one who exhibited the attributes necessary to satisfy the straight shooter. In essence, the sales cycle is a miniature dry run of the long-term relationship.

Knowing the character roles informs you how to act in their presence. You adopt a "tell it like it is" demeanor with a straight shooter, carefully select your words with a hothead, and foster the fantasies of dreamers. You should not believe the schadenfreuder's claim that there is a big deal to be won, and you should expect the people pleaser to give your competition the same compliments that were given to you. Mavens and class clowns narcissistically believe themselves to be uniquely special, so treat them as the center of attention.

> The vice president of IT was a straight shooter. He was the executive sponsor and we assisted him in putting together the business case for approval. He was the traffic cop who got us in front of who we needed and had the power to sign.
>
> —*Top Technology Salesperson*

58. Authority Roles

People's authority does not always correlate to how long they have worked for their company or have been employed in their profession. In reality, selection committee members adopt authority roles in order to influence their colleagues and the decision outcome. Here are the most common authority roles that evaluators assume.

Bureaucrat

Bureaucrats are focused on selection processes and procedures. However, they will use the selection processes for their selfish gain or to exercise their political power. Many bureaucrats are consumed with maintaining the status quo. Most frequently, the best way to prevent change is to stop the purchase process entirely, so that is what bureaucrat customers often try to do.

A sales call with a bureaucrat can be extremely frustrating for two reasons. First, he may use a variety of tactics to dominate you. For instance, he knows that salespeople tend to lack patience and attention to detail and don't like forms and paperwork. He'll purposely exploit these weaknesses to protect himself and his company.

The second reason has to do with how the bureaucrat behaves during the meeting with you. The meeting with the bureaucrat may have been arranged by an underling (midlevel or low-level person) who enthusiastically supports you and your solution. Because he has been championing your cause internally, you are optimistic about your chances of winning the business. However, when you meet the bureaucrat you quickly realize that a purchase will never happen or that the bureaucrat has other ideas about whom the company should do business with. After months of time and effort, all the hopes you had to win the account are gone. This is why you must meet with C-level decision makers early in the sales cycle.

Dictator

Dictator customers are focused on decreeing the company's direction. Whereas a class clown uses humor to keep himself in the spotlight, dictators use unrelenting power to maintain their prominence. These domineering taskmasters are usually interested only in immediate results, what your solution has to offer here and now.

Even if an evaluation team has been assembled under the guise of making an impartial selection, the dictator rules its members through oppression, intimidation, or fear. Most dictators are narcissists (preoccupied admirers of themselves). However, they are typically very polished executives. They don't necessarily broadcast their power or goose-step around the office like a fascist ruler, but they rule their obedient masses with the same ruthlessness. When you shake the hand of a dictator, you are usually shaking the hand of the bully with the juice.

Empty Suit

If you are unsure whether or not the customer you are working with actually has the ability to make a purchase you are probably selling to an empty suit. He may not have the political clout or authority to buy. Therefore, you have to make a calculated decision on whether or not to pursue the business and always try to spread yourself out and meet others within the organization.

Worse yet is when someone says he has buying authority but he doesn't. In extremely large organizations, empty-suit customers protect themselves by hiding behind inflated job titles that are not justified by their experience, knowledge, or ability to lead. While empty suits may be charming and gregarious individuals, they have misconceptions about their own strengths and how the organization views them.

Empty suits are mainly preoccupied with keeping their jobs and this can result in two different behaviors. They can be motivated to find a vendor partner to help them gain power or they can be extremely hesitant to move a purchase forward or to ruffle the feathers of others within the organization. An empty suit will typically make a great impression on the first sales call. However, each subsequent meeting becomes more frustrating if you realize you are wasting your time.

Old Pro

Old pro customers are case-hardened evaluators who have years of experience working with vendors. They are experts at managing the selection process, they know what to expect from the vendors, and they command respect.

You don't exaggerate to an old pro because he'll call you on it every time. Even though the old pro's demeanor may be gruff and cantankerous, deep inside is an individual who seeks friendships. Heavy Hitters love to sell to old pros. The key is finding an intersecting activity you have in common and selling yourself to them by establishing a trusting familial relationship.

He was a hardnosed, old-school executive who worked for the company for 30 years. He was very transparent; he told us how to close him.

—*Top Technology Salesperson*

Proctor

In the academic world, proctors oversee the administration of tests to ensure that none of the students cheat. The business world has proctors whose sole purpose, so it seems, is to ensure that the selection process is followed to the letter.

Whereas a bureaucrat is motivated to stop the purchase decision, a proctor seems more concerned about following the rules of the selection process than the actual selection itself. For example, a purchasing manager who is a proctor will punish vendors who violate the selection process. This obviously creates a challenge because your goal is to implement a strategy that changes the selection process to your benefit. Therefore, you must either be in the account first and attempt to set the rules with the proctor or develop rapport with another higher-level executive, an old pro for instance, so that he can override the proctor.

Pundit

Every group has a pundit—a person who feels compelled to continually parade his or her opinions. On selection committees, these constant critics are the equivalent of a backseat driver. They assail other committee members, find fault with the direction they are taking, and attack vendors with a barrage of criticism.

Pundits will authoritatively pass judgment on you and your solution in your presence to throw you off track. They'll say things right in front of you like "That will never work for us" or "Your competition is better." These assaults are pundits' self-defense mechanism for avoiding a relationship with you (because they favor another competitor) or dissociating themselves from their decision-making responsibilities. Never forget, one of a customer's most prized possessions is his opinion.

Soldier

Corporate soldiers are paid to perform their jobs without question. Soldier customers have the lowest level of power and will dutifully follow orders passed down the chain of command. The soldier's mantra is "Ours is not to question why; ours is but to do or die."

When the CIO tells the IT director what company to do business with, the IT director becomes a soldier who has just received his marching orders. This is why you should always sell at the highest possible level in every account because you want to meet the person issuing the orders, not executing them.

Recognizing the authority roles will provide insight into sales calls during the decision-making process. Is the customer a dictator who will bully the selection committee? Is he a proctor who is more concerned about the rules of the selection than the selection itself? Is he an empty suit who lacks the wherewithal to make any decision at all? Customers' words and actions during sales calls will reveal who they are and what action you should take next.

59. Company Roles

People's titles tell only part of the story about their role within a company. In the business world, selection-committee members take on additional company roles beyond their position on the organization chart. These roles show their true political power and their personal disposition toward their company. Here are the most common company roles that evaluators assume.

Fifth Columnist

Fifth columnists are rebels who are dissatisfied with their personal predicament inside the company. The term "fifth column" originated during the Spanish Civil War and refers to a group of people who clandestinely plan to undermine a larger group. In the business world, fifth columnists feel cheated by their company in some way. They might believe they are not receiving the recognition and respect they deserve.

Frequently, fifth columnists are out to prove themselves better than someone else at their company or to prove that their department is the best in the company. They'll purchase products not only to further their cause but to undermine the success, power, and authority of others inside the company. During the sales cycle, they will frequently identify with and relate to a salesperson more than to their own coworkers. It is actually best to meet with a fifth columnist alone so that he will share his secret plans with you.

Hired Gun

Hired guns are corporate expatriates. They are not emotionally invested in their jobs or completely committed to the company they work for. They tend to select products they believe will help them get their next job. The motto of a hired gun is "There is no such thing as a bad product if it helps you get your next job."

Hired guns are market-share sensitive. They like to do business with gorillas, the dominant players in the market. Therefore, if you sell for a chimp-sized company, you are in an extremely dangerous position when the bully with the juice is a hired gun.

Intern

Interns either will delegate their evaluation responsibilities to others or are the junior members of the selection team so they can't contribute to the selection process. They may be new to the company or profession or lack experience in selecting products.

Sometimes, a high-ranking executive is classified as an intern because he doesn't care to be involved with the procurement process. The project is not important enough to warrant his time and attention. Since the intern doesn't have industry domain expertise or technical aptitude, the bulk of the evaluation work falls on the shoulders of others who are experienced with company operations or low-level personnel who have deep technical knowledge. These people become the bullies with the juice in the account while the executive intern is the emperor. Interns like this typically become involved very late in the sales cycle, after the preliminary recommendation has been made for their review.

Politician

Politicians in a company are smooth schemers who opportunistically maneuver to hold onto or gain power within the organization. They speak with carefully selected words and try to display a professional demeanor at all times. It's not surprising that most higher-level executives are politicians because it requires political acumen to make it to the top.

Politicians are the influential statesmen of companies. They are experienced in dealing with company issues, know how to make things happen, and get their way in the process. They're more polished than interns. They hold their cards close to their chest and won't broadcast their intentions until you have proven that it is in their political interest to do so.

Pollyanna

Pollyannas believe the company they work for is the best, whether it is or not. Usually, they absolutely love their jobs and find good in everyone and everything. Typically, these overly optimistic customers are hard workers and may have spent their entire careers at one or two companies.

Pollyannas have a tendency to ignore ugly facts and underestimate the complexity of the solutions they purchase. They are genuinely excited about the upcoming purchase, and Heavy Hitters are grateful for their naiveté. Obviously, it makes sense for salespeople to mirror their excitement and enthusiasm.

Revolutionary

Revolutionaries are out to create upheaval in their organization. They are agents of change who seek to remake the company's culture, its mind-set, or the way it does business.

As opposed to fifth columnists, revolutionaries have sincere motives and want the company to succeed. For example, they might be trying to change a technology-driven company to a customer-focused one, to reinvigorate company morale, or to enter new markets. They seek solutions that will help them accomplish their revolution. Whenever a new executive joins a company, he becomes a revolutionary who seeks to consolidate his power by creating grand initiatives. That's why you should always keep track of executives on the move and be the first salesperson to meet with them in their new job.

Vigilante

Company vigilantes are extremely pessimistic people who want to protect their company from the claims of vendors. Usually they are eternal naysayers, out to prove that none of the vendors' proposed solutions will work for their company. Vigilantes see their right to voice their opinion as a sacred trust. They take the decision-making process very seriously and vote for the product they believe adds the most value to the company's day-to-day operations and long-term strategy.

Three things keep me awake at night. First is a shift in focus by management. If cost containment becomes the most important priority, then IT becomes an expense rather than a value add. Second is scope control. If you can't break down the work and show you're delivering on it, then once again you are an expense. Large projects are like that. People just say, "Wow, it takes IT a long time." Finally, there's government regulation—whether it is Sarbanes Oxley or one of our foreign companies that sees nothing wrong with shipping products to a country that is against the law here. You have to corral those people and be on the lookout for abhorrent behavior.

—*Vice President of Business Systems*

Vigilantes are skeptical and do not trust salespeople. They'll make every vendor respond to immense RFPs and complete laborious spreadsheets—each product feature and operation has to be fully documented to prove it exists. They'll require meticulous hands-on evaluations of each product and painstakingly documented findings. They won't buy until they are completely satisfied, and when they meet with salespeople, they are cross-examiners as opposed to collaborators like C-level fifth columnists.

Identify company roles so you can understand how each customer perceives himself within the organization. A hired gun wants to be reassured that selecting you will selfishly help his career while a revolutionary wants to know that you are equally committed to the cause he is fighting for. Don't be misled by the Pollyanna's optimism or discouraged by the vigilante's pessimism. Expect the intern and fifth columnist to quickly open up to you and complain about their personal situation while a politician will not confide in you until he feels it's safe.

60. Applying IT Buyer Personas

During sales calls and the selection process as a whole, the role each team member adopts will depend on the roles other members of the decision process occupy. For example, there typically can be only one dictator, maven, and class clown at a time. Selection team members have to assume other roles once these roles are taken. Conversely, a team can have multiple pundits, schadenfreuders, and analyticals. People assuming these roles actually encourage other selection team members to join them.

The roles people take on during the sales cycle determine how you will communicate with them. Most interestingly, these roles can vary from purchase to purchase. For example, a CIO who has a vested interest in the Internet provider his company uses to run its business might be an analytical during the selection process. Conversely, he's a slacker when it comes to the purchase of toner cartridges because he doesn't care.

Perhaps the most important aspect of customer role-playing to remember is that customers do not play the same role with each vendor. For example, an evaluator might present himself as a schadenfreuder and vigilante to you while being a straight shooter and politician with your competitor. Under these circumstances, you will not win this deal. Therefore, you must evaluate not only how selection-team members are relating to you but, equally important, theorize how they are relating to your competitors.

How do you communicate with a person you have never met before? How do you best present your story, and what demeanor should you use to persuade him to speak in confidence with you? These roles help us understand evaluators' dispositions and motivations and the granularity of the information you should present. Why should you segment sales calls by the different customer decision-making roles? Because it will help you strategize, plan, and execute your sales call. Figure 60.1 summarizes the purpose of each buyer persona role.

Information role	Helps determine how you will present information and who should attend the customer sales call
Character role	Prepares your colleagues for the unique group dynamics of the customer's meeting
Authority role	Provides insight into the customer's decision-making process
Company role	Explains the customer's ulterior motives, how he perceives himself, and his power within the company

Figure 60.1 Purpose of determining customer decision-making roles

Some group decision-making combinations are dangerous and unpredictable. Be extremely cautious when meeting customers who are hothead dictators, schadenfreuder bureaucrats, pundit fifth columnists, and proctor vigilantes. One bad move during sales calls with these customers and the account is lost. Conversely, slacker class clowns, believer people pleasers, empty-suit Pollyannas, and soldier interns are extremely bad combinations for another reason. The likelihood that these customers can make a major purchase happen is infinitesimal.

For the purposes of applying group decision-making roles, let's pretend we are part of the sales team working on the Acme account, a Fortune 1000 company that is making a million-dollar purchase of state-of-the-art business software to replace its existing antiquated mainframe software. The Acme decision-making team is composed of Bob Adams, chief information officer; Nancy Smith, director of information technology; Mitch Jackson, project leader; and Mortimer Jones, vice president of purchasing. They are evaluating different enterprise software solutions.

Since the initiative to replace the mainframe software was championed by Bob, we surmise he is the emperor. Therefore, our sales strategy must include sales calls with Bob. This is also a persuasion sales cycle type (see chapter 9) because it has a well-defined selection process and has issued an RFP, and we know we are competing against our two archrivals. We know there is a 30 percent chance the team already has a favored vendor who will win the deal. Therefore, we need to determine if biases exist and build relationships at all levels as soon as possible in order to develop a coach.

Next, we make our assessment and segment buyer persona roles of the Acme evaluators as represented in figure 60.2.

	Information Role	Character Role	Authority Role	Company Role
Bob Adams CIO	Summary seeker	Straight shooter	Old pro	Politician
Nancy Smith IT Director	Intellectual	Maven	Soldier	Pollyanna
Mitch Jackson Project Leader	Analytical	Maven	Pundit	Hired gun
Mortimer Jones VP of Purchasing	Analytical	Hothead	Bureaucrat	Vigilante

Figure 60.2 Buyer persona decision-making roles for Acme's evaluation team members

Bob's a seasoned executive with the business skills and political acumen to lead the organization. Nancy has worked for Bob for seven years and is a maven who understands the details of the daily operations of the department. She's an optimistic soldier who marches to Bob's orders. Mitch is an accomplished technical expert. He's a cocky pundit who has little loyalty to the company. Mortimer is a hard-to-get-along-with numbers guy.

We theorize and prioritize the kinds of stress each person is under. Bob is mainly under corporate citizenship stress. He's worried about cutting costs during tough economic times. Nancy is under pressure from Bob. Bob has mandated that she cut her budget by 30 percent this year. She's worried about how Bob perceives her. Mitch is an analytical who wants to understand every technical detail, so he makes sure they are selecting the product with the best functionality. He suffers from informational stress. Mortimer is consumed with corporate citizenship stress. He's an analytical who wants all aspects of the business relationship documented in the contract. He believes he is the company's fiscal watchdog.

All of the evaluators have different motivations based upon their company roles. As a result, their perceptions of our solution's strategic, operational, political, and psychological value (see chapter 27) will be different. Here are the different values we provide Bob:

- Our strategic value is that we are the most cost-effective solution and provide the best return on investment.
- Our operational value has many aspects: we automate a number of functions that employees currently do by hand, our system is faster so they will be able to process orders faster, and the software has more functionality so user satisfaction will increase.
- From a political standpoint, our state-of-the-art graphical user interface will help improve the image of the IT department within the company.
- From a psychological standpoint, Bob's been worried about the old system for years, ever fearful that it will crash at critical

times of the month and year. Our system will bring him much-needed peace of mind.

Buyer personas enable you to theorize about the people you will be meeting so you can plan your sales call accordingly. You should also adapt your strategy and selling style to match the information, character, authority, and company roles of the person you are meeting with. Prepare yourself with facts and specifications in anticipation of meeting the analytical. Massage the maven's ego during the call. Tell it like it is and don't fudge the truth when meeting with an old pro. Support the revolutionary's goal to become the organization's change agent.

> Every sale is different because there is always a different cast of characters. I map out everyone in the account. I want to know how they think and what they think about me, my competition, and each other. The technology guys can love you and the business guys hate you or vice versa. The most difficult part of the sale is understanding what motivates someone and building all the different relationships so you can manage the account.
>
> —*Top Technology Salesperson*

61. Information Role Buyer Persona Case Studies

The following case studies show how different information roles impact sales strategy. People have different tolerances for stress, anger, and worry. At one end of the spectrum is the person who is always experiencing a crisis. At the other end is the person who is calm and collected even under immense pressure.

If a prospective customer is even-keeled, the sales process will most likely be logical, unhurried, and sedate. Therefore, the salesperson will mirror that behavior during the sales cycle and adjust his sales strategy and selling style accordingly. Here's a case study about Kurt, who is an analytical.

	Information Role	Character Role	Authority Role	Company Role
Kurt	Analytical	Maven	Bureaucrat	Politician

Kurt had worked in the same local government agency for over twenty years. During this time, he had risen to the position of director. The agency was migrating to cloud-based applications.

Kurt was in charge of selecting cloud technology. His environment was structured around order and predictability. Everything, including his appearance, his office, and the process to select the new solution, reflected this.

The salesperson had to make an important decision about whether or not to pursue the business. Based on Kurt's personality, the salesperson knew that he would not be able to accelerate or change the selection process. Kurt's orientation was long term, and there would be no quick decisions.

The evaluation process would be well thought out and lengthy. The winner would be the last vendor standing, the one who exhibited the attributes necessary to have a long-term partnership with the agency. In essence, the sales cycle was a miniature dry run of the long-term relationship.

To develop Kurt into a coach, the salesperson's strategy was to prove that he and his company were like Kurt. He had to adopt Kurt's calm, unimpulsive traits (not an easy task for a high-energy salesperson). First, he adopted Kurt's personal demeanor. Every communication with Kurt was structured and well documented. When meeting with Kurt, the salesperson consciously slowed down his speech and mannerisms from his normal hyperactive pace.

Another part of the salesperson's strategy was to introduce himself to Kurt's other longtime business partners, the members of Kurt's staff. Through these meetings, he gathered more information about Kurt. He was told about a past incident when a vendor tried unsuccessfully to go around Kurt to sell his solution.

He also met with other vendors with whom Kurt had existing relationships. From these vendors, he hoped to uncover any existing relationships that might work against him. He was also demonstrating to Kurt his desire to enter Kurt's world and his network of relationships.

As the sales cycle progressed, the other vendors' patience and commitment to the opportunity waned. They had miscalculated their ability to shorten or subvert Kurt's process. As this happened, Kurt spent more time with the salesperson, which presented more opportunities to build a personal relationship. The salesperson learned Kurt rode horses, had served in the military, and, surprisingly, had been married twice. Kurt ultimately became the salesperson's coach and shepherded the purchase through the agency's bureaucratic sales process.

While an aggressive, high-energy strategy might be appropriate for certain sales buyer personas, the decision to model Kurt in a complementary reactive manner was an equally effective strategy.

At the other end of the spectrum from an analytical is a believer. Here's a case study about a believer named Larry. Larry's been worried about how his department is perceived within his company, so he's devised a strategy to improve its reputation. However, he needs a vendor's help to execute his plan.

	Information Role	*Character Role*	*Authority Role*	*Company Role*
Larry	Believer	Dreamer	Soldier	Fifth columnist

Larry was worried. He had heard talk about outsourcing his group's application development function. Since he had been with the transportation company for over thirteen years, he was angry with his employer and somewhat discouraged by his current predicament. His career seemed to be heading in the wrong direction, and he wasn't aware of what strategic decisions were being made by the senior IT leadership team above him.

One project he had unsuccessfully tried to get funding for in the past was an online reporting application to replace paper reports. He had ulterior motives for completing this project. He knew that once the flexibility of online reports was introduced, it would be well received, and perhaps others would adopt a more positive view of his group's value. Also, the reporting system would become irreplaceable, requiring continual enhancements and maintenance from his team. Larry asked all the leading reporting tool vendors to present their technologies to his team. However, he was more than hoping to find a solution; he wanted to believe that the reporting system would actually be completed. Of course, none of the vendors had any background information about Larry's dilemma.

However, the winning salesperson had a unique strategy for the meeting. Prior to the technology presentation, he met with Larry to further understand his needs. From this meeting, he determined that Larry had three problems. First, Larry's team didn't have enough time to learn the new tools and build the application to meet his schedule. Second, Larry was concerned that his team was not technically capable of completing the project. Finally, Larry didn't have a defined budget approved for the purchase. This information would make any salesperson nervous. Was Larry serious about the purchase or just "kicking tires"? Was there even a project?

The salesperson decided to do something to separate himself from the other vendors. He would change the game and better serve the customer at the same time. While the other vendors would tell Larry how much easier their product was to use, the salesperson would build a prototype of the reporting system. He wanted to show Larry that his project could be completed successfully within Larry's constraints. However, prior to committing the resources to execute this strategy, he completed a background check of Larry. He wanted to know if Larry was the bully with the juice who could push this product through purchasing. By understanding the past projects Larry had successfully managed, the salesperson concluded Larry was not a dud. The salesperson decided that the strategy had an acceptable risk and persuaded his management team to commit the resources to build the prototype.

The other vendors gave Larry and his team a presentation of their company, their product's feature set, and a short product demonstration. It seemed to Larry that any of the vendors' products would meet his requirements. To add to Larry's confusion, all the products were priced similarly.

However, the salesperson's presentation was different. He showed the completed prototype application. Following this, he dissected the prototype, displaying the unique features that had made the prototype so easy to create. Larry's team was excited! The salesperson was invited back the following week to show the application directly to the nontechnical business users within the organization who would ultimately use the reports.

Building the prototype had other benefits. To create it, the salesperson's technical team met with Larry's team to determine basic functionality. This was a much more desirable environment in which to build relationships than the stressful sales presentation.

While the technical relationship was being developed, the relationship between the salesperson and Larry changed dramatically. Larry asked for a detailed proposal for training his team and a bid to build the entire application. Completing these tasks required constant communication between Larry and his team and the salesperson and his. The other vendors were locked out of the opportunity because the salesperson had thought about Larry's end goal, not just selling some software.

The presentation to the business users the following week was a success. They wanted the application—the sooner the better. Money was allocated, terms were finalized, and the project was completed successfully ninety days later.

There is a path to every piece of business. But to find the path, you must walk in the shoes of the customer.

62. Character Role Buyer Persona Case Studies

The following case studies show how different character roles impact sales strategy. People have different capabilities to build and manage relationships within group settings. Some individuals naturally command groups and lead, while others tend to follow. Here's a character role case study about Paul, who is a schadenfreuder.

	Information Role	Character Role	Authority Role	Company Role
Paul	Analytical	Schadenfreuder	Dictator	Fifth columnist

Paul was the manager in charge of information systems security in a well-known financial services company. He had a low level of agreeableness and didn't get along well in groups of people. His main responsibility was to ensure customers' data was safe and secure. The position held a lot of responsibility and commanded equal authority. A breach in a customer's data could have significant financial implications. In addition to the legal liability, the unfavorable press would impact the company greatly.

Paul was a tough-minded authoritarian. He didn't "meet" vendors; rather, he verbally abused them in front of his staff! These staged events were designed to showcase his considerable knowledge and the extent of his authority. Paul didn't trust anybody. He spoke negatively about other divisions of his company and how he would manage them differently.

Developing Paul into a coach was critical. He was the bully who had all the juice. If the salesperson didn't win him over, he wouldn't win the deal. He knew it was pointless to argue with

Paul; nothing would be gained by doing so. Paul would not be swayed by any vendor's logic or reason. He marched to his own drumbeat and he was considered somewhat immature for a person who was over forty.

Paul would choose the solution he believed was in his own best interest. So what did Paul want? He wanted to be a hero. He wanted to prove he was smart. He was seeking the recognition he felt he was entitled to. The salesperson's mission was to ensure that the selection of his product helped Paul achieve his needs.

Paul was considering replacing the company's existing security vendor because of continual product stability problems and the quality of customer support. The product was already in use when Paul was hired, and the company had spent a significant amount of money to purchase and implement it. Knowing this, the winning salesperson worked with his management team to package a very compelling proposal that included a full product trade-in credit and included some implementation services for free. This excited Paul! He would take great pride in boasting to his managers how he not only fixed the problem but essentially got their money back too.

The salesperson continually sold to Paul's ego. At every opportunity, he elicited Paul's feedback, not so much for its own merits but so Paul could hear himself talk about the salesperson's solution. He arranged for Paul to meet with others from the salesperson's company—the technical support manager, the product management team, and various members of the executive staff. So the salesperson's colleagues were subjected to Paul's pontificating, and the salesperson was freed for other tasks. The salesperson even arranged an invitation for Paul to join the customer advisory committee of the salesperson's company.

Paul ultimately became a fantastic coach and an incredible champion. He was sold on the salesperson's company as well as the product. Finally, someone was treating him with the respect he deserved. Later, he even met with the president about the possibility of joining the salesperson's company. Paul wasn't such a tough guy after all.

Selling to an optimist is easier than selling to a pessimist like Paul. Here's a character role case study about Bill, who is a dreamer.

	Information Role	Character Role	Authority Role	Company Role
Bill	Summary seeker	Dreamer	Old pro	Revolutionary

Bill is the director of information technology for a business unit of a multibillion-dollar conglomerate. He wanted to make his mark, not only within his organization but also within the parent company. Bill's vision was to change the way the company did business by employing technology strategically throughout the organization. His goal for his unit was to become the model for all the other IT organizations within the company. He had deployed the latest products in his attempt to build his technology showcase. To drive his agenda, he was constantly meeting with his own team as well as the other departments within the organization to rally them around his cause.

After meeting with Bill, the salesperson truly understood the depth of his conviction to accomplish his goal. However, the salesperson had a major problem as Bill's approach was not conducive to using his solution. He had to challenge his methodology and change his way of thinking. Instead of focusing on product features and functionality, the sale to Bill would have to be at a more strategic level. He had to offer Bill a better way of achieving his vision and expose the risk of the direction he was considering.

To accomplish his goal, the salesperson used his management team and key company experts extensively during the sales cycle. They shared business philosophies, industry trends, and best practices. They also made site visits to several accounts to show their solution in action.

These efforts changed Bill's mind. He needed comrades who not only believed in his vision but, more importantly, would help him successfully execute it. Partners who weren't afraid to tell him the truth would keep the project on track. As a result, Bill viewed the salesperson's company as an integral component and the only one that could help him achieve his dream.

63. Authority Role Buyer Persona Case Studies

The following case studies show how different authority roles impact sales strategy. Salespeople wear many hats. In some situations, they are the customer's friends. In others, they are the promoters of the company's vision. Sometimes they become the human encyclopedia of all the facts about the company's products. Here's a character role case study about John, a pundit.

	Information Role	Character Role	Authority Role	Company Role
John	Analytical	Maven	Pundit	Vigilante

John was an extremely difficult person to sell to. He was the vice president of information services for an outsourcer of computer applications. John had been a low-level technician and had worked his way up to the executive level. His technical expertise made him even more intimidating to vendors.

He was a realist who based his decisions on facts rather than ideas or emotions. He was interested only in discussing the here and now. With every topic, he carefully selected his words to reflect their accuracy. He wanted nothing but the facts.

With John there wouldn't be any detailed discussions about the company's vision or any deep personal conversations. The topic would always be the product—the way it worked, what features it lacked, and the details about the underlying technology that most customers would consider minutiae. However, John needed to hear all the particulars.

Developing John into a coach involved several critical steps. First, the winning salesperson never went alone to a meeting with John. He always had his system engineer or other technical team members on hand to help answer John's questions.

Second, the salesperson and his team gave only definitive, truthful answers to John's questions, responding with the same precision as John used. They wanted to maintain their credibility. The team members edited their usual optimistic product claims to mirror John's conservative demeanor.

Third, they always worked with John's best interests in mind. They wanted him to know both the features and limitations of their product. It made no sense to sell John a product that didn't meet his requirements. Rather, it was important that his expectations were set correctly during the sales process. They arranged for a detailed on-site technical evaluation of their product and provided technical resources to assist him.

During this evaluation process, an interesting change in John began to occur. He began to openly criticize the other vendor's sales tactics and honesty. Also, he uncovered many flaws in the salesperson's product. However, instead of criticizing the product and declaring it unsuitable, he worked with the salesperson's team to find workarounds for these limitations. John was now the salesperson's coach.

While Paul was an extremely diligent evaluator in a leadership position, a soldier follows orders as part of the chain of command. Here's a character role case study about Lou, a soldier.

	Information Role	Character Role	Authority Role	Company Role
Lou	Slacker	Class clown	Soldier	Hired gun

For the past five years, Lou had worked as the system administrator responsible for database operations at a medium-sized electronics manufacturer. Lou was not the type of person who was intensely focused on his career. He was a happy-go-lucky guy who seemed to do the minimum to get by. This also applied to his interest in technology. While he understood concepts, he did not seem particularly interested in mastering the details.

Although he was part of the evaluation team, he was not a key influencer of the group. In team meetings, his only contribution was an occasional wisecrack courtesy of his dry sense of humor. He was not a mover or shaker who called the shots. In short, Lou was an obedient member of the team who followed the direction set from above. In spite of this, the salesperson made a special effort to get to know Lou.

Acknowledging Lou's traits, the salesperson arranged unusual activities that were outside the work environment. To become better acquainted, the salesperson took Lou to lunch at eclectic restaurants and invited him to his company's local events. The salesperson was normally an intense person, but he suspended this personality characteristic when he was around Lou. Over time, this "odd couple" actually found they enjoyed each other's company.

None of the other vendors paid any attention to Lou, as they considered him trivial to the decision process. In addition, none of the vendors were able to develop a coach out of anyone else on the selection team. Lou was the only coach to be found. For the salesperson, Lou developed into a great source of information about the company's political environment and how the sales process was progressing. While the other vendors were flying blind, the salesperson knew who was for and against his product and what objections he had to overcome. He knew the prices bid by his competitors. Lou even told the salesperson he had won the deal before it was publicly announced.

64. Company Role Buyer Persona Case Studies

The following case studies show how different company roles impact sales strategy. You can expect a very exhaustive sales cycle when a person with a high level of conscientiousness and protectionist instincts is leading a selection process. Here's a case study about Michelle, a vigilante.

	Information Role	Character Role	Authority Role	Company Role
Michelle	Analytical	Maven	Bureaucrat	Vigilante

Mr. Johnson was the chief information officer of a multibillion-dollar publicly held medical device manufacturer. He was the prototypical executive: confident, capable, and successful. However, one huge problem in selling to Mr. Johnson was that it was impossible to meet with him personally. For purchase decisions, he had several trusted lieutenants who did most of the data gathering and analysis.

Mr. Johnson would become involved only very late in the sales cycle, after the preliminary recommendation had been made for his review. Until that time, the salesperson would have to work within the established process. In the salesperson's case, he was able to find a coach in one of Mr. Johnson's direct reports, Michelle, the vice president of applications development. She was much easier to gain access to and meet with.

Michelle made every vendor respond with an immense RFP and complete laborious spreadsheets. Each product feature and operation had to be fully documented. Following the responses, Michelle performed a meticulous hands-on evaluation of each product and painstakingly documented her findings. It was clear that Michelle felt the decision process was a direct reflection of her competency.

It wasn't until Michelle was completely satisfied with the salesperson's product that her demeanor changed from cross-examiner to collaborator. Suddenly, Michelle was strategizing with the salesperson about presenting her recommendation to Mr. Johnson. Michelle scheduled the meeting with Mr. Johnson to present her decision and asked the salesperson to attend. The salesperson knew the deal was won if they made it successfully past this final hurdle.

Michelle planned every detail of the presentation. The salesperson was fearful that Michelle's decision could be overruled, and Michelle was fearful the salesperson would somehow embarrass her. They discussed the demeanor of the participants: both salesperson and coach had to display confidence and professionalism, along with the etiquette expected when meeting a person of Mr. Johnson's stature.

The salesperson and his manager arrived early to meet Michelle at Mr. Johnson's office. The salesperson was nervous, and while the meeting seemed like life or death to him, it was just a small item on Mr. Johnson's daily calendar. They had been allotted forty-five minutes of his time. Unfortunately, Mr. Johnson was running late and their meeting was pushed back a half hour and shortened to twenty minutes.

Mr. Johnson opened his meeting with an overview of his expectations. He then asked a series of high-level questions about the salesperson's company, product, competitors, and customers, which Michelle and the salesperson answered together. However, rather than being subjected to the grueling interrogation that he expected, the salesperson felt this meeting was more ceremonial. Michelle's attention to detail had already won the deal.

Sometimes, not losing the deal is a key part of winning the business. You have to know when to keep your mouth closed. The next case study is about a politician named Tom.

	Information Role	Character Role	Authority Role	Company Role
Tom	Intellectual	Straight shooter	Old pro	Politician

Tom was the senior director of the information technology department of an educational institution. He was an engaging, interesting person who was friendly, outgoing, and easy to talk to. He was even a past member of the Screen Actors Guild. Tom's background didn't match that of most IT people, yet somehow in his past he had become involved with computers.

Tom's world was more political than technical. He spent the majority of his time meeting with various deans and placating them. His department was staffed with younger employees who had minimal business experience. While Tom did not get deeply involved in detailed technical issues, he clearly was the bully with the juice and approved every decision within the department.

The salesperson's first impression was that Tom might be bored and unfulfilled by his job. When the salesperson tried to talk about his products, Tom kept changing the subject back to the salesperson by asking personal questions about his family and where he grew up. Tom wanted to be liked, and this was not a typical sales call.

However, what many salespeople would have viewed as small talk was actually a key part of Tom's decision process. Tom was trying to determine if there was a personal fit between him and the salesperson. For Tom, this was an important business prerequisite. The salesperson mirrored Tom and asked him the same type of personal questions. Tom described his childhood in the Midwest, his affinity for the Chicago Cubs, and his desire to retire in a few years. As a result, a meeting that should have taken forty-five minutes lasted over two hours.

Many additional meetings would follow where products would be discussed in addition to personal matters. But the most important aspect of Tom's sales selection process was already decided; he liked the salesperson.

If you are unsure whether a customer is your friend or a business acquaintance, apply the barbecue test. Would you invite the person to your home on a Sunday afternoon for a barbecue with your family and close friends? The more important question is, would your customers invite you to *their* barbecues?

PART V

Personal Communication Strategy

65. Situational Dominance

The concept of situational dominance has three distinct sales applications. First, it is core to the personal communication strategy used during customer interactions. Second, it plays a key role in formulating sales cycle strategy as it relates to when provocation or alignment is used. Finally, it is used to drive sales team strategy and manage internal resources. In other words, situational dominance can be applied to sales calls, sales cycles, and how you direct the sales team.

Customer Interaction Strategy

In every customer conversation you will find yourself in one of three places. You can be in a submissive position, where you are not respected and the customer rejects or ignores what you say. When you are in this position, the prospective customer thinks of you solely as a salesperson who is trying to sell him something. You can be in an equal position, where the customer respects you and is interested in hearing what you have to say. Or you can be in a dominant position, where the customer accepts your arguments, internalizes them, and then acts on them. Figure 65.1 illustrates the three situational dominance positions.

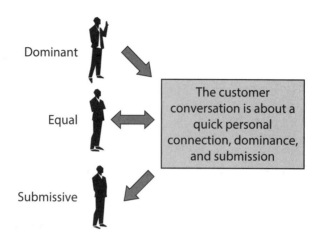

Figure 65.1 Situational dominance positions

A successful customer conversation starts by recognizing that a quick personal connection occurs between people based mainly on nonverbal communication and physical appearance. How long is it before a prospective customer makes an initial assessment of whether or not he likes you during your first sales call? The answer is between 30 and 180 seconds, according to my research. Then, he'll spend the next 10 to 18 minutes of the meeting validating whether his preliminary decision was correct.

Situational dominance can be thought of as gaining the willing obedience of the customer. The customer listens to your opinions and advice, internalizes your recommendations and agrees with them, and follows your course of action. This is based on the lasting impression the customer has of you.

A salesperson's goal is to gain dominance over a willingly submissive customer. While dominance is commonly associated with brute force, this is not the case in sales. It's simply how people judge others. People are continually sensing whether their position is superior to yours, relatively equal, or inferior in some way. In turn, this impacts what they say during conversations and how they behave. A relaxed dominant salesperson speaks freely and guides the conversation as he confidently shares his knowledge and opinions. He is in control. An anxious submissive salesperson is forced into reactive behavior and his tendency is to operate under the direction of the customer, never being in control of the account.

> It's not the number of deals you are working on that's important; it's the number of deals you are in control of.
> —*Top Technology Salesperson*

While some dominant people will surround themselves with submissive people, most dominants want to associate with people whom they perceive as equals. Equals converse with relative ease. One of your most important goals when meeting with a customer is establishing yourself as an equal at a minimum. That's why you need to master the technical specification language and the business operations language of your industry described in chapters 42–43. Only by knowing the customer's company goals, business problems, technical frustrations, and personal aspirations will you be able to explain how you can address them.

> If all the solutions we are evaluating have the same payback, it becomes a sales job as to who can sell best to our upper management. What you say and how you say it is truly what sets you apart.
> —*Chief Financial Officer*

Obviously, a salesperson who can employ a wider range of dominant traits can sell to a wider range of customers. Knowing which trait to draw upon is determined by your sales intuition. For instance, in one account you might display an optimistic attitude to instill optimism when the evaluators are nervous and scared. In another account you might display outward skepticism, forcing the customer to explain why he believes his company will actually make a purchase. In both circumstances you have established dominance.

You probably have used a wide range of attributes to establish your dominance, depending on the customers you have met with. That's a fundamental trait of Heavy Hitters. They behave in a way that makes them dominant, even if that means they must behave submissively. For example, the case study about Paul in chapter 62 showed an example of a salesperson consciously employing submissive behavior to establish a dominant position later.

Every account has an equilibrium point of dominance versus arrogance. It's the point where the customer respects your conviction and is not offended by your demeanor. Even though you promote your agenda with determination, you are not considered pushy or overbearing.

However, at times you have to confront the customer directly—in some situations you have to challenge the customer's beliefs, process, and decisions for his own good. This takes courage and conviction as the quotes below show. Furthermore, you have to become comfortable with very uncomfortable situations.

> The RFP came out and it was geared for our competitor. We declined the RFP twice. They thought I was being rude, but I had to change their process for them to see our value. We said, "We want your business, but we have to do it this way." The main contact that worked with us was not our biggest fan, and the CIO slapped our hand and said, "If you work this way, we don't work with you." It was a very risky strategy. We endured months of demos and antagonistic meetings. But if it wasn't for this strategy, we would have never closed this account.
> —*Top Technology Salesperson*

We basically told them that their "baby was ugly" and their system was a mess. They were shocked and protested. I thought we were done, but three weeks later they called us back.

—*Top Technology Salesperson*

You have to address the elephant in the room. I confronted them point blank: "Why aren't you talking to us anymore?"

—*Top Technology Salesperson*

You can use two basic approaches to establish dominance during sales calls. The direct approach is based upon personal prowess, while the indirect approach is based upon finesse. The approach you should use depends upon attributes of your personality. Now it's time to measure your situational dominance. Read the following questions and select the answer that suits you best.

Let's pretend you are having a hallway conversation with three colleagues. Do you usually

(A) remain silent the majority of the time, letting others speak;

(B) speak for an equal share of the conversation; or

(C) find yourself talking the majority of the time?

Using the hallway example above, if someone said something you disagreed with would you typically

(A) remain silent;

(B) challenge the person to explain himself; or

(C) confront the person directly?

When speaking with colleagues, are you someone who

(A) carefully edits your words;

(B) tactfully speaks your mind; or

(C) is completely open and honest with all your thoughts?

Your number of A, B, and C answers represents your situational dominance from low to high. If you answered all Cs, that would indicate a naturally high level of situational dominance.

Conversely, all As would be associated with an extremely low level and Bs a medium level.

If you have a naturally high level of situational dominance, you are typically well suited to use a direct approach. This approach is based upon first establishing yourself as the focal point of the purchase. In essence, the customer is buying into your credibility, your personal experiences, and your ability to help him accomplish his goals.

If you have a naturally low level of situational dominance, you are probably better suited to use an indirect approach. This approach is based on establishing the capabilities of your company and products as the focal point to move yourself to the position of being an equal. For example, a salesperson with low dominance who transitioned his career from a technical position into sales can have an equally dominant presence as a seasoned sales veteran. However, he has to use a different approach. Instead of projecting a powerful presence in person, his deep-rooted technical understanding of his product draws customers to follow him and makes him dominant.

Sales Cycle Strategy

In chapter 12 we reviewed the three paths for working on an account. You can be in alignment and agree with how the customer intends to solve his problem or achieve his goal. In this case you submissively *follow* the customer's lead. You can be *adaptable* and gradually transform his thought process over time till he considers you an equal who is operating in his best interest. Or you can use *provocation* to dominate the customer and completely change the customer's selection criteria or sales process. Remember, "dominant" is not a negative term. It simply refers to someone following your advice and recommendations.

Sales Team Strategy

The concept of situational dominance also applies to how the salesperson manages the presales resources that are involved in a sales cycle. The salesperson should control and coordinate all meetings, presentations, and technical evaluations. He is in charge of the company resources that are assembled to win the account, regardless of their departmental origin, including management, engineering, support, consulting, marketing, and product management. The salesperson should be the prospective customer's main point of contact for all customer communication. In essence, the salesperson has to establish dominance internally within his own company.

The salesperson is responsible for defining the products that will be proposed and ensuring they match the customer's needs. As the team leader, he confirms to the rest of the project team that the customer is qualified from a business and technical perspective, motivates the team, and takes responsibility for the overall relationship with the customer and ongoing account satisfaction.

The presales engineer is mainly responsible for understanding the customer's technical profile and presenting the company's technical solution. The system engineer conducts the process that determines the level of technical fit between the vendor's product and the customer's technical environment. The system engineer is also responsible for solution design, product evaluation, and implementation of the project. Members from other departments, such as consulting or support, may also perform certain tasks at the system engineer's direction. Most importantly, the system engineer is responsible for the technical relationship with the customer and the ongoing technical satisfaction with the product. In this role of a customer advocate, the system engineer represents the customer and facilitates meetings with the technical support department.

Here are some interesting customer quotes to consider.

I'm going to say this bluntly. Tell the sales engineer to shut up and let the salesperson do his job. The engineer hijacked the discussion. I'm glad he was enthusiastic about his product, but there was no room for discussion about our needs. For some customers, this may be the way they offset a less-than-robust salesperson who was not in control. However, they should realize what works with one customer may not work with another. They would have a better chance to win if they did.

—*IT Manager*

Their salesperson was a typical sales guy who wanted to make a sale. The engineer knew what he was talking about and could answer questions. Since I come from an electrical engineering background, I asked technical questions and the engineer gave answers I liked. I had good interactions with the engineer. I didn't really like the salesperson.

—*Director of IT*

Vendor A's sales team was best. It was evident the sales rep and engineer had worked together for a long time. There was a synergy between them that gave us the confidence to buy their products.

—*Chief Technology Officer*

66. Personality Traits of Top Technology Salespeople

Over the past decade, I've administered personality tests to better understand the characteristics that separate top technology salespeople from their peers. The findings indicate that key personality traits directly influence top performers' selling style and ultimately their success. Below, you will find the main key personality attributes of top salespeople and the impact of each trait on their selling style.

1. *Achievement orientation.* Eighty-four percent of the top performers scored very high in achievement orientation. They are fixated on achieving goals and continuously measure their performance in comparison to their goals.

   Selling style impact: political orientation. During sales cycles, top sales performers seek to understand the politics of customer decision making. Their goal orientation instinctively drives them to meet with key decision makers. Therefore, they strategize about the people they are selling to and how the products they're selling fit into the organization instead of focusing on the functionality of the products themselves.

2. *Curiosity.* Curiosity can be described as a person's hunger for knowledge and information. Eighty-two percent of top salespeople had extremely high curiosity levels. Top salespeople are naturally more curious than their lower-performing counterparts.

   Selling style impact: inquisitiveness. A high level of inquisitiveness correlates to an active presence during sales calls. An active presence drives the salesperson to ask customers difficult and uncomfortable questions in order to close gaps in information. Top salespeople want to know if they can win the business, and they want to know the truth as soon as possible.

3. *Modesty.* Contrary to conventional stereotypes of successful salespeople as pushy and egotistical, 91 percent of top salespeople had medium to high scores of modesty and humility.

Furthermore, the results suggest that ostentatious salespeople who are full of bravado alienate far more customers than they win over.

Selling style impact: team orientation. As opposed to establishing themselves as the focal point of the purchase decision, top salespeople position the team (presales technical engineers, consulting, and management) that will help them win the account as the centerpiece.

4. *Lack of gregariousness.* One of the most surprising differences between top salespeople and those ranking in the bottom one-third of performance is their level of gregariousness (preference for company and friendliness). Overall, top performers averaged 30 percent lower gregariousness than below-average performers.

Selling style impact: situational dominance. Situational dominance is the ability to gain the willing obedience of customers such that the salesperson's recommendations and advice are followed. The results indicate that overly friendly salespeople are too close to their customers and have difficulty establishing dominance.

5. *Lack of discouragement.* Less than 10 percent of top salespeople were classified as having high levels of discouragement and being frequently overwhelmed with sadness. Conversely, 90 percent were categorized as experiencing infrequent or occasional sadness.

Selling style impact: competitiveness. Casual surveys I have conducted throughout the years indicate that over 85 percent of top performers played organized sports in high school. There seems to be a direct correlation between sports and sales success as top performers are able to handle emotional disappointments, bounce back from losses, and mentally prepare themselves for the next opportunity to compete.

6. *Lack of self-consciousness.* Self-consciousness is the measurement of how easily someone is embarrassed. The by-product of a high level of self-consciousness is bashfulness and inhibition. Less than 5 percent of top performers had high levels of self-consciousness.

   Selling style impact: aggressiveness. Top salespeople are comfortable fighting for their cause and not afraid of rankling customers in the process. They are action oriented and unafraid to call high in their accounts or courageously cold call new prospects.

7. *Conscientiousness.* Eighty-five percent of top salespeople had high levels of conscientiousness, whereby they could be described as having a strong sense of duty and being responsible and reliable. These salespeople take their jobs very seriously and feel deeply responsible for the results.

   Selling style impact: account control. The worst position for salespeople to be in is to have relinquished account control and operate at the direction of the customer or, worse yet, a competitor. Conversely, top salespeople take command of the sales cycle process to control their own destiny.

Not all salespeople are successful. Given the same sales tools, level of education, and propensity to work, why do some salespeople succeed where others fail? Is one better suited to sell a product because of his background? Is one more charming or just luckier? The evidence suggests that the personalities of Heavy Hitters play a critical role in determining their success.

67. Meeting Someone for the First Time

Meeting new people is stressful. If you watch strangers meet you'll notice that they are on guard. We typically don't have to worry that someone is physically threatening; we have to worry if they present a psychological threat. Therefore, we try to ascertain whether a stranger is in a dominant, equal, or submissive position in comparison to ours. Next, we try to find out what we have in common by discovering intersecting activities. Finally, we try to classify the relationship into a familiar pattern so we can decide how we should behave and whether we should invest more time with the person. The sequence is shown in figure 67.1.

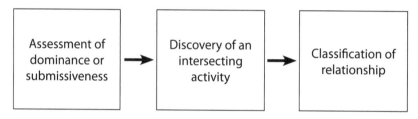

Figure 67.1 The process of meeting a stranger

The instinctual comparison of dominance tends to occur quickly when people meet. But what makes someone dominant? Dominance can be the result of a diverse set of attributes. When two people talk at a party, one person may be better looking, more intelligent, funnier, wealthier, or better respected or have a quality that the other person lacks, such as kindness, generosity, humility, aggressiveness, assertiveness, or selfishness.

> I have sales reps who come in here and would rather look at the floor than talk to me. It's like they are scared of you.
> —*General Manager*

The natural course of a conversation between strangers is for them to find out what they have in common. Through intersecting activities, people display their personal interests, character, and temperament and express their value systems. Intersecting activities create shared bonds and reduce the level of stress involved in meeting someone new. Intersecting activities play an equally important role in sales calls. Regardless of whether the salesperson or the customer initiated the meeting, the first intersecting activity is the sales call itself. It is the first point in common between the salesperson and the customer.

You can use the first intersecting activity (the sales call) to find *personal* intersecting activities. By doing so, you develop rapport and begin the process of building a personal friendship. In essence, you try to relieve the stress caused by the typical dominant-submissive meeting between a customer and a vendor by turning it into a conversation between equals.

All people have outside interests, hobbies, and personal pursuits by which they display their personalities, beliefs, and values. Think about all the potential non-business-related subjects you can discuss with your customers—for example, cars, movies, wine, college, dieting, music, pets, investments, marriage, horse racing, golf, books, professional sports, raising children, and cigars.

You can easily identify intersecting activities of customers by observing how they have decorated their cubicles or offices. Pictures of family vacations, mementos, awards, degrees, and other personal artifacts convey their interests and the attributes of their personality.

Always engage the customer in a personal conversation about the intersecting activities you have in common. By doing so, you develop rapport with the *entire* person, not just the *business* person—building the foundation of a personal friendship that sets you apart from the competition.

Once the strangers establish who is dominant and they have searched for what they have in common, each person tries to characterize the relationship by placing it into one of the categories of familial relationships he or she is familiar with, such as a relationship with a father figure, big sister, best friend, or son.

What intersecting activities do you like to talk about with customers, and how would they classify their relationships with you? Customers are personally evaluating you during the first few minutes of a sales call and making an initial judgment about whether they like you or not. Think about how you can use the process of how strangers meet to your advantage. Equally important, think about the lasting impression you want them to remember you by.

68. The Better Sales "Person"

At the root of dominance is the "Better Person Syndrome," which is based on the theory that people will naturally gravitate toward people they feel are better than themselves in some way. In this respect, the Better Person Syndrome helps explain the old saying that opposites attract.

The theory also applies to sales. When customers are choosing between two similar products, they will not always buy the better product. Rather, their tendency is to buy from the salesperson they believe is the better person. So while one salesperson may have a slightly better product and be more proficient in explaining its features and functionality, in the end the customer will buy from the person who has the personal attributes the customer most admires. (Obviously, if one product is light years ahead of another, then the Better Person Syndrome is neutralized.)

Some customers will gravitate to a friendly and responsive salesperson. They admire and respect these qualities. Others might enjoy being around an aristocratic salesperson in cufflinks and a monogrammed dress shirt. Perhaps these customers behave and dress in a similar way and have some deep-seated desire to be like him. Because people admire different qualities in other people, every sales call is unique.

> All things being equal, I'll go with the company of the salesperson who established a relationship better—someone I felt comfortable with—because at that point it comes down to trust in the guy calling on you and his company. Is it a fellow I know I can do business with? Someone I might have some camaraderie with? When we're done with the business day can we enjoy the evening without him trying to sell me at ten o'clock at night?
> —*Chief Information Officer*

Your situational dominance in any setting is dependent upon the submissiveness of the person you are talking with. It is not a measure of how easily you overpower the person. Rather, it depends on the traits that the other person respects, admires, or does not possess. For example, a customer may be submissive to a salesperson's industry expertise, technical aptitude, or product knowledge. Many people become submissive when they perceive a salesperson to be better looking, more charismatic, or more enthusiastic than they are. For instance, I know several vice presidents of sales who will hire a good-looking salesperson with average sales skills over a great salesperson who is not so attractive.

Most customers tend to gravitate to salespeople who are similar to themselves. They want to be surrounded by competent, successful people. However, opposites attract as well. For example, very meticulous, no-nonsense customers sometimes bond with lackadaisical, carefree salespeople who are their exact opposites. These customers seem to be hypnotized into a submissive position. One of the best technology salespeople I know of was the most unorganized, lackadaisical, smart-mouthed goof-off I ever met. However, a certain cross section of executives absolutely adored him because he always said exactly what was on his mind in the most politically incorrect way. Surprisingly, the executives he bonded with were usually straight-laced, button-down CFOs and CIOs. I think they found his uniqueness intoxicating compared to the personalities of the staff members they had to deal with daily.

Now it's time to do a quick exercise to help you discover what makes you dominant in customer meetings. The list below includes just a few of the wide range of dominant traits that people respond to submissively. As you read the list, think about when you used one of these attributes to put yourself in a dominant position over your main contact (who was probably a midmanagement or lower-level person) at a recent account you won. Recall not only the account but the specific person who responded to you submissively and followed your lead.

Athleticism	Humor	Product knowledge
Business knowledge	Industry expertise	Professionalism
Charisma	Integrity	Sense of humor
Cleverness	Open-mindedness	Seriousness
Curiosity	Optimism	Technical aptitude
Empathy	Organization	Thoughtfulness
Enthusiasm	Passion	Tolerance
Friendliness	Persistence	Trustworthiness

A good salesperson takes the time to understand my overall environment, speaks to me about the areas where they have strengths as opposed to attempting to be the solution to all of our problems, and is patient in terms of managing the relationship and right circumstances for us to take our relationship deeper. A good salesperson is easy to be around, makes you feel comfortable, and thinks like you do.

—*IT Director*

69. Customer Relationships

We all have many different types of personal relationships. We have friends, family, coworkers, and neighbors. When we meet someone new at a party, we decide if we like the person and whether he or she might become a friend or is more likely to remain a distant acquaintance.

This classification also happens on sales calls. However, each customer may have an entirely different perception of your character. For example, you may be characterized as a friend by one customer and an acquaintance by another. You could be a little brother to an older customer or a big brother to a younger one. You could be thought of as a father, lover, uncle, cousin, or even an enemy. Here are some possible characterizations:

Best friend	Father figure	Lover
Big brother	Girlfriend	Mentor
Big sister	Grandparent	Mother figure
Boyfriend	Husband	Son
Buddy	Little brother	Soul mate
Daughter	Little sister	Wife

When I ask salespeople to explain their selling style, the majority say, "Consultative." Unfortunately, every salesperson competing for a deal is trying to be a consultant. You need to establish a stronger relationship. Depending upon your background, you may want to be the trusted father figure or the soul mate the customer is searching for. Whatever it is, don't be solely a consultant.

Knowing whether you are a customer's submissive little brother or a dominant mother figure and when to act like a mentor plays an important role in the sales call.

> There wasn't anyone on the evaluation committee who liked the salesperson. While we ranked his company at the top and would have preferred his solution, no one was excited to buy from him so we went with the alternative. You have to have relationships to do business with our company.
> —*Director of Application Development*

70. How Customers Receive and Transmit Information

You have developed a lifetime of experiences that are unique. These experiences, both good and bad, have shaped your perception of the world. Through your senses, you are constantly adding to your cumulative knowledge of how your world functions. As you accumulate new experiences, they are edited and influenced by your history. As a result, it is accurate to say every person functions in his or her own unique world. Your world is your own personal reality. You use your "word catalogs" to catalog your experiences and describe your world to others. It is also the methodology by which you ascertain correct interpretations of a message and associate complex psychological meanings.

Through language, we represent our thoughts and experiences. We use words to represent the sensory experiences of sight, sound, touch, taste, and smell. The map we use to describe and interpret an experience is based upon one of three word catalogs—visual, auditory, and kinesthetic. "Visual" refers to pictures and imagery, "auditory" refers to sounds, and "kinesthetic" refers to touch and internal feelings.

Most people use one word catalog more frequently than the others. This word catalog has become their default, or "primary," mode of communication. You can identify someone's primary word catalog by listening to the adjectives, adverbs, and nouns he or she uses in conversation.

People whose primary word catalog is based on sight will describe their experiences in visual terms. They are likely to say, "I see what you mean," "Looks good to me," or "Show me what to do." People with a primary word catalog based on sound will say, "Sounds great," "Talk to you later," or "Tell me what to do." People with a primary word catalog based on feeling might say, "I've got it handled," "We'll touch base later," or "I don't grasp what you mean."

Three channels of information continually bombard your brain with information: visual, auditory, and kinesthetic. You can't turn off your senses. You can't slow down your vision, turn off your sense of touch, or silence your hearing. Your mind has had to adopt a strategy to assess and prioritize incoming information. While you were born with a tendency to prefer one stream of information over another, during your childhood you adopted the channel processing strategy your mind uses today. Figure 70.1 below represents how people receive and transmit different streams of information.

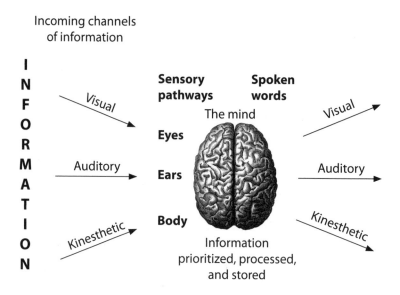

Figure 70.1 How people receive and transmit information

Some people have a more dominant ear (the one you use when you talk on the telephone), a dominant leg, and even a dominant eye. Similarly, people have a dominant, primary word catalog. A word catalog is the mind's method of gathering information, accumulating knowledge, and recording experiences based upon the visual, auditory, or kinesthetic senses. Your word catalog is also responsible for the association of psychological meanings to words. Your dominant word catalog might be visual, auditory, or kinesthetic. You also have a weaker, secondary catalog and, finally, a recessive catalog.

Your primary word catalog is your "default" method for accessing your catalog of experiences. It is the catalog used most often. People with a visual primary word catalog think in terms of pictures, those with a primary auditory word catalog think in terms of sounds, and those with a primary kinesthetic word catalog think in terms of feelings. Your secondary word catalog is your next strongest method for accessing your catalog. Finally, your recessive catalog is your least used and least developed access method.

You can tell what people's word catalog wiring is by noting the adjectives and verbs they use in their conversations. An adjective is a word used to modify a noun, and a verb is an action word. However, some words can be used as either a noun, verb, or adjective, and this usage will significantly change the interpretation of the word catalog. The sentences in the left-hand column represent a visual, auditory, or kinesthetic usage, while those in the right-hand column do not imply any particular word catalog:

Don't *glare* at me.	The *glare* of the sun was intense.
Map out your account strategy.	Please hand me the *map*.
Please *watch* your mouth.	His *watch* is broken.
Focus on the problem.	The camera has automatic *focus*.

The italicized words in the sentences in the left-hand column are verbs that imply a particular word catalog. Although the same words are used in the right-hand column, they are used as nouns. As you know, a noun is a word that describes a person, place, or thing. In general, nouns do not imply any particular word catalog.

People with a primary visual word catalog will use visual keywords more frequently than auditory or kinesthetic words to describe their experiences. Here are some examples of visual keywords:

Beaming	Demonstrate	Frame	Imagine	See
Bleak	Diagram	Gaze	Light	Shine
Bleary	Diffuse	Glance	Look	Show
Blight	Disappear	Glare	Magnify	Sight
Blind	Discern	Glimpse	Map	Snapshot
Bright	Display	Graph	Murky	Spectacle
Brilliant	Distinguish	Hallucinate	Observe	Spot

Chart	Dreary	Hazy	Outlook	Stare
Clarify	Emit	Highlight	Perspective	Survey
Clear	Expose	Illuminate	Preview	View
Cloudy	Fade	Illustrate	Reflect	Viewpoint
Dazzle	Focus	Image	Scan	Watch

People with primary auditory word catalogs will use auditory keywords like these in their conversations:

Accent	Bark	Denounce	Note	Say
Amplify	Berate	Dictate	Paraphrase	Shout
Articulate	Bicker	Digress	Persuade	Slur
Ask	Blare	Discuss	Plead	Snap
Assert	Boast	Drone	Profess	Sound
Attune	Cajole	Edit	Promise	Speak
Audacious	Call	Giggle	Quiet	Spell
Audible	Chime	Hum	Rave	Talk
Backfire	Chord	Implore	Recap	Tell
Back-talk	Crunch	Loud	Retreat	Vague
Banter	Cry	Noise	Ring	Yell

People with primary kinesthetic word catalogs will use kinesthetic keywords like the following:

Ache	Catch	Hard	Pique	Smile
Bash	Chafe	Heart	Plug	Smooth
Bask	Chew	Heavy	Post	Spit
Bat	Choke	Hit	Press	Squash
Bend	Chop	Hold	Pull	Sticky
Bind	Clinch	Impact	Push	Stink
Bit	Cough	Impress	Queasy	Strike
Blink	Crawl	Irritate	Rough	Taste
Boot	Draw	Kick	Rub	Thaw
Bounce	Feel	Leap	Scratch	Throw

Bow	Friction	Mark	Sense	Touch
Breathe	Gnaw	Move	Sharp	Walk
Caress	Grab	Nip	Smell	Weigh

From this point forward, we will refer to people with a sight-based primary word catalog as Visuals. Similarly, people with sound-based or feelings-based primary word catalogs will be referred to as Auditories or Kinesthetics.

71. What Is Your Word Catalog Wiring?

What is your primary word catalog? Here's an exercise that will help you understand how you are wired. Print out the last ten business e-mails you sent to colleagues within your company and the last ten personal e-mails you sent to friends or family. Write the letters *V, A,* and *K* across the top of a piece of paper. In the left column write "Work," "Personal," and "Total." The chart should look like figure 71.1.

	V	*A*	*K*
Work			
Personal			
Total			

Figure 71.1 What is your word catalog wiring?

You are now ready to perform a "VAK keyword count." Examine the e-mails and circle each occurrence of a visual, auditory, or kinesthetic word. Remember to circle the word only when it is used in the context of an action or description ("you *light* up my life," not "please turn the *light* on"). As you circle the words, add a tally in the appropriate column. The chart may look something like figure 71.2 when you are done.

	V	A	K
Work	III	ⅢⅡ I	III
Personal	ⅢⅡ	ⅢⅡ ⅢⅡ	ⅢⅡ IIII
Total	ⅢⅡ III	ⅢⅡ ⅢⅡ ⅢⅡ I	ⅢⅡ ⅢⅡ II

Figure 71.2 Sample results of a VAK keyword count and VAK pattern

Did you notice a difference between the tallies from your work and personal e-mails? Most likely, the language in your work e-mails is more androgynous and technical; therefore, the counts will be lower. Were the counts evenly dispersed or clustered under one catalog? In the example above, the person's word catalog wiring is primary auditory, secondary kinesthetic, and recessive visual.

The first step to broadening your appeal to a wider audience and becoming more persuasive during sales calls is understanding how you are wired and whether you are a Visual, Auditory or Kinesthetic. How are you wired? Are you a primary Auditory, Visual, or Kinesthetic? Did you notice a big difference in keyword counts between your work and personal e-mails?

Now conduct VAK counts based upon the e-mails sent to you by the key contacts for the most important deals you are trying to close. Compare their VAK counts to yours and think about whom you have the best and worst rapport with. Most likely, you share very similar wiring with individuals with whom you enjoy harmonious communication, and you're wired differently from those with whom you have tenuous relationships.

Whenever you meet with someone, perform a VAK count to determine the primary, secondary, and recessive word catalogs of the person you are talking with. You don't have to count for the entire meeting or conversation—just until you have a basic understanding of the person's wiring.

As you begin to perform VAK keyword counts, you will notice some patterns developing. There are three major types of VAK count patterns: balanced, strong secondary, and dominating primary as shown in figure 71.3. The strengths of the three catalogs in the balanced pattern are relatively close. However, the strength of the catalogs are different in the strong secondary pattern, where the visual word catalog is far weaker than the auditory and kinesthetic catalogs, and in the dominating primary pattern where the visual word catalog is strongest.

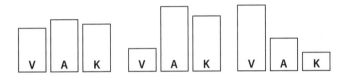

Figure 71.3 Balanced pattern, strong secondary pattern, and dominating primary pattern

Balanced communication is a key attribute of effective persuasion. Balanced communicators create better rapport. They don't limit themselves by speaking exclusively from a single word catalog. They connect with Visuals, Auditories, and Kinesthetics equally. Therefore, a balanced speaker naturally reaches a broader audience.

People use all three word catalogs, just in different amounts and priorities. For example, a person might use visual words 60 percent of the time, kinesthetic words 25 percent of the time, and auditory words only 15 percent of the time. The strength of each of your catalogs and the order in which you use them can profoundly impact your ability to persuade during sales calls. Therefore, you must know your word catalog usage and determine whether you have a balanced, strong secondary, or dominating primary pattern.

In addition to the VAK keywords, catch phrases, descriptions, and clichés also reveal a speaker's word catalogs. For example, "sizzling hot" is most likely to be said by Auditories. They hear the sizzling sound. Upon hearing this phrase, Visuals might picture a grill with something sizzling on it, and Kinesthetics might think of a finger actually touching the grill (particularly if they have burnt themselves in the past). "Keep your fingers crossed" is usually said by visuals while "hindsight is 20/20" is said by Auditories.

Pay attention to the sayings and clichés used by customers during sales calls to them. They will help you determine a customer's word catalog wiring and whether he is a Visual, Auditory, or Kinesthetic. Ultimately, they will help you understand and think like your customer. For example, if the customer tells you, "We'll look at the numbers and get back to you," you could reply, "Let me show you a couple of areas of cost savings that might not seem so obvious." When the customer says, "We want more bang for our buck" you might respond, "Tell me what sounds fair to you." If he comments, "We're weighing all the possibilities," you might come back with, "What can we do to tip the scale in our favor?"

72. Learning Styles

Since every salesperson is an educator, doesn't it make sense for you to understand how different types of people you must influence like to learn? A person's word catalog wiring typically influences the manner in which he or she likes to learn. Here's a quick test to help you determine your learning style. Circle the letter following each question that best applies to you.

1. When driving to a new customer address for the first time, I like to:

A. View printed directions or watch my GPS

B. Ask the customer for directions or listen to my GPS

C. Use my strong sense of direction in conjunction with maps or directions

2. I like to learn about the new products my company is offering by:

A. Viewing product information and watching presentations

B. Listening to someone describe the product and talk it through with me

C. Using the product or having someone demonstrate how it is used

3. To learn the features and benefits of a new product, I like to:

A. Write them down so that I can refer to my script in the future

B. Repeat them and practice saying them aloud

C. Rehearse through role-plays or pretending that I am with a prospective customer

4. At sales training sessions I:

A. Take notes on important topics so I remember them after the meeting

B. Like hearing discussions about important information

C. Like participating in exercises and role-playing

5. When making an important customer phone call:

A. I may have prepared a list of topics or notes to remind me of what to say

B. I tend to talk more than I listen

C. I like to move, walk around, or doodle on a paper during the call

Now add up the number of As, Bs and Cs you have circled to find your primary, secondary, and recessive learning styles. The As are visual learning style, Bs are auditory, and Cs are kinesthetic.

Incorporate the different learning styles into your sales call strategy. Make sure you have a PowerPoint presentation to show visual customers or be prepared to show them how your product works by drawing on a whiteboard. Auditory customers are more likely to want in-depth conversations, so be sure to bring along your colleagues who can answer all of their detailed technical questions. Kinesthetics tend to prefer hands-on demonstrations and trial product evaluations and will become frustrated with vendors who are unable to provide them.

73. Short- and Long-Term Memory Cues

You are constantly accessing your short-term and long-term memory. However, it is much easier to access your short-term memory. Accessing your long-term memory is harder and slower. In computer terms, short-term memory is your RAM, while long-term memory is your hard drive. Much like a computer's disk drive, accessing your long-term memory requires some "mechanical" movements, and access to long-term memory can be seen. Conversely, short-term storage is accessed "electronically" and is therefore unobservable.

Amazingly, by observing people's eye movements, you can follow the mechanical movements of the brain that happen when they access their long-term memory. By watching their eyes move, you can determine if they are making pictures in their mind, listening to themselves speak, or experiencing feelings. From this information, you can determine their word catalog wiring and the primary language they use. Most importantly for salespeople, you can learn how to sequence customer questions so specific movements are triggered in order to determine a customer's truthfulness and your future likelihood of winning the deal.

The brain is a widely distributed neural network with information and memories stored throughout. Eye movements are believed to cause the left and right hemispheres of the brain to better interact with each other. For example, the right hemisphere may maintain information that the left hemisphere requires to retrieve a certain memory. Eye movements to the left activate the right brain hemisphere, and eye movements to the right activate the left hemisphere.

When remembering pictures, people will move their eyes up to the right, keep their eyes straight while defocusing their pupils, or move their eyes up to the left. When remembering sounds, people will move their eyes straight to their right, down to their left, or straight to their left. People will move their eyes down to the right when remembering feelings.

Before we go further, it is important to define the two different types of long-term memories. Some long-term memories can be recalled precisely (precise memories), and some memories are recalled by creating, constructing, and comparing images, sounds, and feelings (assembled memories). Assembled memories will usually cause a different eye movement than precise memories. For example, a Visual might move his eyes up and to the left when asked how many bridesmaids were in his wedding because he's mentally viewing a picture from his wedding album. But the same person may have to look up and to the right when asked to name the church where he was married. Because he couldn't precisely visualize the name, he had to construct the answer and use his imagination to picture the wedding license, the pastor, or the front of the church. Assembled memories require the use of imagination in order to fill the gaps of missing information.

Eye movements reflect the inner workings of the mind. Let's suppose people are asked, "What was the best day of your life?" Visuals may start searching their memories by looking for stored pictures before finally deciding on a specific day, such as the day their first child was born. To search their memory banks of pictures, their eyes would move up to the right, move up to the left, or look straight ahead with the pupils defocused. Once retrieved, the picture could then trigger the feeling they had of holding the baby for the first time. Their eyes would move down to the right to get the feeling. Finally, to recreate the entire experience, their eyes may move down to the left or right to actually recall the sound of the baby crying. This is called a "search loop." Their eyes initially went to their primary system, then their secondary, then their recessive. They were trying to find a mental tag (by sifting through different pieces of information) that would help them bring back the entire memory.

While some people will make very obvious eye movements, other people's eye movements are very subtle and consist of quick glances away from you. Some people have to blink to think. They have to close their eyes for a second to retrieve information. In this case, you will be able to see the bulge of their pupil and iris on the eyelid as the eye moves. The main point here is that you have to pay close attention and look for subtle movements as well as obvious eye movements.

There is also a very rare group of people that I call "Masterminds." One or two out of fifty people have the uncanny ability to instantly recall exceptionally detailed autobiographical memories and past personal experiences, even though they may have occurred decades before. Even though most of the Masterminds I have ever met have been Visuals, they don't seem to make any eye movements at all.

The mind is an incredibly complex system, and there will be exceptions to the general rules above. For example, left-handedness impacts eye movements about 50 percent of the time based upon my observations. Since only 10 percent of the population is left-handed, this means that 5 percent of the people you meet may be wired in reverse. For example, their kinesthetic (down to the right) and auditory (down to the left) eye movements are reversed.

When you first meet a customer, ask questions that require long-term memory access: When did you start working here? What did you do before you started working here? Where did you grow up? What was your first job here? The eye movements made while answering these questions will help you get a preliminary idea of the customer's word catalog wiring.

At this point, you may be skeptical about whether eye movements can really explain what is happening in the brain. Try the following experiment. However, before you start, you will need to find a mirror because this exercise is much more meaningful when you can watch yourself.

Below, you will find a list of questions. All of these questions are intended to make you access your long-term memory. As you read each question, try to follow your eye movements. Specifically, concentrate on where your eyes move first to "search" for the answer and make a notation of it. Use *UL* to reflect upper left and *UR* for upper right. Write *SL* for straight left, *S* for straight center with no eye movement at all, *SD* for straight with defocused pupils, and *SR* for straight right. Write *DL* for down left, and *DR* for down right. Also try to pay specific attention to the exact position of your eyes when you actually "find" the answer.

1. What did you have for dinner last Friday?
2. What was the name of your third-grade teacher?
3. What was the worst sales call you ever went on?

4. What account that you closed are you most proud of?

5. What was the license plate number of your first car?

What happened? Did you have to look away from your reflection to answer a question? Where did your eyes move first?

Let's examine the questions further. They are all date dependent and designed to access your long-term memory. However, it's possible that some of the answers were in your short-term memory. It depends on you. If you're reading this on Saturday, it's easy to remember what you had for dinner yesterday. However, if you're reading it on Thursday, the answer may be in long-term memory.

The key to successfully understanding customers is to first establish their baseline movements. Baseline movements are the customers' default nonverbal communication style. For example, at the beginning of a sales call you could ask nonthreatening questions that invoke long-term memory in order to establish the baseline eye movements. These questions could be about date-dependent experiences or minutiae and hard-to-remember details. For example, how many employees worked at the company when you started?

74. Final Advice

Most salespeople don't like to read. You see, your brain was built for talking. It was not designed for reading. While speaking comes automatically and is a natural part of the brain's development, reading is a skill that must be learned. It requires three different areas of your brain to work together in close coordination. So it's unlikely you'll read this book in its entirety. Therefore, my final advice is to go through the book and read all the customer interview excerpts. You'll be glad you did, and I'm sure it will help you create your own *magic*.

> Ultimately, the quality of the vendor's relationship really comes down to the quality and work ethic of the account executive. The extent to which the salesperson makes it his business and makes sure everything at his account is going well will dictate the quality of the vendor relationship. I can point to times where we had a crackerjack account executive who made sure that everything was under control and that all parties are kept in constant communication. This person is an advocate for us on his side and makes it smoother for us no matter what is going on behind the scenes in his organization. My experience is the most important determination of whether we will have a successful relationship with the vendor than all the other things combined. Now the product still has to work and the services still must be rendered. But if that account executive is really taking ownership, it can become quite magical.
>
> —*Chief Information Officer*

Index

About the Author

Steve W. Martin is the foremost expert on sales linguistics, the study of how salespeople and customers use language during the complex decision-making process. He began his career programming computers. Through working with computers, he became acutely aware of the preciseness and structure of language. In addition, programming is built upon models—verbal descriptions and visual representations of how systems work and processes flow. Models enable repeatable and predictable experiences.

Early in his career, he was also introduced to the concepts of neurolinguistics (the science of how the human brain constructs and interprets language). After working as a programmer and data processing manager, he transitioned his career into software sales. He realized that he could build models to create successful relationships based upon customers' language and thought processes. Without any sales experience to speak of, he was the number one salesperson in his company for the following four years.

Steve went on to be a top sales producer for a billion-dollar software company and was promoted into management to imprint his sales strategy model on other salespeople within the organization. As vice president of sales, he successfully trained his technology salespeople on the sales strategies and communication skills that are necessary to close large accounts.

Steve is the author of the critically acclaimed Heavy Hitter series of books for senior salespeople. His books have been featured in *Forbes*, the *Wall Street Journal*, and *Selling Power* magazine. He is also a frequent contributor to the *Harvard Business Review*.

A highly sought-after speaker and sales trainer, Steve is both entertaining and provocative. He has worked with hundreds of companies. His clients include IBM, Oracle, Lenovo, HP, AT&T,

EMC, PayPal, McAfee, Cadence, Akamai, Riverbed, TELUS, Solidworks, SunGard, NEC, Nimble Storage, and Cornerstone OnDemand.

When not working with his clients, Steve teaches sales strategy at the University of Southern California Marshall MBA program. He is a proud recipient of the USC Marshall Golden Apple Teaching Award presented to the professor who has had the greatest impact on students as voted by the members of the graduating class. Please visit http://www.stevewmartin.com for further information.

Notes and Action Items

Notes and Action Items

Notes and Action Items

Notes and Action Items